NICK CAVE

The Birthday Party and other epic adventures

ROBERT BROKENMOUTH

Edited by Chris Charlesworth
Cover designed by Michael Bell Design
Picture research by Robert Brokenmouth & Nikki Russell
ISBN: 0.7119.5601.4
Order No. OP 47826

Exclusive Distributors:
Book Sales Limited,
8/9 Frith Street,
London W1V 5TZ, UK.

Music Sales Corporation,
257 Park Avenue South,
New York, NY 10010, USA.

Music Sales Pty Limited,
120 Rothschild Avenue, Rosebery,
NSW 2018, Australia.

To the Music Trade only:
Music Sales Limited,
8/9 Frith Street,
London W1V 5TZ, UK.

Every effort has been made to trace the copyright holders of the photographs in this book but one or two were unreachable. We would be grateful if the photographers concerned would contact us.

Printed in the United Kingdom by Biddles Ltd

A catalogue record for this book is available from the British Library.

CONTENTS

FOREWORD

DURING MY RESEARCH FOR THIS BOOK, I spoke to a large number of people, jogging many memories, opening old painful areas. Some carry a sense of loss, and I learned much about perception, emotional freedom, discovery and inhibition.

Everyone has their own truth. So who can you believe? All? Some? None? Why not others? Who chooses? How? Everyone has their own truth. The quickest way to destroy the human spirit is to deny that truth, repetitively.

There are hundreds of *great* anecdotes about The Birthday Party; spending more time on daft, intense, sordid or tragic stories would've detracted from the essential truths of the band, and from my reason for writing: the music.

The examples and anecdotes I've chosen are primarily there to pace the text, add insight and offer a sense of intimacy and familiarity with these people.

The more one learns about Nick Cave the less an enigma he seems, always his own self – albeit one formed early. I'm not a mate of his, nor do I idolise him. He's an interesting, funny guy; a man whose career is well worth following.

Along the way the band's guitarist Rowland Howard told me: "A lot of people who're incredibly creative are really introverted, and sometimes their public persona is very different. When somebody comes up to you in the street and expects you to entertain them; says, 'Hello', and expects you to be wildly funny and hilarious, or say something devastatingly philosophical, it's really horrible. It used to happen to me a lot, so I imagine it would happen to Nick an incredible amount. Towards the end of The Birthday Party I stopped going out because so many people would corner me. People would expect outrageous stuff from you, and be really offended when you failed to provide it."

Acknowledgements

I RECEIVED A LARGE AMOUNT of selfless assistance from many people while researching this book, and I must thank them. A special mention must be made of Rowland S. Howard and Phill Calvert for ridiculous amounts of patience and for enduring a seemingly endless battery of questions at the most awkward times. I wish also to express my gratitude to Andrew Browne, Kitty-Mae Carver, Tony Cohen, David Gerard, Helena Glass, Dave Graney, Mick Harvey, Barbara Kerr, Genevieve McGuckin, Shane Middleton, Wendy Munro, Nancy and Fiona Pew, Maira Poletti, Joan and Josephine Pugh, Rob Scott, and Mary and Ross Waterman.

This book is dedicated to the memory of Tracy Pew.

"It is no business of the artist to educate the public."
(from 'Artist and Public', *Times Literary Supplement*, 17 August, 1940.)

PROLOGUE

THE AUSTRALIAN DRAUGHT

THE AUSTRALIAN MUSIC SCENE of the Sixties and early Seventies was forever hampered by sporadic, second-hand information on overseas music and fashion trends, and by a record industry for whom the 'safe bet' was always the preferred option. Imported rock records were expensive for punters, and without the backing of a major label it was unlikely that a local act would prosper. As a consequence many young Australians of the time were unaware of the more progressive music emanating from the US and UK.

As the Seventies progressed Australia was swamped by American values and attitudes. A recognisable and socially acceptable Australian identity had yet to develop fully. "The yarts" as Barry Humphries' ocker-diplomat Sir Les Patterson describes them, felt this lack of direction strongly.

Countdown, Australia's overtly camp teenypop programme, was arrogant in its pimping of the next big thing from overseas, self-conscious in its attempt to straddle 'Ozrock', the more mature Seventies 'progressive' chart music and disco. Hugely popular, it promoted everything new with a grotesque disregard for quality or taste.

Above all, pop music was pub-friendly, with bands providing backing music for entrenched mating customs or having a few beers. The American music of the cultural underclass, R&B and soul, was the traditional soundtrack for an average Aussie on a night out. In Australia, popular culture is so artificial, our history so slap-dash, that it displays roots that are almost a tacked-on afterthought. Frankly, we'd rather be watching the footy or cricket with a tinnie and a pie.

In 1976 everything changed. An underground movement interlinked the great open spaces of this sprawling continent. Like the rave scene in the late Eighties and early Nineties, punk in Australia was about people discovering hitherto unrevealed musical and artistic potential, aided and abetted by drugs, freedom and information. In Dubbo, The Reels were beginning a lengthy career annoying punters in small bars. In Brisbane The Saints were rocking up a storm at legendary parties held in an abandoned house and pissing off the local authorities no end. In Sydney, Radio Birdman, Australia's first thrash band, carved out a legend, one of the first bands to utilise feedback within their *sturm und drang*.

These were alien bands and alien sounds, outside the convenient marketing slots that the music business had established for Boz Scaggs and Elton John.

The alternative music scene developed as a means of questioning established values. Like their UK counterparts, Australian punks were fascinated by trashy clothes, gay styles and nonconformist behaviour, without fully understanding the import of what they were doing. Leather jackets, male earrings, eyeliner and shades were adopted as accessories, making attack out of what was really an inverted self-defence. A scornful local media pounced on the superficial aspects of the scene, ignoring the cultural changes that were taking place among the young, overlooking the new influences pouring into Australia via the UK and US.

Each Australian city developed its own scene. Sydney's harder, grimmer approach was practical in crushing R&B into new forms. The brutish X could have developed nowhere else. Perth was open and carefree, isolated, producing the powerpopunk of The Manikins, The Victims and The Scientists. Brisbane's The Four Gods and Super K were witty and knowing.

Melbourne, the hub of artistic pursuit in Australia, was the only place that could have given birth to bands like Tsk Tsk Tsk, JAB or The News. Unusual or varied music was readily available compared to the indifference of other major cities (a friend of mine once searched the record shops of Adelaide for a copy of 'The Velvet Underground & Nico', eventually finding it in the comedy section). A small scene developed in Melbourne and everyone knew each other.

For years the scene consisted simply of those you'd meet at a gig or down the pub. Then, slowly, a genuine scene began to develop despite the limitations, most notably the shadow of UK punk which was just beginning to rear its confusing and regimental head. Would-be punks of similar persuasion all met at a variety of venues: gigs, parties, barbecues, art galleries, drug dealers' hang-outs, pubs and cafes.

Rose Tattoo toured Melbourne, as did X. Like The Saints and Radio Birdman, these two powerful, intense bands helped set a yardstick against which future Australian 'punk rock' would be measured. The scene was small and everyone knew each other. It was cosmopolitan too, from hippies in flared cords to the average suburban bloke with a suntan and stubble, from surfies in tank tops and thongs to hoons in lumberjack shirts and sneakers, art school students in dinner jackets and thin ties to lecturers and mums . . .

Little cliques and mannerisms appeared, and over the months, intensified. Where previously only women and gender-benders would dress up to go out, dress codes evolved across the scene. Mythical, darkened evening courts with their jesters and royalty developed; they were artistic refugees from another world. Each Christmas another new wave of ex-school children stumbled into the half-light of the pubs, where blue clouds of tobacco and dope smoke hazed in great lowering cushions. They would take in the exotic smell of grass, illegal yet readily available, get drunk and enjoy the thrill.

This mysterious underground, where anything was possible and everyone was an intellectual, contrasted sharply with the school scene for many of the newcomers. The Australian private school system, run largely by diligent clerics from religious orders, encouraged questioning thinking. Bringing on healthy, youthful curiosity while aiming to preserve the status quo, the private system unwittingly fostered an alternative Melbourne scene based on middle-class youths questioning middle-class values, rather than the working-class values apparently underlying the UK punk movement. These Aussie kids had money, could afford the weird imported records by Faust, Can, The Velvet Underground, Television and the like. Taking in Leonard Cohen and Alex Harvey alongside Neu and Captain Beefheart was no platform for the under-privileged to fight for freedom, rather a place to hide from what their parents saw as their own impeccable cultural integrity.

The new music made for rebellion; acquiring it became a seditious act – emotional, intense and non-political. In such a small scene bands could have a disproportionate influence on their peers. Animation and competition helped the development of bands like The Young Charlatans, JAB, Crime and The City Solution and many others. They were a village of foreigners encamped in a strange new city. The English punks provided plenty of role model material but no-one followed them. Australian punks did as they pleased. The Melbourne scene was fragile and distinctive.

Like the music itself, the UK papers – *The New Musical Express*, *Sounds* and *Melody Maker* – came in three months late too. Hip Australia has seen Hip London through a filter of time and distance for over a century. Those who were hungry for input either struggled to seek it out or created it themselves. The philosophical aspect was as important as the increasingly varied dress sense. Their music was a reflection of the scene.

For the outsider, the development of the Melbourne scene looked like bland posing rather than the testing of values and rules by a minority group of self-styled intellectuals. Serious, thin young men in dark clothes would gather in The Crystal Ballroom to discuss literature, Dostoyevsky, Voltaire and Rimbaud. They talked politics, too, but less so – the human condition, the personal politic was the thing to be seen with.

Then there were drugs . . .

Drug use in Australia really began with Vietnam, as disaffected soldiers came home with seeds of marijuana and discontent. By 1970 there was a huge increase in use. Films like *Easy Rider* helped the tide along. By 1973 opium, grass, hash, hash oil, heroin, and speed were all available. Acid came in a variety of forms – Blue Babies, Orange Barrels, Purple Haze and so on. Australia is a very alcohol-friendly society, and beer and wine are both cheap. Everyone knows someone who has a home brew on the go, and drugs slotted easily into this culture.

Drugs, communes, sex, drinking and driving . . . punk served as a sort of rowdy finishing school, a lackadaisical vehicle for a generation of dynamic youth. As the influences of The Stooges, Velvet Underground and MC5 grew, so the scene fostered its own dark cultural secrets. By 1977, The Saints and Radio Birdman had toured their assaultive, hard-swirling, suburban outcast rock through Europe and into the UK. To Australians, The Saints and Birdman were more tangible than the theatrical UK punks. Both bands helped forge the Melbourne scene, symbolising a heady, dramatic, exit from the monosyllabic Australian rock circuit. Opportunity was rife, even if both bands did break up in England.

A precedent had been set, and The Boys Next Door set out to break the still cooling mould.

I

Out After School
(Melbourne 1976–1980)

The Boys Next Door started in Melbourne in 1974, their line-up consisting of Phill Calvert (drums), Nick Cave (vocals), John Cochivera (guitar), Chris Coyne (sax), Mick Harvey (guitar) and Brett Purcell (bass). They were the 'posh' Caulfield Grammar 'rock band', a muck-about thing.

Nick Cave has described his childhood and early adolescence years to many journalists. He grew up in the Victorian countryside, first at Warracknabeal, and then at Wangaratta. After a few unbecoming incidents at Wangaratta High School, where his parents worked, Nick was sent to board at Caulfield Grammar High School in Melbourne's suburbs. There seems no doubt that he was a charismatic tearaway who left his mark wherever he went. The nomadic alien provocateur of The Birthday Party learned his style early but that doesn't explain Nick's extraordinary ability to drive himself where no-one else would even think of going. It was clear that he possessed significant qualities of determination and self-belief that were unusual in an adolescent.

Phill: "Beaver Mills also boarded at Caulfield Grammar. Beaver and I were really good mates; he was a bad, bad kid, and I was a 'goody-two-shoes' type. The boarding house kids were always the bad-arse mess-you-up guys. There was this fight between Beaver and Nick. Nick was the art-house wimp guy who painted and all that stuff; Nick was just not gonna win this fight, it was just no-contest, but . . .

"Nick's incredible under adverse conditions, he has incredible strength when he's under duress. It's this absolute driven animal-type strength. I just could not believe it when the teacher broke it up, Nick was winning, he was on top and he was gonna kill Beaver.

"Another time, at a party, Nick was being the class clown, pushing people into the swimming pool. Me and several other people decided that Nick was goin' in. Nick latched onto the leg of a twelve foot by six foot slate-bed billiard table – and he was just *not* going in. Like, ten guys couldn't pull him off. His energy is driven on a different level; it wasn't to do with whether or not he was gonna get wet, but that he was gonna *lose*."

Nick had been writing poetry since he was twelve, and although he could play the piano well enough to hold a tune, he had also been in the school choir and felt that singing was the best way to express himself musically.

Mick Harvey's father was a preacher, Nick's folks were academics. Phill's dad, who had knocked about the world before migrating to Australia with his wife, was a painter and decorator.

Phill: "I always enjoyed working with Mick, he was a good counter-balance for me when I was trying to control the situation where I knew it wasn't being productive for the band. I might express that in an over-emotive or clumsy way, but Mick would be able to steer it around in such a way so that what I was saying made sense, or he'd be able to get the guys to do what needed to be done.

"I think Mick knew that he was really good as a collaborator and an organiser, and that that's where his strength was. Mick's become very good at music, he understands the fabric of it, where it's going, and what it's doing, whilst he's dealing with it. He has a very good vision of how things will end up while he's working on them.

"The good thing about Nick is that even in the middle of him being the star there are still those moments where he turned to you and said, 'Come on, let's go do this!', which was just like, 'Well, let's just go and be naughty!' Not really bad, but playing at being bad. There was always that level of camaraderie."

Like most private schoolboys of the time, the Caulfield Grammar boys were surrounded by authority figures who ordered their lives with discipline. Some escaped to the sports field, some buried themselves in schoolwork, others rebelled, and the most outward form of rebellion was in hair length. The longer, or the more dramatic, the hair you wore, the more rebellious and the more accepted you were among your peer group.

Acceptance is always important, and authority is always alien. School photos from the 1975 Caulfield Grammar yearbook show the usual 'police-suspect'-like line-ups of young louts squinting awkwardly into the camera, or slouching, nettled, amongst their fellows. And they *all* have hair past their ears. Mick, Phill and Nick were no exception.

Since sport and schoolwork were part of an anonymous haze, the school band was formed from an assortment of arty misfits. Phill Calvert had been learning drums since his first year in primary school, and from the age of 10 was taught by Les Taskin, who used to drum for the Moscow Circus. "He helped me a hell of a lot," says Phill.

They were pretty awful at first, their musical ability typical of beginners. Phill was the most accomplished musician at this stage, his reliability doing much to keep the band together.

They played covers: 'Johnny B Goode', and about seven or so Sensational Alex Harvey band covers, including 'Framed' and 'Midnight Moses'. Harvey was a favourite of Mick and Nick's at the time. When they played – two or three shows a year by some accounts, more than double by others – it was at school dances (Caulfield Grammar or its sister school, Shelford, a Church of England Grammar school for girls), barbecues and parties.

Naturally, the band wasn't regarded as a long-term proposition so when school finished it never really 'split up' as such, since no-one was concerned about its future. Shortly after the final school year, in early 1976, Tracy Pew replaced Brett, who'd drifted away.

Tracy's parents split up when he was 15, and he went to live with his mother, Nancy, and sister, Fiona, then aged eight. Tracy learned clarinet at school for a couple of years and was apparently very good. He was also good at drawing – he'd take a subject or an image and give it an unusual twist; for example, his character 'Edward' with his hands tied behind his back to a log, which strained the gag in his mouth, on his knees with a tear in his eye before a woman in stockings and stiletto heels, or what could be a self-portrait gazing at his own image in a mirror, the boy with no face, whose t-shirt is torn but the rips don't match the mirror image.

Nancy Pew: "First Tracy began talking about it, then he went out and bought this fellow's bass. He'd go and see 'the schoolboy band' with his girlfriend before he joined them. They used to practise out in my shed, and they weren't too bad about the noise. I think the Caves got the worst of it, they used to be down the back in their garage."

Phill: "I'd known Tracy for a long time, he was always in

trouble at school. He was always pushing things a little and he was a very smart guy.

"Tracy certainly had an incredible capacity for knowledge. He was well-versed in literature, and he had a good frame of reference on music. He didn't channel his musical listening tastes into what he thought he should be listening to, and he liked things because he was Tracy and he bloody well liked them. He certainly liked to drink, he was into drugs to a degree but in a very minor way. He was very much into his girlfriends.

"He didn't need to practise his instrument, he just played it when he needed to, and through that he got good. He was a bit rough and tumble, but inside he had a heart of gold . . . and I miss him very much.

"When we first started, all we wanted was to play gigs, our own music, and have people go, 'Yeah, this is good music', enjoy what we were doing and come and see us."

Tracy was an interesting addition to the band; intelligent and well-read, he fitted in well with the band's perception of themselves. His quiet personality belied a powerful will which rarely showed itself.

As 1976 developed, the band became less of an occasional hobby. Everyone had their own particular way of handling their personal situations which were later to become a part of the fusion reactor which fuelled the band.

Nancy Pew: "People seemed to like Tracy a lot, considered him a good bloke. He never made a point of showing how well read he was, he was a bit reticent about that. He did read a lot, I have hundreds and hundreds of books here that belonged to him. He kept things very much to himself, he was a bright child; when he was two he had an enormous vocabulary. You could have a conversation with him; he wouldn't talk at you, but with you. He was very interested in the world around him, and he used to talk to you about it. When the news came that John Kennedy had been shot it was about 7am, we were having breakfast. Tracy burst into tears and said, 'Why did somebody have to do that to him?' He was six at the time, you don't expect a six-year-old to have that understanding."

Phill: "Mick was in the band at school, but we felt Mick wasn't up to speed or interested or whatever, and so we replaced him with Ashley Mackevicious. Mick took lessons from Bruce Clark, a very good Australian jazz guitarist. Mick took what he wanted and turned it into his own thing. After an open-air battle of the bands at Mount Waverley, Mick came up and said 'I'd like to play with you guys again.' He had more drive than Ashley, so Mick was back in.

"After John Cochivera left, and after Mick had rejoined, when our 'Roxy Music' phase had died away towards the end of 1976, we were back down to me, Mick, Tracy and Nick. We had more of a cause to hook onto. The musicians of the future are the fans. That's how I became a musician. Most people I know in the industry became singers or guitarists or whatever after being the guys who thrashed about furiously and sweat themselves to death. Like Nick in the front row of Birdman gigs. We all used to do that. We'd dance like crazy."

As interest in the new music developed, long hair became passé, a badge of the stultifying old world. New music spoke of dumping such uniform tastes so the new men cut their hair short to appear different, thereby attaining acceptance within their own small but snowballing scene. The band followed suit.

They rehearsed during 1976, playing parties, barbecues, and a few gigs; sometimes turning up to ask if they could play. They didn't have a name, so when they were asked, whoever was around, often Nick, would come up with a spontaneous name and one of these, The Boys Next Door, stuck. From August 1977 they were The Boys Next Door. They outgrew the name fairly quickly, but it didn't seem to matter.

Phill: "The first gig was at a church hall in Ashwood. Mick's father was the Reverend. Mick organised it through the church's youth group. We'd rehearsed at the church hall in the adjacent rooms. Nick's sister Julie was there with some guys, and some skinheads turned up and they were making trouble, jostling people and so on. A fight broke out and Nick jumped off the stage and got involved because Julie was in there somewhere and he was trying to drag these guys off . . ."

Their support band was The Reals, comprising Nick's brother Peter on drums, Garry Grey on keyboards, Ollie Olson on guitar, and Tracy's best mate Chris Walsh on bass. When Ollie left The Reals became The Negatives with Mick Holmes on guitar.

The Boys Next Door began using the independent booking agency Nucleus, and tried out several short-lived managers. They were already playing music that warped into punk but they had an intuitive grasp of the complexity of creating a decent song, and they were intent on producing music of which they could be proud. Rehearsals were ongoing, a well-established part of their lives, and were taken seriously. The novelty of being in a band actually playing in front of people other than their mates, vanished fairly quickly.

Their dislike of established rock trends, which they shared with many of the English punk bands, was matched by a rowdy pop sensibility. Popular rock of the Seventies was regarded by the scene as top-heavy, derivative sloth, with little or no passion or relevance. But the Melbourne scene couldn't have numbered over 350 at this point.

The most influential Australian bands on the scene were The Saints and Radio Birdman. They shared a contempt for the dreadful tedium of suburban Australia, particularly The Saints whose passionate stance seemed to espouse casual violence. Their legendary live shows brought together many people with similar attitudes who would not otherwise have known about each other. Radio Birdman also brought people together in the same way, but their impact was different. With a stance one step removed from the immediate culture of 'Orstralia', they were a wildly thrashing band. The Saints had a threatening poise that Birdman did not but Birdman were important in the most simplistic sense: in your face, intense, immediate.

Phill: "The Boys Next Door were so good early on because we were involved with something people didn't want to be involved with. The people that wanted to be there gathered other people around them for support and strength, and they brought the crowds in. Mick got me onto Birdman, who were very important to me . . . Tracy once got arrested in Frankston with Rob Younger on the back and Deniz Tek on the front of his motor scooter."

Mick Harvey: "There used to be a lot of people who'd come to every gig. It stayed between 50 and 150 people turning up to our shows. If we started playing very well occasionally, it got up to 200, and then we'd play a bad show and it'd go down. It was really noticeable how, when we'd play well, playing three times a week, we'd start going through a good patch. We noticed that the audience had gotten bigger, and then we'd play a really bum show in front of 200 or 300 and all of a sudden no-one was at the next show; they'd decided we were woeful.

"The Melbourne audience was very faithful and remained

enthusiastic throughout, although over a period of time the audience changed, and it also depended on what area of the city we played. There were certain elements who remained faithful throughout the years when we were just playing around Melbourne."

Nick went to art school during 1976 and 1977, obtaining consistent 'A' grades for his work in the first year, and displaying the influence of Brett Whitely, a popular painter. He began experimenting with extremes of expression, including juvenile expressions of sexuality, and offended one of the art teachers. He found pleasure in forcing someone to witness an expression which they clearly disliked. During 1976 and 1977, art school and The Boys Next Door were equally important to Nick, but when the art school failed him at the end of 1977, the band became pre-eminent.

It was a time of emotional expansion and experimentation for the band. Although the mainstream Australian rock media treated 'punk' as novel and slightly loopy, The Boys Next Door took themselves more seriously, were more vigorous, more interesting and they caught more eyes. Among them was Rowland S. Howard who played with The Obsessions and wrote reviews for punk fanzines and *RAM – Rock Australia Magazine* – which started out as a rather sleazy Sydney-based national weekly underground magazine with Suzi Quatro on its first cover. In the late Seventies it grew from strength to strength, examining the scene in each major city, albeit comparing each to Sydney. Rowland liked The Boys Next Door, especially Nick, and in the February 1978 issue of the *Pulp* fanzine he described The Boys Next Door as "the best practising rock 'n' roll group in Melbourne".

They weren't a punk/new wave band. Although, like most of their contemporaries, they had borrowed inspirations and attitudes from English and New York punk, The Boys Next Door were firstly a rock 'n' roll band, playing to entertain the crowd, and later a band that followed its own nose, regardless of whether the audience might like it or not. They began to develop their own persona, their own codes, particularly Nick, whose performances became more dynamic and intense as he gained in confidence. They'd always enjoyed their crowds' response to them, and they began to experiment. An overriding need within the group was to inspire the audience to 'let go', to create as much chaos and drunken revelry as possible.

Rowland Howard: "I saw their second gig at Swinburne College of Tech, organised by Bruce Milne. I was supposed to be playing with The Obsessions but we didn't have a drummer, so it was The Reals, The Babeez and The Boys Next Door. I remember thinking that The Boys Next Door were very entertaining, but all they seemed to be doing was versions of Ramones songs, and 'Gloria', which went on for twenty minutes. Musically they were pretty woeful, but it was a spirited performance."

There is a much-bootlegged tape of this gig and it is obvious that the band are trying to provoke a reaction from the crowd. It was probably a fun gig, but the music is pretty dreadful. "Nick told me this was the best night of his life. He'd played a gig, got drunk and got laid," recalls Rowland.

Their third gig was on September 14 at The Tiger Room. "It was a cool, hip musos venue run by Laurie Richards, it was great," says Helena Glass.

Keith Glass: "I was playing a Wednesday night gig with The Living Legends at The Tiger Room in Richmond, and we were getting a crowd of gobbing punks who had nowhere else to go. We didn't play the music they liked, they used to spit at us and say, 'Play faster!' We'd have guest bands on because there was really nowhere for anyone to play.

"We were all five or six years older, which seemed like a lot. A friend of mine, Jenny Bakes, worked at the record shop I owned, Missing Link, and had her hair done next door at Merrivale, where Phill Calvert was a hairdresser. She said, 'My hairdresser Phill works in this band, maybe you can get them to play the guest spot on Wednesday night'. So Phill came to the shop and gave me an information sheet on the band, so I invited them.

"They brought along 40 of their friends so Laurie Richards was thrilled and gave them residency for about four months, before the 'new wave' people outnumbered the 'old wave' people, when we said, 'We'll go and play somewhere else'.

"Laurie Richards offered them more gigs, too. They were pretty embryonic, but I was impressed by Nick, who had an Elvis sorta thing about him; they had a really good sense of humour and didn't give a shit about much at all, it seemed. They were trying to create their own clichés, but trying to avoid the obvious clichés of the time.

"The whole thing sort of grew from there, and the Suicide label developed out of that whole Tiger Room scene. We're talking maybe 100 people a week showing up. It wasn't a big deal, and it was very opportunistic of Barrie Earl, an old-style rock 'n' roll-type, to pick up on it. It was a very cynical exercise, him going to Mushroom and saying, 'Hey, we can make a few quid out of this, let's do a rip-off of a punk label *à la* Stiff Records'. They grabbed all these bands and recorded them at Alan Eaton's studio for a week and bunged them all out, with stupid gimmicks like chewing gum."

Helena: "Keith was immediately impressed with Nick, and, in his fervour to realise the band's potential, perhaps ceased to think clearly about the other parts of his own life. A lot was sacrificed on the altar of this cult. Keith and I were older than the band, we had a parental image; they thought we'd supply all their needs *now*!"

Michael Gudinski's Mushroom Records gave the go-ahead to set up the new subsidiary label, Suicide. Mushroom bands used the Premier booking agency, and The Boys Next Door made use of what was on offer.

The concept of 'Australian rock', The Easybeats and The Seekers notwithstanding, was largely a contradiction in terms until Mushroom Records, owned by Gudinski, helped make the idea acceptable to Australians. Until bands like Skyhooks, Daddy Cool and Sherbet became popular in the earlier Seventies, rock was made overseas and distributed locally. The Seekers were a fluke, The Easybeats a forgotten fad.

In England, where punk was now attracting a lot of press, major labels were snapping up punk acts in a frenzy so as not to miss out, and making quick profits in the process. So Mushroom checked their local gig guides, contacted a few bands they thought were punk enough and put a contract in front of them. There was a minor furore over the contracts, which held all participants, including The Boys Next Door, to a 'future publishing rights' deal, but it could have been much worse. Those recorded were Teenage Radio Stars, JAB, X Ray-Z, The Boys Next Door, (Brisbane's) Wasted Daze, The Survivors and The Negatives.

They recorded their tracks around October/November 1977. Greg Macainsh, the bass player and the prime mover in Skyhooks, produced The Boys Next Door tracks, loaning Tracy his 'naked female torso' bass.

Apparently other record companies had been interested in

signing The Boys Next Door, but not the other 'Suicide' bands, or the punk movement. In order to distance themselves from punk, they began to dress more sharply on stage, wearing suit jackets, ties and shirts.

Barrie Earl became their manager, and tried to guide them towards his idea of what a band needed to be to gain credibility and support. Premier Artists booked most Mushroom bands, and they toured with their 'label-mates' to the outer suburbs and large towns, like Geelong.

Earl's approach was 'complete control' over the band to effect the most favourable impression, but the bands felt pressured to record what the company wanted to hear – nothing too offensive – which missed the point. The Boys Next Door recorded 'Lethal Weapons' but they had stronger songs which could have been used. 'Secret Life', 'Conversations', 'Sex Crimes' or 'Success Story' would all have had a greater impact on the potential audience and represented the band more accurately. They were lucky to have made such an important mistake so soon.

Phill: "If we hadn't done the 'Lethal Weapons' thing, we wouldn't have taken such a strong 'let's do our own thing' stance, and we wouldn't have reached the stage we ended up at."

Keith: "We were at some function, Tracy got down on all fours behind Gudinski, and Nick walked up to him and went, 'Hiya Mike!', and pushed him in the chest. Gudinski went completely over backwards and just about broke his neck."

Despite their reputation for violence they weren't all that violent.

Shane Middleton, their roadie: "They were a bunch of pussies. They're all private schoolboys, a bit like Hugh Grant. Upper middle class, close to peerage, don't know the seamy side of life. In a popular movement, you adapt your looks and behaviour to fit in. That's what they all did."

Phill: "After 'Lethal Weapons', we made some decisions about what we would and wouldn't do and on what levels we would and wouldn't do things. It wasn't laid down like the Magna Carta, just understood. We cut our losses, and went forward."

So far, Nick had been writing most of the band's songs; twisted social commentary anthems with little or no personal sentiment, as if to deny any personal feelings. After Rowland Howard joined, Nick began to concentrate on material focusing more on personal responses, feelings, moods, dilemmas and emotions. Until then, he wrote some pretty strange songs, funny but impersonal, including 'Earthling In The Orient' and 'Spoilt Music', which Rowland describes as being like "a manic polka with falsetto backing vocals".

In February 1978, they played Rundle Mall, Adelaide.

Paul Slater, a fan: "The Boys Next Door were more punk, certainly better than the other bands. They were a lot more interesting to watch. Nick Cave jumped around, shook, danced an awful lot. He attracted the crowd's attention with his constant dynamic motion. Because of this, rather than the noise they made, they attracted a lot more people who watched them with evident enjoyment. No-one danced to them; everyone was pretty intent on watching the band. Phill Calvert was really sharp on the drumkit.

"I remember looking at the set list . . . 'The Laughing Dogs', 'I Need A Million', 'Big Future', Alice Cooper's 'I'm Eighteen' was on there. 'Sex Crimes' was funny. Nancy Sinatra's 'These Boots Were Made For Walking', 'Masturbation Generation', 'Can't Do It', 'Funny, Isn't It?', 'Who Needs You', 'World Panic' and 'Boy Hero'.

"The usual rock 'n' roll line up, but they made a pretty big sound with it. The police ordered the power to be pulled for playing 'Masturbation Generation', and Nick had to reintroduce it as 'Frustration Generation', but sang it with the proper lyrics anyway, which was hilarious. The police didn't seem to pay any attention."

Mick: "I remember the police stopping it. I don't remember them asking us to change anything about what we were playing other than the volume."

Dave Graney, a pop singer: "The Boys Next Door were the sensation, they were full of ideas and they looked so great. I'd moved to Adelaide from Mount Gambier; they all looked very exotic to me. I was addicted to reading overseas rock magazines, so I could see a lot of things. Mick had a fantastic Rickenbacker guitar, and they weren't fashionable in oz-rock at all. That was like, John Lennon or The Byrds. Phill had on this wacky piano-key shirt, with the keys down the front. Tracy Pew looked great, playing this semi-acoustic bass.

"They were doing quite long, elaborate songs, like 'Earthling In The Orient', and 'Masturbation Generation'. The police always felt obligated to go up to the rock group and tell them to turn it down, and there'd be this cheap drama. The crowd would listlessly watch, and the singer would have to, y'know, deal with it, and we'd check out what the singer would do in this situation. Of course, they couldn't do anything, they'd have to turn it down. Tracy and Nick were up on this balcony '*sieg heiling*' at the police; it was quite funny."

Mark M, a fan: "Nick was so dynamic, always striking a pose. He wore eyeliner, which made his body look more emaciated and scarecrow-like than ever, nattily dressed in a suit and white shirt and no tie. He'd look elevated, helpless, enraged and finally alien by stages.

"Mick was a pretty cool guitarist, he obviously liked the idea of pushing his range of expression as far as he could. Mick got into the songs quite a lot, lashing out at the sound like he'd never get the chance again.

"Tracy looked like a young schoolboy out for the night with his suit jacket, tightly knotted tie and collar askew. He'd play almost without effort, slipping in with the band easily, but there was always something about him. He seemed occasionally distant. His bass sound was kinda funky, tough and sinewy.

"Phill set a cracking pace behind the kit, always checking out Tracy's lines and clocking the crowd – what or who was he always looking for? Nick? Tracy? His place in the song? Nick, the perfect antagonistic young rake, would abandon the mike stand and use it as a prop, like Mick Jagger or James Brown. He'd twist and wrench himself into each song, contorting his on stage self to express the importance of the lyrics . . . although I thought his performance overshadowed any of the lyrics."

Jo C, sales manager: "I've got vivid but hazy memories of Tracy looking so dapper and cool; he was very prominent, he didn't keep to the background.

"Mick used to have this great sinister snarling guitar sound that just rushed over the crowd. He'd do these inventive solos within the songs; he was a very busy and strong presence on stage. Same with Phill, but you never see a drummer. I was often close enough to notice him, and he laid down a rhythm with a vengeance. He was a great drummer and still is.

"Nick moved a lot on stage. He created this strange comic persona; at times he moved almost like a vulnerable puppet might. He'd shake spasmodically, buck in the middle like a hinge with his fists clenched, stand up, shake again, and then stop, looking vaguely stunned. I recall one night Nick wearing a handcuff on each wrist with the chain cut, as if he'd just escaped from a remand centre or something, but wearing a bow tie and a suit of some description. That juxtaposition was very funny. At the time I thought of The Boys Next Door as a gutsy, stylised glamour-influenced band wrapped in a spiky cloak of danger."

Dave Graney: "They were always rivetting performers, they were fantastic to see, they stood out from the rest of ozrock in Adelaide. Adelaide wasn't large enough for someone to cultivate a mysterious, tubercular side to their character."

Other songs in their set included 'Maybe Zone', 'Joyride', 'Conversations', 'All This Fuss', 'Secret Life' and 'Success Story', 'Show Me A Sign', The Velvet Underground's 'Caroline Says'. I think 'Can't Do It' and 'Who Needs You' were Mick Harvey's.

Rowland recalls that Nick sold 'Big Future' to older Australian musician, Ross Wilson, for a stubby of beer.

Rowland: "Nick told me how Anita had stayed at his house, and, coming back to his room from a shower, she was reading his words to 'Joyride'; 'People down in the city square/They're losing their minds and they're losing their hair/Yeah yeah yeah', and he was mortified that she was laughing at them, saying 'This is stupid'. He then went out of his way to write to impress Anita; the band was becoming more than a joke and a hobby, and it hadn't been necessary for him to apply himself seriously before. Suddenly Nick was meeting people who expected more of him."

From December 1977 to June 1978 Rowland was in The Young Charlatans alongside Janine Hall, Ollie Olsen and Jeff Wegener. They made a considerable and important impact on both the Sydney and Melbourne scenes, breaking up after about fourteen gigs, ten or eleven in Melbourne.

Mark: "They were pursuing a form of music which had been largely unknown in Australia, and most of the people who saw them liked them immediately, their attitudes and approach to their music were extraordinary. A type of open-ended acceptance of things, coupled with a dislike of routine for the sake of routine."

Mick: "The Young Charlatans were quite popular. They could've done really well if they'd stuck it out a bit longer. They should've made a record; they would have made a great record; it would have been a cult thing."

The Young Charlatans had a significant effect on the developing scene, walking several steps away from generic punk and introducing a striking power and approach previously unheard in the decade of Australian plod-rock.

Mark: "'Shivers' was the only song released by the band (on Fast Forward #8 cassette magazine), and was not what they sounded like. In comparison with their other material, 'Shivers' is fairly sedate and pedestrian. You had to be there to see the different directions all ripping at each other. They played some astonishing songs."

Ollie Olsen formed Whirlywirld, and is still an active performer; Jeffrey Wegener and Janine Hall joined The Laughing Clowns.

Mick: "All these bands started off in Melbourne at the same time, and there is, although I don't get involved with it, a very strong level of competition between the people who started off at that time. In the late Seventies there was a very bad competitive streak. It can be healthy, but usually it isn't."

Phill: "Most of the other bands in town were either not as keen to play as much as we were, or not as good. We wanted to play, and we figured that people wanted to see us, and it was a lot better than rehearsing."

'Lethal Weapons' had an immediate, chastening effect. Ashamed and angry at the way in which they had been manipulated so effortlessly, they wanted atonement, to demonstrate that there was more to them than throwaway tracks. Unable to gauge public response, partly because there was so little of it, and self-conscious over such a public mistake, they were embarrassed about the record and the false impression it gave of them.

As a result they began to concentrate more closely on a musical direction that reflected their interest in progressive/art rock, artists like Bowie, Roxy Music and Alex Harvey. But their most important influence was undoubtedly each other. They fed off each other's egos and weaknesses, picked up on what each was listening to, discarding what they disliked. It was a period of tremendous discovery and personal innovation. Ideas bounced about, forming cliques of musical intent which stewed for months at a time; fans of Lee Hazelwood, Nancy Sinatra *and* The Stooges!

Individual rediscovery of old records and soundtracks, mixed with the flow of ideas and concepts picked up from friends led to a frenetic burst of confused creative activity. Music wasn't the only means of expression. Apart from Nick's interest in art, there exists an unfinished film, apparently based on The Doors' clip for 'The Unknown Soldier', made by Tracy, Mick, and Nick.

After 'Lethal Weapons', some bands received more assistance than others. The Melbourne scene split into various camps, almost 'the bands who'd signed', and 'the bands who hadn't'. The News (previously The Babeez) had refused to sign an offered contract, yet they were undoubtedly a viable proposition in terms of a larger market.

There was more to this than petty jealousy, and other divisions on the scene developed over the ensuing years. Some felt that their creativity and ability had been bypassed, and crucial lines were drawn in the dust for the boys from the wrong side of the Yarra to spit over.

Those linked with experimentation and socio-political subversion were on one side, and those more concerned with a combination of expressionism and sheer hedonism on the other. No prizes for guessing which faction group The Boys Next Door were in.

Phill: "At first I drove our gear in my car. Then the gear lived in Nick's parent's garage. Either Shane Middleton would cart the gear or, later, the Nunna boys would shift it about. We'd finish a gig, load the gear into the van with the Nunna boys, off their brains from dancing all night into an absolute sweat, and drive off to some party. We'd consume more piss, then drive the van back to Nick's parent's place at four in the morning, trying not to let the dog out, y'know, put all the gear in the garage 'very quietly' and roar away into the morning."

By 1978, Radio Birdman and The Saints were derided for their mythological roots (rock 'n' roll as explosive device) and for taking the 'easy way in', although their popularity continued to grow.

What else was happening? US bands were making more of a mark: Pere Ubu's 'Modern Dance', and then 'Dub Housing', Devo, Suicide. Blondie toured in 1978 with some success, and at the end of 1978 burst into the mainstream with 'Plastic Letters' and their huge disco single 'Heart Of Glass'. The Voidoids, Television, The Cramps, Talking Heads, Patti Smith, The Ramones as well as legends like The Velvet Underground and The Doors. All this was part of The Boys Next Door's music library.

Inevitably ambition outstripped ability, and the 'Suicide' bands slowly split up. As attitudes and cliques hardened, more distinctive rivalries developed, mirroring the scene itself, which attempted to force its differences and identity on the gawkish crowd surrounding it. The vague idea behind it was to effect a change in moral attitude, the consequences of which weren't well thought out. But it was a great prank, in that typical Aussie shit-stirring-deadpan-pseudo-savage-macho-outlaw tradition.

The Boys Next Door had established their musical policy of frequent change and adaptation fairly early on, and their skill at altering their textures of sound always challenged their audience. Australia's limited music press was unprepared for the abruptness of that change. The band pushed against creative limits without regard for the needs of the audience, much less the tender skin of the Aussie rock critic. They felt the audience should love what they were doing for its very self, rather than loathe it because it was new and alien.

Playing more frequently during 1978, they took a residency on Saturday afternoons at the Crystal Ballroom in St Kilda. Inevitably The Boys Next Door encountered the drug/art culture centred around St Kilda.

The Crystal Ballroom was a hotel, not a pub, adopted by the scene, who formed a sizeable chunk of the bands who played there. There was a dining room where a classical quartet played in the evening, a chandeliered ballroom where the main bands played and a small lounge where other bands could play as a warm up. Each band had a room and people would wander from one band to another. An atmosphere of middle-class manners decayed into seedy, intellectual squalor.

Helena: "The Ballroom was a fabulous moment in Melbourne's cultural history."

St Kilda was a lively area of Melbourne near the beach, with a reputation as a nightspot for those seeking out extremes. The scene wandered into an area already inhabited by prostitutes, junkies, backpackers and alcoholics. St Kilda was a melting pot, and the band dived in.

It was a very attractive area visually, although no-one respectable wanted to live there, as it was perceived as too down-market. St Kilda had venues where a poor band could play, along with cheap rent, an alternative cinema and several cheap second-hand book and clothing shops.

Rowland and Genevieve McGuckin would often sift through rubbish and find German identity papers and the belongings of the recently deceased. Most of those who lived there appeared to be German Jews and European refugees. In cafes and bars people exchanged horrific stories of fleeing Nazi Germany.

It would have been unusual for The Boys Next Door not to mingle with this strange culture and they soaked up its rich, cosmopolitan fumes as eagerly as they embraced the general hedonism of the times.

Ross Waterman: "I was at an age where you went out and saw bands, and there were so many good bands around. But something had to be particularly brilliant to sustain my attention . . . I wasn't going along to listen to just anything, I was searching for something that strongly affected me. From day one, it was bloody obvious that The Boys Next Door, their music and particularly Nick's voice, was leaps and bounds ahead of anything else around at the time. Nick was up against some pretty stiff competition . . . La Femme, Bohdan X, Jab, and The News."

Andrew Browne: "The bands were really young. The Teenage Radio Stars were all 20 or under. I remember Molly Meldrum on *Countdown* promoting the whole Melbourne 'new wave scene' and The Teenage Radio Stars. But The Boys Next Door always seemed to be trying something a bit more serious, attempting to push things a bit further; not necessarily to please their audiences.

"The audience was mostly middle-class kids who'd moved into the city; to St Kilda or wherever. People were conscious of being different and individual so they enjoyed bands that tried to be more artistic or creative in what they were doing. So you'd see the same group of people in the audience all the time. They were all into music, painting, lots of diverse interests."

Such was the province of The Boys Next Door, where they began their development into the somewhat schizoid creature called The Birthday Party. Dedicated to artistic expression, and to experimentation, they wanted it all . . . now!

One of the great Australian pastimes is 'shit-stirring'. It takes many forms, usually remarks or written statements which are moderately inimical, often deliberately confusing or plain insulting. Nick,

Rowland, Tracy and Mick all practised this. In the best shit-stirring the victim cannot win. The degree of damage inflicted depends entirely on the savagery with which the game is played. It's a cruel game, but it establishes a power-based relationship between people. The Birthday Party was very much a power-based relationship.

In such a competitive atmosphere, a game of constant one-upmanship can be practised to the detriment of honest, open communication. Depending on the situation, it can result in a tragic end to a friendship. Shit-stirring is also linked to the Australian concept of mateship. It is impossible to imagine The Boys Next Door or The Birthday Party, or indeed The Bad Seeds, without this convoluted concept within the working structure of the band.

The punk ethos that Nick, Tracy and Rowland adopted also embraced a musical direction that was becoming more codified; increasingly a reflection of their immediate surroundings. They were the 'decadent European bohemians' located in Melbourne. Then there was Nick's deadpan delivery.

Ross: "I went to a party at the Cave residence in Caulfield. After staying the night, I continued to stay with my friend there for two weeks. During that time I saw The Boys Next Door at the Victorian College of the Arts. I was knocked out, couldn't believe it. But I was able to see Nick as an individual before I knew about his musical talents, so when people got interested in him for his 'personality' – as reported by the press – I wasn't.

"I'd seen what Nick was like at home, and didn't have any preconceived notion of how he should behave. I'd see him zipping around the house; the thing that stands out the most is that he was such a funny guy, he had an amazing sense of humour, really perceptive . . . One day he was sitting in the lounge room writing, and to me it was just amazing that a person was sitting down in a lounge room scribbling notes; just being creative. For a little while I sat there and watched him, and then he got up and went to this little room.

"I heard him playing, so I followed him to this tiny room with a piano in the corner and stowed into another corner was this rickety-looking table. On the corner of the table was this four-foot-high clown which Nick had apparently made, sort of a bust, from the waist upwards.

"I'm standing there looking, and I thought 'If he's going to do that for a while, I'll make myself comfortable', so I went to sit on the corner of the table, which just collapsed, and this massive clown just fell to the ground; it was unfired clay, so it broke into a million bits. He didn't even stop what he was doing, he just looked over his shoulder and said, 'I always hated that fucking thing', and just kept on playing.

"That was his attitude, and in years to come I was to realise that that was very indicative of his attitude to things. I think Nick rejects something because he isn't satisfied with it. Even if other people like these things, that's not good enough, he has to do things for himself. He was quite happy to see a work of his smashed if he wasn't happy with it. Although it was a pretty awful clown, you could see the Expressionist nature of the clown, the happy clown, the sad clown, so you could see why he'd made it.

"Over the time I was there, I realised that Nick had a lot on his mind. This guy wasn't wondering what he was going to be doing that afternoon. One day I was looking through some photographs and he came in and said, 'They're no good'. This was the first time he'd actually started a conversation with me.

"I said, 'Well, I can see they're not so hot', and he said, 'These are much better', and he showed them to me. I realised at that stage that he liked having his photograph taken. He didn't just make judgements about himself in the photographs, but commented on the quality of the photograph and the overall effect. The photographs he showed me could have been blurred or whatever, but he was looking for the intrinsic quality within.

"He was never angry at anything the whole time I was there. All I remember him being was genuine, funny. He'd walk into a room and with a few lines people could be laughing. It wasn't just a 'ha-ha I've just told a joke' thing, but him being himself. Every time I've seen him on stage, he cracks me up, he's the ultimate comedic persona."

Nancy: "I knew a lot of the venues because I'd drop Tracy off and sometimes I'd pick him up, and there was always amps in the back of the car. I've carted them to universities, recording studios, gigs . . . none of the boys had cars at first, although Phill did buy one.

"Phill was always the most charming and the most delightful. He would always make a point of coming over and saying hello. The band used to call me 'Mrs Pew', and then I became 'Nancy' when they got a bit more sure of themselves."

* * *

'Lethal Weapons' was released in March 1978. Critical reaction was mixed, often dismissive, though most critics seemed to prefer The Boys Next Door. By this time, they'd changed their set completely, and Rowland began to join them at the Tiger Lounge to play 'Shivers' (slightly faster than the later recorded version) and a few other songs.

Ross: "Suddenly they weren't doing the familiar songs anymore, the ones that we hung out every week to hear. They'd made up a new set, and they didn't particularly care about what the audience wanted to hear, whereas I think most musicians think they're there to please the audience."

They toured the eastern states to promote the album; Adelaide, Tasmania, Melbourne and Sydney and a few outlying towns. Mushroom released their first single, 'These Boots Are Made For Walking' b/w 'Boy Hero'. 'Boots' was an alternative radio favourite. Much more Australian poppy/punk stuff was being made but 'Boots' was superior by far.

'Masturbation Generation' seemed simplistically punk, but it's more complex than that. 'Boy Hero' was an indication of the direction the band were heading in at the time of recording. New Romantic-ish, three years before Duran Duran. Poppy, with Mick's thoughtful, almost delicate, lyrics, it also became an independent radio favourite.

Phill: "Suicide was supposed to be like the Stiff Records of Australia. It didn't work because there wasn't a big enough audience to support it."

Home-grown punk was not chart material, and the album 'bombed', a lost cult landmark. The first 4,000 copies were pressed in white vinyl, but only 1,500 more copies were pressed in black. The scene mostly agreed it was an important record, an essential Australian purchase. Most Australian cult records were made by fairly well-established bands who'd never had the luck to be signed to a major.

The point was made in some circles that Suicide was ripping off the artists concerned. The principal claim was that the label tried to monopolise all 'alternative' music for itself while keeping a chunk of the profits. No competition means maximum profit. If the movement took off, the label had all the 'punks' under contract.

'Lethal Weapons' succeeded in typecasting alternative music in Australia, playing a significant role in the development of this music over the next few years. Few bands or individuals linked to that record continued in music, but it did give the bands national exposure which they never would have had without affiliation with a major.

In June 1978 The Boys Next Door recorded 'Brave Exhibitions' for Suicide. Of the 12 songs recorded for this album, six would subsequently appear on the first side of the later 'Door, Door' LP. The lost songs were 'Secret Life', 'Sex Crimes', 'Conversations', 'Earthling In The Orient', 'Spoilt Music' and a Rowland and Nick duet which "absolutely horrified the engineers" (RSH), consisting of Rowland enthusiastically but inexpertly pounding the piano with Nick singing something quite possibly improvised over the top.

Mick: "Some of the songs weren't too bad; we just decided at the time which songs, maybe mistakenly, were the best."

This recording was more representative of what the band was currently playing, but the attitude within the band at this time was that they felt that they had generally lost their direction. It took the entrance of Rowland S. Howard to rejuvenate their creative juices.

Phill: "In December '78 we went to Sydney with JAB for a tour, leaving after two sets at Melbourne's Bombay Rock, driving two station wagons. Crime opened for us at Blondies, and they were a pretty cool bunch. I remember Nick picking up a lot of Simon's expressive gestures, like burying his head in his arms. They broke up shortly after, and Simon and Harry changed the line-up (Crime II) after they came down to Melbourne around May or June 1979 and picked up Kim, the saxophone player, and a keyboardist.

"Any band we liked, we gave support work to, like The Laughing Clowns or The Go-Betweens. That way our bill had bands that we liked on it. That's the way you honour a band the most. You don't want a shitty band on your bill so you can blow 'em offstage, you want a good band to add to the atmosphere, to say 'we give this band our stamp of approval, 'cause this is what we like'."

Mark: "A mixture of guitar noise blended together like warm fuzz intercut with sparkling, jazzy sax which was just totally unheard of. Each song was unique, distinct. Concentrating on the music and each song . . . well, the band demanded a certain amount of attention from the audience. Simon seemed to be interjecting his lyrics when it felt appropriate, rather than having a set musical order."

Mick: "I think Crime And The City Solution had the most impact on The Young Charlatans and The Boys Next Door. Not many people showed a lot of enthusiasm for Crime . . ."

Quite taken with Simon's unique approach to performing and song writing, Crime And The City Solution made an important impact on Nick, Rowland and Mick. Lyrically and physically loose, the songs appeared to flow from Simon's soul, semi-structured and flexible, the centrepoint of converging emotions, expressed by musicians more bent on interfering with the songs than keeping them rock-steady.

Rowland remembers Simon's performances with the first two Crimes and comments that "both Simon and Nick saw things in each other that they wanted to be"; that Simon's movements on stage were very different to what he was to do later with Crime III. He apparently moved in a "semi-flamenco, balletic manner, which looked uncontrived and as if Simon were entranced".

It was later suggested that Nick had 'copied' Simon's on stage style. Not true. Nick was influenced by Simon (the 'Shivers' clip – the way Nick behaves with his arms is pure Bonney), but had been inspired by Simon's realisation of some mutual attitudes towards performing – that being on stage and singing is a performance, that a gig can be an event; a performer has more free rein than the confines of either the gig or a song.

Nick did not take to Simon's yearning, melancholy sensuality. Listening to the second side of 'Door, Door' is revealing for those who hold the 'copycat Nick' view, but Rowland had great influence on that side and the band's next few releases would reveal a wide variety of different influences.

The Boys Next Door had a five-year deal with Mushroom/ Suicide. The booking agency Dirty Pool offered The Boys Next Door a deal which would see them touring the country supporting other more established artists in the Dirty Pool stable. Had they taken this option they might have become marginally more popular, but wide exposure to potentially hostile crowds in unfamiliar territory would have pressurised them to tone down their repertoire, to 'please the crowd' and the industry.

The offer came at a time when they were in a state of flux. Prior to Rowland actually joining, they were tinkering with more modern, serious pop. When Rowland finally joined, the band twisted and squirmed. Rowland's manner of writing could either be intensely personal or utterly detached; sometimes, from the point of view of the listener, it is difficult if not impossible to tell the difference.

While many find 'Shivers' emotional and relate intimately to the song, it was actually an attempt by Rowland to write the most commercially acceptable song he could. The first couplet is evidence of this banality: "I've been contemplating suicide/But it really doesn't suit my style". The manner in which the song is sung makes the subject matter quite plausible, but no-one depressed enough to commit suicide would decide against it because it might not live up to their image; when people suicide it's because they want to die.

"I was feeling my influences; Rimbaud, for example," says Rowland. "Tracy used to mock me mercilessly and I was generally considered pretentious."

'Shivers' is acutely ironic, drawing power from its delicacy and precision in the wavering morality, but it's not without humour of the 'black' or 'absurdist' kind. Juxtaposing seriousness with trivia is a familiar device in comedy. There is definitely a nod towards Lee Hazelwood here.

David Gerard, a writer/editor: "I always thought of 'Shivers' as a hilarious and spot-on depiction of a shallow scenester on any 'arty' scene."

This deliberate chuckle at the inevitability of life and death, the ridiculousness of human behaviour, became something of a misunderstood trademark for them. Pretentious? Sure! But it *worked.*

The Boys Next Door were insular in a street-gang way, outgoing in all ways apart from having unintentionally isolated themselves from a larger potential audience very early on. Their contempt for the ordered world of the conservative rock biz, which begun in earnest around May/June 1978, merely isolated them even further.

Rowland: "There was always anger directed against the band, but after I joined it was more blatant; people suddenly regarded us as 'art-house' dilettantes. People who used to like the band *hated* the band after I joined. They'd call out for 'Boy Hero' and we wouldn't do it, and they'd come up to us afterwards and say, 'You think you're just fucking great, don't you? We're your fans and we're asking you to play this song, and you can't fucking do it!' They were just incensed, because Australian rock bands used to play what the audience wanted them to.

"The big difference between what we did and a band like Whirlywirld was that we'd progress very quickly from one thing to another, but it was a very natural, organic shift. Whereas Whirlywirld would go, 'Okay, now we're *this*.' "

Paul Goldman, film-maker: "A lot of people perceived The Boys Next Door as being like that, slavishly copying things from overseas; they didn't see that they were shifting organically at all. In my immediate circle of friends, I would get so much shit from people, and I would spend all night justifying them and people just couldn't see it. They'd think the band were copying this stuff from England; look at the way they dress; they're pretentious, stuck-up, smug bastards."

Rowland: "We were! But the way we dressed around the time of 'Door, Door' predated the later New Romantics in England. We wanted to get away from punk and its constrictions."

From the outside, The Boys Next Door were becoming increasingly like a strange creature in a zoo – fascinating to watch, but you wouldn't want one in your home. A bit too disturbing. Blame Rowland for bringing out the latent art-thug in the rest of the band.

Nick had already focused his lyrics towards extremes of behaviour ('Sex Crimes') in his own wickedly funny manner. Rowland's material sparked more of a direction for Nick, bringing an ironical, blackly humorous outlook into sharper relief. Rowland does comment, "we were all fucked up in those days."

The usual aim of music is to communicate using a recognised set of linguistic codes. The Boys Next Door were attempting a form of communication, but they weren't satisfied with the set of codes being used. So they began to use aspects of other codes, and many thought they had little to offer. They were rightly considered pretentious – but without an artistic pretension to achieve a unique form, that form would seldom be reached. To educate the public would give the game away, destroy the urban enigma before it had a chance to fester into a social confusion.

Adding another member had been on the cards for a while, and although Ian 'Ollie' Olsen was under consideration at one point –

he was Nick's original choice according to Phill – Rowland joined the band around late August or early September 1978. As they developed they met Rowland's implicit creative challenge, and upped the stakes of the game by not immediately absorbing him. For a long time, Rowland felt like an outsider.

Rowland: "Before I was in the band I could never understand why everyone was so rude to Phill, because he seemed inoffensive and nice enough. When I joined the band I was nice to Phill, and I was the only one in the band who was nice to him a lot of the time, and he treated me with contempt. As I responded to him in kind, the nicer he became. It's difficult to treat someone with respect when they don't treat themselves with respect. He had the unfortunate habit of saying the wrong thing.

"For example, Phill was driving me, Nick and Tracy to St Kilda or something. I think Nick and Tracy were drunk, and they gobbed on the inside of the roof of his car, and Phill said, 'Hey, guys, don't do that, this isn't my car'. So their immediate response was to gob all over the interior of the car. Now, if he'd left it at one gob, it would've stopped a lot quicker, but because of his interjection, it carried on for a long time, ten minutes or so. It was pretty vile. It wasn't uncommon for us to be extremely cruel to anyone who'd allow us to be cruel to them, but people have to play a willing part in that game."

Mick, although an equally noisy and probably more competent guitarist, adopted a different approach. Instead of competing with Rowland, his guitar shovels the whole racket forward, like an Eskimo whipping a team of huskies. The dogs can't hear the driver too well over the rush of the sled and the noise of their own progress, but they are constantly aware of the driver's urgency.

Rowland introduced several guitar devices, including an octave divider which gives the guitar a much fatter sound. Rowland recalls that some new ideas were resisted quite vigorously by the band, like Tracy showing up at rehearsal with a 6-string bass with a tremolo arm. Mick told him to "get rid of it"; presumably it was 'too rock 'n' roll establishment'.

Rowland was as interested as Tracy in experimenting in any way possible, so he told Mick that he was going to buy a guitar with a tremolo arm. Mick was "amused but horrified", but the sound Rowland produced silenced the doubt.

Rowland: "Prior to me joining, they were much more 'straight' in direction. I was brought in by Nick, and I superceded Mick's position; all of a sudden, I was the guitarist, and Mick . . ."

Paul Goldman: "Mick would spend more time at the side of the stage playing his dinky little synthesiser."

Rowland: "And that must have been hard for him, but his reaction was 'I don't care. I'm not looking for attention. I don't care if I don't get to play in the songs, if I don't get to play guitar, I don't care if someone else sings all the backing parts because I'm just happy for the group to be as good as it possibly can be.' But of course he fucking cared."

Phill: "Rowland brought a fistful of good songs, a lot of new material, which gave us things to feed off. He gave us stuff we agreed and disagreed with. There was already a healthy respect between Nick and Rowland, and it gave us a good lift.

"He also affected the decision to record another side of songs for the album, because we couldn't represent the band like that; Rowland's influence had to be represented. He added a lot to the band, but I think once he was there, fulfilling the initial role he was intended to, he just couldn't keep up with the pace of where Mick and Nick were going."

Rowland: "There were songs of mine that we did that never made it onto record; there was a whole period of the band's song writing that also never made it onto record, such as 'Mouth To Mouth', and my 'Grand Illusions', 'Whatever It Means', 'The Wrong Person', 'Mad About The Boy' and 'AKA'. The only Young Charlatans song we did was 'Shivers', although The Young Charlatans did do 'Whatever It Means' once."

Mick: "It's a shame we didn't record some of Rowland's songs properly. Nick responded well to the challenge of having another songwriter in the group. I think it affected his writing style somewhat. Maybe around late 1978 there was a change, 'cause we'd gotten more pushy."

Rowland: "Shortly after I joined the band, I think I led Nick in a direction that Tracy considered to be pretentious and ridiculous. Tracy's reaction to this was to immediately behave like a complete blundering oaf in direct proportion to us; however ridiculously fey and effete Nick and I became, the more earthy Tracy became. That led to him falling out of favour with the band for a while I think.

"Tracy came up with a couple of songs, too. I remember one which he presented around this time called 'Bound For Glory'. It was stylistically similar to 'Roman Roman', and Nick's 'Spoilt

Music' ("Einstein's theory of time and space/Never meant that much to me"). It was rejected by the band, I can't remember why; I think it was dismissed pretty much out of hand. It wasn't that what Tracy had come up with was bad, but it was out of step with what we were trying to achieve."

Robert: "Do you think Tracy wasn't encouraged to produce anything for the band?"

Rowland: "Yes. I don't think that that was how his persona was perceived. It was thrust upon him as much as anything else. But Tracy was . . . the first time I went round to his house, I walked in and there was beer cans all over the floor, *Playboy* magazines, and he was sitting there reading Plato's *Republic*.

"Tracy really didn't like people who overtly displayed their intelligence. Although he was a very intelligent person, he liked nothing more than taking the piss out of people whom he thought were being pretentious. But, when you'd least expect it, he'd come out with some incredibly intelligent comment."

Nancy Pew agrees, and can recall a visit to one of his earlier homes where she found a similar blend of girlie mags (kicked under the sofa), beer-cans and literature.

Genevieve McGuckin: "When Tracy wasn't drunk, he was a charming, witty gentleman who was interested in literature. As The Birthday Party went on, he just exaggerated himself, to the point where he looked like something out of The Village People."

Rowland: "He came to rehearsal one day wearing a balaclava in the middle of summer, and he was so drunk he was incapable of speech. I remember he walked in two hours late and he didn't speak to anyone, just very drunkenly unpacked his bass. We'd start a song and about 30 seconds later he'd join in, but from the beginning. When he finally took his balaclava off, he looked like a World War I flying ace. He'd had his head shaved up past his ears and parted in the middle; he'd started having his hair cut like that but had stopped half-way through, it was extraordinary. He had a very perverse attitude to the way he looked. He'd deliberately give himself haircuts and things which would de-emphasise the fact that he was really handsome. Girls always found Tracy really attractive.

"There was a period where Tracy was in extreme disfavour because he thought Nick and I were being incredibly precious, which we probably were, and he felt that it was his job to deflate us at any possible opportunity, and he'd act like the most moronic person alive, like cutting his hair in a way he knew we'd hate."

Nancy: "Tracy went through a stage where he gave up eating because he was a much bigger build than the rest of the band. He had enormous willpower, and he slimmed right down because he felt he was too big and muscular to be among them. Later, when they were in England, he must have decided to capitalise on what he had, and just be big."

Tracy was creative and intelligent, but within the band he was allotted only a thin stream of creative opportunity. Phill and Mick were able to contribute far more. Apart from drumming, Phill set up gigs and looked after the gear. Mick had a say in songs and arrangements, and contributed to what Phill was doing. Nick and Rowland wrote most of the songs, both sang and played an instrument. Tracy 'just' played his bass. Given his later success at university, Tracy probably felt creatively stifled within the band.

When Suicide fell apart, their contract defaulted to Mushroom. Undeterred, during late 1978 and early 1979, The Boys Next Door became more popular with the fringe element of the 'rock' scene. The music papers tended to ignore the band's potential and charismatic performances. But they wanted to be noticed, and they'd begun to be more aggressive, putting themselves in the public and media eye more frequently.

Paul Goldman: "I'd started to see bands during 1978. I got into the Swinburne Institute of Technology at the beginning of 1979, and I realised how important the band were. I identified very strongly with the aesthetic of the band. The Boys Next Door were different, they always tended to galvanise a reaction. They were the nexus for a whole lot of things going on. There was an enormous amount of opposition and very few people realised there was something important going on."

Ross: "Split Enz were playing a lot around the colleges and they were what people liked; wacky, but mainstream wacky, not seriously unhinged . . . the mainstream audience would see The Boys Next Door as wankers because they were attempting to do something creative."

The Boys Next Door could be seen at a pub where you'd pull up a seat in front of them and watch.

Andrew: "Yeah, at the London Tavern or Hearts, or at smaller places, you'd get a small crowd, 20 or so. A lot of bands played residencies, so a few people tended to go and see them regularly, but if The Boys Next Door were playing a big show at, say, the Crystal Ballroom, you'd get a lot more people going . . .

"When I first saw them, they struck me as being very self-conscious, attempting to be arty. Nick's movements, there was a lot of skipping around and these deft hand movements . . . You could see the influences of David Bowie and Roxy Music and so on. Rowland and Nick seemed to be at the centre; Rowland was doing some really great guitar, all of his early guitar was great.

"A lot of this ended up on 'Door, Door', but they were introducing more discordant elements. I was struck by their sound; they were the first band I saw in that era that was different to Australian rock music."

Phill: "We did a few covers: 'The New York Dolls' 'Personality Crisis' and Iggy Pop's 'China Girl'. We were playing to two men and a dog, a late afternoon show, doing 'China Girl'. With the line, 'I feel tragic/Just like Marlon Brando', Nick was crawling around on the floor with his shoe on his back, singing, 'I feel tragic/Just like Julius Marlowe'. (Julius Marlowe was a popular brand of shoe.)

"At the Rex Hotel in King's Cross in Sydney, there was a white piano on the stage, and one of the girls in the audience had these clear plastic slipper-type of things; y'know the plastic that makes your feet all sweaty? Nick got one of this girl's shoes, filled it with champagne and drank it out of the shoe."

Mark: "Many of the girls at their gigs used to wear black, dark and white contrasting make-up, an archetype of femininity and drop-dead serious horror movie attitude. As if they'd constructed identities that no-one could approach because they were so extreme."

Maria J, a fan: "A lot of what we were doing was perceived by the general public as somehow *wrong*, and although we were never stoned by an angry mob, some of the more edgier elements got aggro at us. Young blokes seem to need a target to exercise that chip on their shoulder, and with our dyed black hair and anti-good-little-girl make-up, we were yelled at and accosted a fair bit. We wore make-up, but we weren't pretty. The older blokes didn't tend to get too aggro unless they'd had a few beers.

"We'd show up to see the band and be surrounded by imminent hostility and distrust; although some of the people were really tolerant. I say 'we', but it was really me, a couple of friends and a bunch of other people who did likewise."

Helena: "Phill was the 'tryer' who made phone calls, picked up the equipment, had a car, picked up the other guys, hired the lights, got the gigs and did the slog-work."

Nancy: "Tracy said to me on a couple of occasions that it was always left to him and Phill to pack up the hired amps and return them."

Phill: "By late '78 we were using 'Groper' to run the truck and his P.A. Groper couldn't drive, so Shane used to drive the truck, so all the band would have to take home was their guitars; although in Tracy's case, he'd always say, 'Take the bass' – he only used it for rehearsal or a gig. Shane did lights and roadied for us until we left for England. Our crew worked very hard for us for very little money so the band could get to England.

"A drummer has to have a big enough car to hold the kit, and since you can squeeze in the amps and stuff as well, you can kinda end up being the roadie. I like to know things are right. It's very hard to just not bother, to walk on stage and presume that it'll all happen. Unless I have a killer crew, I will personally check all my equipment before I go on stage, otherwise I'm not confident that everything's how it should be. "

Keith Glass: "Missing Link was originally conceived in 1977 as a retrospective label which would issue material from the Sixties and Seventies which was no longer available. The first few releases were obscure Sixties bands, a collection of Melbourne rockabilly and a compilation of indie singles, but with the developments of a local music the label's policy changed and they signed up The Boys Next Door, Whirlywirld, La Femme, Laughing Clowns and many others. Along the way they had a surprise top ten hit with The Flying Lizards and licensed overseas releases from The Dead Kennedys, The Residents, Snakefinger and Young Marble Giants.

"The record shop was going well, so I was looking to release stuff on my label which mirrored what was going on, like Ian Olsen's Whirlywirld, which was the first record I put out in that area, in June 1979.

"I was always friendly with Phill; they'd done 'Lethal Weapons' which was a real problem for them because it had so many shortcomings. I felt that The Boys Next Door had more long-term worth, although there wasn't much evidence to show that they did. They seemed to have something that little bit extra."

Phill: "We were always interested in Keith's record store because it was a Mecca for import records. Missing Link had done promotional stuff for other bands, run gigs and so on, so we were interested in being tight with that. Also, our situation with Mushroom was in a real mess. We were forging ahead and making some really good music but no-one was supporting it apart from a small scene.

"I was working in the record store part-time and Keith came back from England in January or so, 1979. He took me aside and said, 'I want to talk to you'. We went and got a coffee, and he said, 'I want to manage the band and I want the band in England within a year'. 13 months later we flew out.

"We decided we wanted to make challenging, interesting new music just prior to Keith taking us on. We decided that we weren't going to do the older type of stuff, we were more into the post-punk thing."

Keith: "I was selling this stuff that nobody else was, and if we were to do any recording on Missing Link, then this was the area to get into. I said, 'Look, why don't I try to do something for you?', which was how I got into managing them.

"I went to Gudinski and said 'Look, I'm going to manage the band'. 'Shivers' was going to come out as a single, I said, 'Why don't we put a picture sleeve on it?' He said no. We did the cover, showed it to him, he still said 'No, the single's never going to sell'. Up to the end of vinyl that single was still in the Festival (distribution) catalogue; it wouldn't have been in there if it wasn't selling, and nothing else they released at the same time would have been."

Phill: "The Melbourne scene was getting challenging, we were developing more of a 'no rules' approach. It was like we were coming off a springboard at the end of punk. People were listening to Magazine and Siouxsie and The Banshees, and the totally bent stuff like The Red Krayola, Pere Ubu, The Pop Group and Captain Beefheart. There was also a pop sensibility, like The Gang Of Four, whose songs were totally aggressive but the tunes were really chirpy.

"That was also one of the reasons why we decided to take Rowland into the band. Mick was very much in favour of Rowland, and he did a lot of work teaching Rowland all our songs. I never got that friendly with Rowland because he hadn't been through all the other stuff that I had with the other guys; it took me a long while to get to know him.

"We would've kept gigging if Keith hadn't come along, because no Australian record company would've seen that what was going on in England was good for a band like us.

"After Keith became our manager the band got five bucks each per gig, and the rest of the money went in the bank for airfares. Even with the amount of touring that we did, we didn't make enough to do that, and Keith made up the shortfall; we had one-way tickets when we went to England. Keith sent us the money for the tickets to come back to Australia and organised for the gear to come back too."

Mushroom label mates Split Enz went to England in 1978. Well-known in Australia with a minor hit or two, they took their painted faces and clownish antics to the English, where they were received with bemusement and vitriol. In the face of such hostility, what response would the increasingly bizarre head-fucks of The Boys Next Door produce?

Phill: "The thing I like most about The Birthday Party is that we did it all pretty much on our own terms, although Keith helped a lot to get us into the situation where we could do it. Everything was more joyous when we left Melbourne. When things soured so much later, everyone kinda forgot how we got there in the first place."

Shane: "I was probably more attuned to what they were on about than they realised. They seemed to underestimate other people's abilities to understand what they were into. Had they been able to drop the pretence, they could well have become more successful than they actually were. I've never asked them if they ever wanted to be commercially successful; it takes a lot of hard work to be in that league.

"After Keith began booking their gigs, the Skyhooks connection was dropped with some relief. They also used independent booking agency Nucleus. From late January, when the Tiger Lounge shut down, they played a residency at The Crystal Ballroom, again under Laurie's management."

Paul Goldman: "David Thompson and I would talk to Nick about books, and two days later Nick would have the fucking book in his pocket, reading it. David and I were the best-read people I've ever met for our age at that period, and Nick would sit for hours listening to David talk about books; David was the first person to talk to Nick about William Faulkner in detail, and American gothic."

Nick's lyrics were now becoming more wilful, playful, more Dadaesque, and showing influences like Pere Ubu. Nick and Rowland were both good songwriters in their own right. Mick was writing less because Nick and Rowland wrote better songs. This upped the ante in the creative stakes. Nick and Rowland weren't at loggerheads, but would work off each other. This was a private, unofficial poker game amongst friends.

It was necessary for Nick to produce lyrics that would impress Rowland, and at the same time Rowland had to come up with a tune or interpretation of Nick's lyrics that would satisfy Nick. Rowland would come up with songs that Nick felt he could sing, Nick would sing Rowland's lyrics in a way that satisfied Rowland. An intense desire to better what they'd done before, to challenge themselves, seeped into their gigs.

Phill: "Mick had written songs besides 'Boy Hero', and Rowland wrote a lot of songs when he was younger. When he joined the band that really spurred Mick and Nick . . . this guy appears who's a prolific songwriter with ten great songs that really suited the band and we all wanted to do his songs. But after those ten songs, we got like two a year, although he did co-write with Nick.

"Nick's way is, 'Here's the bones and here's how it kinda goes', and then everyone has a good old whack at it, and you come out the other end with a song. Rowland would say, 'I've got this song; this is my part; Mick you go like this; Phill, play like this' – and he'd indicate a style or a feel."

Side Two of 'Door, Door' was recorded in January, at AAV in Bank Street, South Melbourne. Meanwhile, the band's set changed dramatically, and their direction, their metabolism, speeded up.

Tony Cohen: "They came to Richmond Recorders and I was the house engineer. They'd done the first side of 'Door, Door' and they were miserable about it. They filled up the grand piano with bits of metal; mike stands, paperclips, anything they could lay their hands on. They were waiting for the engineer to come in and just spew. I came wandering in, looked at it, and said, 'Ooh, that'll sound interesting'. They looked at each other and said, 'He'll do!' I'd formed an immediate rapport with them because I didn't growl at them. I was always willing to try something new."

Rowland: "One of the main problems we had with 'Door, Door' was that it wasn't done live. It was done bass and drum, one guitar at a time, then vocals. Mick and I, in our sheer stupidity, thought that that was the way you had to do it. While we were doing it, Nick was going, 'Can't we just record it like a band?', and we were knowledgeably going, 'No, Nick, you have to do it this way!', even though we knew absolutely nothing about it.

"Nick was completely right. The whole second side of 'Door, Door' wasn't live; the songs didn't really sound as precious as they do on the record."

Tony: "Apparently in their earlier recording, the producer had told Nick to enunciate, and Nick was horrified. When I was recording them I said, 'Just sing how you sing', which is the way I work, I let people express themselves how they do naturally. I learnt so much about what I do from all those years of having so much time to experiment."

Paul Goldman: "Keith always seemed to be in the studio. Once he went out at 3am to get Rowland a Telecaster, just so Rowland could get a sound."

Rowland: "I vividly remember Keith saying to us that 'You can't do this, it's too over the top; it's painful to listen to, you just can't do it', when we were doing 'Hee-Haw'."

Phill: "We did a lot of trying to push it to see how far we could go. We used to ensure that our P.A.s had a lot of horns, 'cause we liked to drive a lot of top end live; we had white lights pointing into the audience's faces. We were trying to cause an affront against the people who were watching, to see how much they would or could take at any one gig, and then see what you got back."

The same attitude spilled over into their private lives. They were playing a more challenging music, as well as gigging a lot more, often several times a week in front of receptive, friendly, regular fans. The wider public's reaction was so predictable, ranging from simple booing to the mute ignorance of a cold crowd on a national support slot. Occasionally the reaction was quite intense.

Ross: "That (early 1979) Skyhooks concert . . . what'd you play, five songs before you were kicked off?"

Mick: "Yeah, that was a bad decision by Greg. He got worried about how popular we were with the audience and got his roadies to get us off stage. Skyhooks weren't very popular and I think most of the crowd were there to see us."

Phill: "When we supported international 'new wave' acts it was because the touring promoter would say, 'Shit, we need a new wave band to support this new wave band, um . . . The Boys Next Door'!"

Rowland: "Nick was incredibly funny on stage in those days. He'd say the funniest things between songs, he'd improvise the lyrics to the songs, as much making fun of himself as anyone else, 'cause we were playing three times a week. We were playing at Bombay Rock, which was a horrible rock industry place, a singles bar, and everyone there hated us. The bouncers were all seething to kill us. These big Mediterranean, long-haired, pot-bellied retards with skin-tight flares had been heckling us or something, and ignited Nick's wrath.

"He said, 'Put the spotlight over there, over there on Fatty and his friends. Stand up, Fatty, let's all take a look at you', which the lighting guy did. And Nick proceeded to humiliate this guy and his friends . . . I can't remember what he said, but it went on for a very long time, and it was very funny and everybody in the place was laughing.

"They then colluded amongst themselves for revenge, and the best thing they could come up with was that they would pretend to forgive us, give Nick a glass of piss, and Nick would think it was beer. And he probably did. But when they held it out to him, he kicked it and it went all over them. We found out later that the glass had actually contained piss because somebody had seen them pissing into it."

Paul: "The only other person I've seen like that is Dave Mason of The Reels. He'd single someone out in the crowd and either humiliate himself or that person."

They gained a reputation for self-destruction and seemed to have an aversion to being accepted by a large group of people.

Rowland: "It never to occurred to us that we would be successful, and we knew that if we were to become successful, it certainly wouldn't be through Bombay Rock. There was no reason for us to be worried if we insulted the clientele there. Our motives for doing things were completely different from the motives of other people. The group was an extension of our lifestyles, our sense of humour, our whole world-view. If it had something to do with rock music, it was for different reasons to what had gone before. We took offence that people seemed to think that if you were intelligent, you had to act intelligent all the time, and that you had to be . . . consistent. What we thought was great rock music was full of contradictions and inconsistencies.

"Early on, we were all big fans of Bowie, Roxy Music, Alice Cooper and Alex Harvey who were all entertainers, but we wanted to take it a step further. We didn't want to take off our make-up when we got home, we wanted to be the same on stage as we were on the street, and if we acted differently it wouldn't be because we were putting on a show for people. There are a lot of flaws to what I'm saying because you do perform for people. But we were showing off a lot of the time on the street . . .

"It's hard to explain because we never talked it through that much, and until we left for England, we were very reliant upon each other. A lot of groups, like The Rolling Stones, look like gangs but aren't. We were a gang in the same way that, say, The Stooges looked like a gang and were a gang."

Well-accustomed to alcohol, some of the band also tried marijuana and speed on an occasional basis. Drugs were part of the scene and the lifestyle the band were pursuing. To make too much of it is to misunderstand the climate they were in. The illegality of it was a naughty-boy spur, the act of having to acquire them was in itself an adventure, exploring the forbidden and unknown.

Rowland: "Nick tried heroin sometime in 1979. Nick always drank and took speed a lot. He'd tried heroin a few times before introducing it to me through a friend who was a part-time user. Heroin came at the right time for me, and for an extended period of time I was able to take it on a daily basis, leading inevitably to a habit. The effects of speed and alcohol can be devastating in concentrated amounts, but since heroin lets you keep going and makes you feel good without apparent side-effects, it's easy to keep taking it if the supply is there."

The band toured to support 'Door, Door'. From April 1979 they were in the process of slowly shaking off the perception of art and rock being a deathly serious business, giving way to more earthy, baser instincts, and allowing more random elements to form an integral part of their music. But the more the boys pursued the music, the more challenging their situation appeared. They believed their music effected a powerful social reaction, partly on record, but definitely on stage. Their newer songs were more open, looser, and the group abandoned imitative rock for a more spontaneous, anarchic sound. Even their touring posters show the band elegantly wasted and thin.

The band would stuff up a gig or a promising prospect by being their own wayward selves. Their self-referential behaviour was not restricted to the stage.

Keith: "I was up the front of the plane, they were down the back. We were delayed for some reason, and Nick gathered up everyone's airline food and created this monster, came up to me and presented me with it, whacked it down on my tray, and there I am looking at this . . . mound. Everyone around me was quite startled, wondering what was going on.

"(Nick) is an idiot! But most people don't realise it. He's prepared to be a complete buffoon, and people don't get it, they think he's Mr Cool. But he's prepared to be a complete idiot. He is a complete idiot! He's been a complete idiot on stage for years. When I first saw them I thought they were the funniest band I'd ever seen. I used to have tears rolling down my face at performances, and all these people would be right into it! It wasn't a parody, but they had elements of every form of music in there, all these sorts of juxtapositions of images.

"I played them all this country music, Nick always liked Johnny Cash, the George Jones thing and the death song thing; Gene Vincent's 'Catman'. When I was a kid it was the scariest song I'd ever heard. 'What the fuck's a "catman"?' They grabbed that, they were grabbing things from anywhere and utilising them to their own purposes."

Rowland can vividly recall Nick's driving excursion in Tasmania in the early morning of Friday, May 4. "We were invited to this party, which was really bad, and Nick and I were the last people there along with this girl who was the host. The rest of the band weren't there, being much too sensible to go to a party in Hobart. Nick wanted to keep drinking, so she said, 'I know this all-night bar'. Nick had half this girl's record collection stuffed under his jumper, and he says, 'Can I have the keys?' She says, 'Can you drive?', and Nick says, 'Of course I can drive'."

Robert: "Had he ever driven before?"

Rowland: "I think so . . . he'd probably driven Tracy's car for about 500 yards or something; he certainly didn't have a licence. So we got in the car and off we go. Every time we get to an intersection we spin violently, and this went on and on, and eventually we get to this pub. We walked in and everyone in the pub was a policeman in uniform. So we walked out again.

"On our way to some other place, we were going very fast, screaming around corners, 360 degree turns at every intersection. The car was nearly rolling, and we were narrowly missing any object that was anywhere near the road. We had something to drink with us, so Nick was getting drunker and drunker.

"After we'd nearly killed ourselves many times, I said, 'Look, I'm getting out and I'm going to the hotel. Goodnight.' So I walked up the hill, and about a minute later I heard this huge '*crash*' and I thought, 'I'm not going to go back there to be confronted by some hideous mess, I'm going to go home and go to bed'. I was just too drunk and too tired to see my best friend's head knocked off. I was so drunk when I got to the hotel I passed out. Everyone thought this was mercenary of me, but there's a limit. Besides, I'd been telling him to stop for an hour and that he was going to kill us, so I thought, 'Well, if he's done it, then it's his own fault'.

"We were supposed to leave Hobart that day, and after a while somebody said, 'Where's Nick?', and my brain churned into life, and I explained. When he turned up we were told he'd driven the wrong way down a one-way street, straight into a police car, and when they leapt out of the car and confronted him, he jumped over into the passenger seat, and said, 'I wasn't driving'. And then he got out of the car and ran away. So they took him down to the station and beat him up for a while, and told him never to come back to Tasmania."

Keith: "It was a fairly square pub-rock audience. Nick and Rowland had found this girl who was somehow arty-punkish, everyone was very normal down there. So off they drove in her car.

"The story I heard was, that at 2am, with the girl unconscious in the back seat, with Nick driving, they accidentally hit one police car, and then drove the wrong way down a one-way street and got nicked by another police car. The police locked Nick up for the night, not realising he'd bumped another police car earlier.

"I heard about this in the morning and went down. No-one else came down to the court with me, and Nick came out of the nick, sat with me and he was absolutely shitting himself. He knew he'd done more than just drink-driving with no licence, driven the wrong way up a one-way street. The important thing was that he'd smashed into a police car. But they didn't put these incidents together; the girl had disappeared, presumably she slept the night in the car, woke up and drove home – we never saw her again.

"It was pretty tense in the courtroom that morning. I think he was fined $100 and placed on a good behaviour bond, and he was quite relieved."

Shane: "The Tasmanian tour was very good, if incredibly weird. We had people in little pubs down by the waterfront near Constitutional dock chanting, 'The Boys Next Door walk on water', ripping the town up while we packed up the gear, went for a pizza and off to bed. 'Fuckin' locals, who gives a shit?', y'know?"

"For some reason, Phill was getting up everyone's nose. We were a close-knit family; it didn't matter if you were a roadie, we were all rock-stars. And we were very sorely tempted to do things that rock-stars do. We were sleeping in a room with lots of beds, like a big dormitory. We trashed the room, it was just fantastic. Phill ended up with every piece of bedding material in the room on top of him, with everyone else on top of that."

The music was a reflection of their lives, not a creation they could wipe off like make-up. Without this dangerous, prankster dark side to their personal lives, their music would have lacked its threatening aura.

Less than two weeks after the Tasmania dates, a support slot to The Sports was set up in Canberra. All the band had to do was arrive and play. Mick, Rowland and Phill drove together and Nick and Tracy travelled in the back of the truck, with some beer to make the journey less arduous.

At some spot on the Hume Highway Tracy and Nick opened up the back for a piss in full view of the car behind, which contained the wife of the chief of police in the next town. "Nick and Tracy were never ones to lie, even if the truth made them look extremely foolish," recalls Rowland. "They told me they masturbated for something like twelve miles."

They drove through the next town, but she didn't. Her husband chased them down the road, they were arrested and held overnight, blowing out the gig before bail could be organised. Bail, on the 15th (Nick) and the 17th (Tracy) of May at the Gundagai courthouse, was $102.50 *each*, the charge: "Indecent

Manner". Fines of $200 *each* indicate more than just an expensive piss . . . the ex-lead singer of The Sports, Steven Cummings, was awarded Most Popular Australian Alternative Solo Performer in 1991 at the Australian Music Awards and commented, "I would've liked Nick Cave . . . (to have won this instead of me)."

'Door, Door' shows where they were headed, and is something of a landmark in Australian music. The band thank their girlfriends . . .

Helena: ". . . the people close to the band who don't get rich or famous cop the downside. You don't need me to mention the Anita Lane influence on Nick and the band. Everything about her was great. Keith and I really thought she was something."

Paul Goldman: "From speaking with Anita and Genevieve, they are the unsung heroes of that band."

Rowland: "They had an enormous influence . . . Nick got into Flannery O'Connor through me and Gen. At one stage, Nick, Mick and I were all in love with Genevieve; Nick and Mick would probably deny that. When we met Gen, she wrote songs, played guitar and piano. She had a level of technical proficiency and a vision that was greater than ours, she'd been exposed to stuff that was much more sophisticated than anything we'd been exposed to. She was incredible, she was driven."

Maria: "The album was more than it seemed. It had that youthful exuberance which so many bands tried to achieve and couldn't. Something else was seeping out, something that shifted and moved stealthily; not in the beat or rhythm, but in the spaces in between. It left a kind of lingering uneasiness after I'd listen to it; the cover probably didn't help. 'Door, Door' was totally unlike most Australian music, the band were regarded as weird."

The band's rising cult status, the record's hard and serious edge and its pop appeal tended to make 'Door, Door' popular and easy to accept by the scene. The first side seemed more like exercises in songwriting than actual songs but there is a distinct change on side two where the bass becomes an integral, almost textural, part of their driving force. Rowland's guitar hovers and hums, often suggesting physical pain, and his fatalistic codas which repeat in a weird gleeful melancholia emphasise the lyrics. You can't dance to this stuff; the uptempo parts lay emphasis to lyrics or tone, not dancefloor rhythms.

The deceptively childish nursery rhyme piano on 'Dive Position' provides a dizzying and shaky sense of unease. 'I Mistake Myself' is an essay in understated power, with its quiet, evocative bass and its insidious, stealthy guitar sliding all around. Rowland's guitar marries the innocence of familiar children's themes with a heavy sense of mortality. In parts, but especially on 'I Mistake Myself', Rowland's guitar chimes the hours almost like the chimes of a clock; very fatalistic, regretting that so much can't be changed. It's the simple guitar phrases which make the band into something else again, offsetting the lyrics in unexpected ways.

Had The Boys Next Door stayed in this area long enough to develop it, their future would have been very different. But their direction was sealed; their personalities ensured that whatever they produced would be a result of continual feedback with each other.

There is a gentle tenderness to the opening of 'Shivers', with its insidious nursery rhyme feel. It is a very moving song, even if Rowland did remark that it wasn't about anyone in particular.

Dave Graney: "Every time I saw The Boys Next Door, they were different to their latest record. 'Door, Door' was really schizophrenic, they'd changed so much live since recording it."

Paul: "In May or June, I had to do a 'TV studio assignment', and everyone else was doing pretend current affairs programmes and documentaries. I thought this was a waste of time, so I got the band in to make these music videos. We did 'After A Fashion' for the first half of the day, which was them playing against a white background. As an afterthought, we did 'Shivers'. The band changed what they were wearing, and I decided to shoot it on very long takes against a black background, because we were running out of time, which is why the video looks the way it does. I directed, and the lighting cameramen were David Thompson and Evan English, David Thompson was the editor and my girlfriend Lucy McLaren was kinda the producer.

"Then we cut it, then I think Keith and the band saw it, and someone suggested I take it into Mushroom, so we quickly organised that, and after showing it to him in his office, Gudinski said, 'Well, I want to use it, it's mine', and I said, 'Well, no it's not, it belongs to Swinburne', and I pointed out that it was on non-broadcast quality tape, and he said, 'Can you get it so I can use it on *Nightmoves*?' which was a music show on Channel 7 or 9 late on Saturday nights. I think Gudinski effectively owned the show. I rang Gudinski back and told him how much it would cost, and that I didn't know if I could do this as I could get into trouble at Swinburne. So we all said we'll do it ourselves, and I paid to have all our rushes transferred up to broadcast quality, cut it, and Gudinski gave me a cheque for $500, and it had actually cost me about $460 to do it all, and it was shown on *Nightmoves*. I was suspended from Swinburne for two weeks because I'd breached a copyright, and Swinburne were going to sue Mushroom, even though half the staff really liked what I'd done. It didn't stop them from letting me back in the studio later to do 'The Hair Shirt', which we also did as a studio assignment. Nick came in a couple of days before we shot it and we built the set, like a poppy Doctor Caligari. We raided the props store, there were all these door frames and window frames and chairs painted in primary colours which we hung from the ceiling around the band. We moved the camera so fast that it was just demented; we used one camera and rushed it across the studio. We knocked Tracy over once and Nick quite a few times; we had two people all day just pushing this huge pedestal camera at great speed across the studio, which they weren't designed to do at all. It was only shown at the Ballroom."

Phill: "'Enemy Of The State', which was released on Missing Link cassette 'Rare Trax – From The Archives' in 1983 or 1984, was recorded at a session Keith set up in a 16-track studio. We went in and cut some punky stuff; we were going to release it under a pseudonym, The Torn Oxbodies."

Rowland: "'Enemy Of The State' is an Ollie Olsen song. It was completely demented. We started doing this song of Nick's 'Show Me A Sign', a fairly punky song. It was really ridiculous, fast and energetic and nothing like anything we were doing, and we were doing it out of sheer perversity.

"For some bizarre reason we came up with the idea of recording 'Show Me A Sign', and Keith wanted us to do two songs. So we ended up recording that fucking song 'Enemy Of The State'. I think it's a really rotten song, and I mentioned it as a joke, because it was written by Ollie, and Nick and I really disliked Ollie. It snowballed out of control. 'Show Me A Sign', was much better.

"We were recording it in this rotten studio where hardly

anything worked. The engineers were two Italian heavy metal brothers, with really long hair, who thought we were *crap* musicians and couldn't understand why we were recording these songs that we thought were *stupid*. The whole thing was beyond their comprehension . . .

"I remember vividly that Nick and Phill had a head-butting contest in the studio and virtually killed each other. They ran at each other from opposite sides of the room, leaping into the air at the last moment, slamming their skulls together like mountain goats in a fight to be king of the tribe or something, until they were extremely sorry individuals, both standing there nursing appalling headaches, no doubt losing an enormous number of brain cells."

Paul: "I used to see The Teenage Radio Stars at the Ballroom, and there'd be no-one there. I spent a night with Nick and Tracy at the Ballroom watching The Teenage Radio Stars. Upstairs they used to have this big table so you could make yourself a hotdog – in accordance with licensing regulations the Ballroom had to provide food as well as alcohol. They had this huge pot full of hotdogs, those really red slimy ones, and a plate of bread. Well, Nick and Tracy and I took all the hotdogs out of the pot and went and stood right in front of Sean Kelly and James Freud; James used to spend a lot of money on looking great. There they were playing, so earnestly, these rotten songs and there was no-one there. We got the hotdogs and were pouring sauce on them and throwing them at the band, and James started crying."

Phill: "There was a more disgusting incident. Shane from La Femme and Tracy collected Tracy's Great Dane's turds and pelted The Teenage Radio Stars with them. There was a rumour that the turds were human, because they were so big."

With the demise of The Teenage Radio Stars, the 'Suicide bands' had all collapsed. The public didn't seem interested in their local 'new wave', so The Boys Next Door were pretty much left in the cold. They toured Adelaide in June.

Phill: "We did this gig upstairs at the Princes Berkeley in Hindley Street."

Shane: "There was a big front bar and heaps of people. The stairs were fucked, we couldn't get our gear into the room above, where the band were going to play."

Phill: "So we loaded in and out from the balcony onto the roof of our truck and then from the roof of the truck down onto the truck's tailgate. After one gig we went to a nightclub. We were dancing, but we'd be doing really silly dances, annoying the other people and making them get off the dance floor. Me, Nick, Rowland, Tracy and sometimes Mick; Tracy had some great ones, he had a great dancing style. We got thrown out for dancing too violently, offensive dancing.

"Our burly and very capable roadie took exception, and he made a point of trying to get back in, and they wouldn't let him as they knew he was with us, and I think they pushed him around a little. He went back to the truck, and he got the tyre lever, quite a big piece of metal, and went back and smashed up a few chairs and a bit of wood panelling and stuff, and drove back to our hotel. When we woke up the next morning the truck's tyres were slashed."

Rowland: "Nick still does that silly dancing. The last time he came round to my place in London, he and Gen danced for about an hour, until they were both completely exhausted, and Nick does this series of comedic routines, doing absurd dances, but he's incredibly vigorous, he has an enormous amount of energy, he's a very hardy person."

Phill: "Our roadies were very loyal . . . they sometimes used to crew in suits, Shane and David. They'd get very hot! Or they'd wear black jeans and black skivvies . . . they'd have a uniform for the night, complete with identity badges or name tags with little photo-booth photos of themselves on."

Shane: "The violence was all inside it. Real violence, well, there were certain people that still get up my nose regardless, I see a few of them in the street. They don't incite me to violence these days, they incite me to . . . pity, probably, because it was always there. Some people just like gettin' hit, y'know? They like getting in your way, they like fucking with you, and they like getting hit. If that's what you want . . . then you get it. Drugs and shit, when you're taking lots of amphetamines and drinking heaps of piss, and doing this and doing that, fuckin', you just go fuckin' crazy.

"People died . . . for one reason or another. Being almost locked in at Adelaide Zoo with Tracy . . . we were talking to a mandrill, the ones with the red faces. We were talking to him, sharing a couple of cans with him."

Paul: "There were a group of people who realised the band were really important to their lives and beyond that."

Rowland: "It was a very mixed group of people. These young Greek girls would see us every time we played; they were conservatively dressed, didn't appear to drink and loved the band. More than that, they cared about us as people, it was extraordinary."

Ross: "In Melbourne, Nick used to ask the audience, these people who were Tuinalled out of their minds, to get up and dance. Everyone was too self-conscious to do that. When there's twenty people at a gig and four or five people get up and dance, you become a spectacle.

"But they suddenly stopped asking people to dance because they realised how bizarre it was . . . 'here we are trying to push it to the edge, we're not playing our old songs that everyone recognises, yet we still expect you to get up and dance'. They'd begun to change their whole attitude to what part the audience were playing. There was always the need to progress, which is good . . . you could say it was pretentious, but it was their attempt to constantly create new sounds and to stretch the sound, to change it."

Keith: "We were pretty pissed off that 'Shivers' didn't have a picture sleeve; they were on their way to do it on *Countdown*, and Meldrum rang me up and said, 'We can't have the band on because the producers said that you can't use the line 'I've been contemplating suicide'. Meldrum apologised, but they couldn't do *Countdown*. The Boys Next Door's appearance for 'Boots' and having The Saints on once was *Countdown*'s total contribution to assisting the movement which eventually shaped the future of Australian music."

Andrew: "They played 'Shivers' on *Hey, Hey It's Saturday*, a kid's Saturday morning TV show. After that, I went to Missing Link to buy a record or something, and the band were all there, slagging off the host, Daryl Somers."

This contempt for the media, the world outside, strengthened the band from within, but their attitude discouraged industry support.

Nick's performances were becoming more and more physical, and he began to stretch the limits of what was accepted on stage. In combination with the experimental and enthusiastic scene, and the 'punk rock attitude', as well as the other distinctive personalities in the band, The Boys Next Door became an ever more invigorating prospect. Keith suggested they do more demos.

'Scatterbrain' was recorded in Phill's bedroom along with about 20 other songs, (including the early, faster version of 'The Friendcatcher' – RB) by the band's mixer, Groper. 'Scatterbrain' was mixed on the end of a recording session for the 'Samurai Star' 7″ by Peter Lillie (of The Pelaco Brothers, Jo-Jo Zep, etc). "We had Mick on guitar, a bass player I didn't know, me on drums, and Rowland and Keith playing guitar," says Phill.

Many bands get stuck in 'the Australian rut'. The major cities are spread out over a large area, with a comparatively small population, and a band can easily play too much. When a band is starting up, it's natural for them to want to play, but playing to the same audience over a period of years can be self-defeating. Even core fans move on. In Australia momentum can die fairly quickly in ways that are difficult to understand in America or Europe, where fresh audiences are the norm.

Not many bands toured Hobart, Darwin, Perth and Brisbane. In the late Seventies, the tour loop went Sydney-Melbourne-Adelaide, plus a few large towns like Mount Gambier, Geelong or Whyalla. If commercial Australia doesn't jump on the bandwagon when the band's happening, the band could play itself too thin, folding into a heap of resentment and dashed expectations. This happens quite frequently, and several world-quality bands which for years played the local pubs and clubs eventually dropped, their energies exhausted, into that deep pool of 'could-a-beens'.

Without some sort of outside support, a band dies a gruesome death in Australia. Would INXS have been successful if not for a determined record company? Undoubtedly The Birthday Party would have foundered without Keith Glass who paid for the 'Hee-Haw' sessions in July.

The band were ignored, ridiculed and loathed all at once by various sections of the music biz, from media to pubs. There were rumours of arrests and beatings, and the mainstream media (*Countdown* on ABC TV, *RAM* & *Juke* magazines, radio airplay) passed them by. Recording offers were made or were reported to have been made, and were turned down for no reason apparent to the small cult who admired their attitude: perversity in adversity.

As information was so scanty, to the outsider it seemed like the band had gone insane. More likely, they were increasingly ambitious, confident of their own abilities and determined to get out of the rut. Reckless adventure offered some escape.

Rowland: "This happened at least three times. The Boulevard was this enormous curve in the road so that you were turning the car steadily for about a minute, and Tracy had this real wreck of an old car, and Nick used to open the door as we were steaming along, and haul himself up onto the roof and just hang there like a big black spider. It amazed me, because nobody could've got me up there for love nor money. There was a time when he came a cropper, and that was my fault, largely.

"We were at the Tiger Lounge, and there was this older guy about 30 who was very straight and very normal who was a dentist. He was saying how wonderful he thought the band was, and I think we'd been taking Serepax or one of those hideous moodal drugs."

Robert: "And you'd been drinking."

Rowland: "Oh, it goes without saying; you didn't just take Serepax. So we baited this guy until he drove us to this party, and on the way Nick climbed out onto the roof. And I said to the dentist: 'Why don't you slam on the brakes really quickly?' And he did.

"Nick flew off the roof of the car, slid along his back, skidded along this sort of cobbled road, which took big chunks of skin off the nodules of his spine. I don't think he was wearing a shirt at the time, or if he was, he wasn't afterwards. And he's never forgiven me. Quite frankly, I didn't imagine that anyone would be so stupid as to follow my orders. That could have been the end of it all, there and then.

"Nick enjoys taking risks. He probably wouldn't take a risk if he thought he'd wind up dead. Nick doesn't have some asinine 'death-wish', but a craving for more . . . it's as if real life just doesn't measure up, so he feels obliged to increase its sensory qualities."

Paul Goldman: "In The studio I thought they were arrogant and smug. At that time, the creative axis of the band was Rowland and Nick. I think the only reason they got anything done was Phill Calvert, he was kind of the boot-boy, trundling around, bringing the gear in . . . he was more the outsider in the band. He was very close with Keith and Helena, and it seemed to me that Keith exploited that, because he needed someone within the band to keep it on the road, and he was very important to the band for all sorts of reasons. I think the enmity that the band felt was quite important because it isolated them for quite a while."

Rowland: "Phill was like a mole. And we'd play, and then me, Nick and Tracy would wander off and talk to people, and Phill would start picking up the kit and everything; if he hadn't done it, we would've had to do it, but he couldn't bear to see it sitting there."

Paul: "There's something in someone's make-up that lets them do that, but you can't deny that he was important to the band, because at times they seemed to be so fucking disorganised that Phill seemed to be the only one pulling it together."

Rowland: "Phill never organised things *per se*, Mick organised things, and Phill did the dirty work."

Keith: "Mushroom weren't interested in doing anything with the band, so we took it upon ourselves to record at Richmond Recorders. We made these fairly experimental tracks, with the band picking up influences by the week . . . Pere Ubu would have been the prime influence on the 'Hee-Haw' EP. I played that to Gudinski, which was a thrilling experience, and he didn't look too confident, so I said, 'What about we put it out ourselves, Michael?', and he said, 'Oh, okay', which was my plan from the beginning."

Gudinski realised, correctly, that Australia was never going to take to The Boys Next Door. 'Door, Door', had sold 2,000 copies, a meagre quantity for a band with such a high opinion of itself. Mushroom was probably glad to see the back of what could have been an expensive liability. The band hadn't received any royalties for 'Door, Door', and they probably didn't expect to see any for some time. Gudinski allowed Mushroom's option on the band to drop that year, rendering their contract null and void.

Mick: "Mushroom started paying us royalties for 'Door, Door' in 1987, after they'd reorganised the company and put someone in accounts to sort it out. They seemed to be honest about not having the figures, they were just disorganised."

The more The Boys Next Door developed away from rock 'n' roll, the less the Australian music press – *RAM*, *Juke* (who described PiL's first LP as "unlistenable") – wanted to know. Potential fans might pick up 'Door, Door', or hear something on the radio, but actually seeing the band was a different experience altogether. Their music seemed totally bizarre, unpalatable and played at maximum volume – unbearably full-on for those who'd come to see this new pop/glam/arty band who'd released this divine new album.

The Boys Next Door belonged to the misunderstood generation, and they embodied the misunderstandings perfectly, enjoying the frustrated response of a crowd who'd come to hear music they thought they understood, only to be forced to deal with something else entirely. Was this even the same band?

'Faint Heart', 'Safehouse' and 'Death By Drowning' all assaulted audiences intent on beer, chords, beer, chicks and beer. The band had no respect whatsoever for the sexually aggressive oz-rocker.

Andrew: "When 'Door, Door' was released, they were doing stuff like 'Death By Drowning', which was completely different from their earlier stuff, the current album! It was much more ferocious, their newer stuff. They started to sound more extreme around the middle of 1979 . . . they were doing some great stuff with that harder, more extreme sound; Tracy's bass and Rowland's guitar both edging off against each other, and Rowland using feedback and other guitar effects.

"They were using staccato sorts of sounds too. With their earlier pop stuff, everything fitted in, melody, chorus, whatever; this was like they were trying to create a tangible emotion, a sort of internal chaos. I was very struck with it. On the music side they were creating all these different levels of sound which were all going in different directions. During 'Safehouse' Nick would start off with his squeezebox, then the band would come in, and there'd be a break halfway through the song where he'd do it again . . ."

Phill: "The band really became The Birthday Party during 'Hee-Haw', when we started getting more arty. We felt we had a mission; we were getting a sound; we were in the studio just to be us, not to fulfill any other requirements. Whatever we did, our audience would take it, we'd dish up something we were working on and they'd still say, 'Hey, that new song, that was great'. They knew our songs really well."

Paul: "The same kind of chaos that existed on stage was afoot in the studio for their graveyard shifts . . ."

Rowland: "But we also knew exactly what we wanted to do."

Paul: "There was a lot of niggling and fighting, disagreement . . . from my experience their discussions weren't at the sonic level, but there was always another level that was being addressed, which was about the effect of the music. I've never seen that with any other band in the studio – The Birthday Party seemed to address what the record was about, what it represented. I can remember Nick, Rowland, Tony discussing how to make it sound horrible, rotten and disgusting."

Rowland: "This wasn't just with 'Junkyard', this was with all our records. Before 'Junkyard', we had rotten noises in among really nice noises, and we realised nobody understood what we were doing, and the only way to get them to understand it was to rub their noses in it."

Tracy's bass was becoming fuller, more rounded; a lyrically intense funk slap. Phill was becoming more confident and precise, layering secondary rhythms and multiple motifs alongside and on top, very be-bop. Rowland created more of a maelstrom with innovative and intense use of feedback.

The band's desire to expand their potential was stronger than ever, but constant gigging around Melbourne and Sydney left them restless. The need for a more receptive situation became paramount.

Over the next six months they did further sessions with Tony, the songs mostly showing up on later singles and the later 'Birthday Party' compilation album.

Tony: "A lot of that stuff didn't work, the 'Hee-Haw' recordings were really experimental. We had no bottom end on the mix whatsoever. Everything had to be treble. Some of those didn't work: 'Mr Clarinet', 'Death By Drowning'. The band were still learning about the studio, too. Nick and Mick would come up to me now and say, 'Okay, Tony, we want this record to be like this', and they'll have some phrase or word to set the mood. With 'Junkyard', it was 'We want trash, we want to sound trashy. Junk, trash, bad sounds, no slick sounds at all'.

"For the 'Friendcatcher'/'Hee-Haw' times, it was all 'thin', absolutely 'thin', all treble. 'Make it all treble, Tone', they said. 'No bass. Everything's got to be trebly'."

Rowland: "Nick would dance and move around to the music during his vocal takes . . ."

Phill: "We wanted to put metal, pots and pans and stuff in the piano and still play it so that it sounded like a crashing car, you can hear it on 'A Faint Heart'. The snare drum on 'Mr Clarinet', that's doubled with Nick and I playing those rectangular metal ashtrays they used to have in banks with 'Smokers Please' written on them, holding them upside down and playing the bottoms with screwdriver handles.

"Rowland wrote 'Running Goat' about this game that he and Harry had played together as kids, which was never recorded."

The band toured Adelaide in late September. Then they announced they were heading to England, where a more receptive audience would be waiting to discover them. They re-emphasised their intention of creating a primal response in the audience. They hoped that after a night of lost inhibitions and lost preconceptions, a creative energy would remain with the audience long after the band had departed.

Mick: "At Bombay Rock, at some horrendous showcase for the Pyramid agency, 'Rocktober '79', we played with Australian Crawl and The Aliens, it was a real music industry do. It was a horrible occasion, disgusting. It was the only night I was late for a concert, the band were already on stage when I arrived. I was late because our roadie didn't pick me up, and I got a taxi to Bombay Rock from St Kilda which, considering I was earning about $10 a week, was an extreme action to take to get there.

"When I arrived, Nick was on stage going, 'Is Mick Harvey there?' In the confusion, someone, Australian Crawl's roadie probably, repatched some of the microphones so nothing worked, half the amps were unplugged from the wall. It was a total mess. The first three songs we didn't get anywhere, so we walked off. It was a really good night for us because it was a disaster, nobody liked us at all, which was good because it was just a bunch of arseholes."

Phill: "The most common fuck-up was to give us, as the support act, less mike channels and less lighting channels, and wind the power amps back three notches. This means the support band look okay, but no matter how bad the headline band, they invariably blow the support away. It's a common option."

Mick: "We reached the limit of our market long before we were able to leave. People obviously didn't like us much, so we had to go further afield. We wanted to do something original for ourselves, and to take that wherever we could."

The Boys Next Door enjoyed being an unpredictable force, a jab in the rear, a thorn which went unnoticed until too late. They'd play suburban dives where their friends might follow. Their music tended to chase all the 'available' girls away, preventing the great Australian male from scoring. They were never actually banned, but flying glasses, insults, and fights were commonplace. A singer is a natural target, and Nick's height tended to intimidate, although he'd usually have a longer reach than his opponent.

Rowland's 'Scatterbrain' was given away at the Crystal Ballroom on October 20, 1979. The flipside was by The Models, 'Early Morning Brain', who also played that night. The Ballroom scene was active and self-promoting. Downstairs you could see music clips or the gig on a large video screen. Bands could use the Ballroom's equipment to make their own clips.

The Boys Next Door demanded a reaction; you either loved them, or you hated them and everything they stood for. Their live set at this time consisted of: 'Let's Talk About Art', 'Shivers', 'Somebody's Watching', 'After A Fashion', 'Running Goat', 'Death By Drowning', 'Cracked Portrait', 'A Catholic Skin', 'AKA', 'The Friendcatcher', 'Safe House', 'Scatterbrain', 'Mr Clarinet', 'The Guilt Parade', 'The Hair Shirt', 'Faint Heart', 'Waving My Arms', 'Red Clock', 'Bones For Borneo' and a few more, perhaps 'Show Me A Sign'.

In June and September 1979 The Boys Next Door played in Adelaide.

Shane: "The first two tours to Adelaide had been pretty good, we'd turn up at a local hot-spot, full of piss and a bad attitude, contempt towards the local yokels and create havoc. We'd parked the truck on an incline because the battery was flat and we had to roll-start it, and I thought I'd best arm myself against the horde of locals that we'd offended at the pub we'd played at. There were all these people bearing down on us, so I grabbed the nearest weapon I could find – it wasn't something you could talk your way out of – they were going to tear us limb from limb. It was probably something I'd said to them, something totally obnoxious and totally condescending. The attitude of, 'We're here to take over your pub, who gives a fuck, we're from Melbourne, blah de-blah and that's that'."

Mark, Paul: "My god. The rhythm in 'Hair Shirt', that was a real clincher. I got to know every beat and danced accordingly. 'Let's Talk About Art' . . . people joined in with the chorus, if you could call it that. Sort of a boisterous holler designed to get your back up."

Nick was very deliberate about how he was moving on stage, but it seemed natural and fitted in with the music. Rowland's movements seemed at odds with the occasional waves of feedback and general row coming from his end of the stage.

They were full-tilt – totally wrapped in and intent on their own creation. Nick was wearing frilly shirts at the time, which was definitely alien to the pub crowd looking for a punker band.

About a third of the crowd in Adelaide walked out fairly swiftly, and another third drifted out more slowly, while others called for the support band to come back on, which was unusual. Their tour poster captures the essence of their music . . . dark, murky, and indistinctly bright by turns; threatening in shade, vulnerable and anxious in examination.

Mick: "We played Festival Hall on 25th November 1979, with Flowers, The Angels and Cold Chisel on the top of the bill – four or five thousand people. I think 'Death By Drowning' did it. I remember this noise emanating from the crowd throughout Tracy's clarinet solo . . . It grew to this rumble underneath the group. When we finished there was this big BOOOOOO coming from the audience which continued for the rest of the show and between every song.

"The first few songs they were okay with. It wasn't going too bad, we were playing alright, they didn't seem to be offended. But 'Death By Drowning' blew it, I'm afraid, and from then on they hated our guts. These people came backstage, going, 'Don't be upset, we thought you were brilliant, they're all arseholes'. 'What?' We weren't upset, booed for most of our concert, we didn't care at all."

Andrew: "Some friends from High School had been to Festival Hall to see The Angels, and this appalling band called 'The Boys Next Door' had been poncing around on the stage and everyone in the audience had been throwing stuff at them; as soon as they were off the 'proper' music came on.

"I became familiar with the songs they were playing . . . they always seemed to introduce a new song each time you saw them. They were all great shows."

Ross: "At some of their bigger gigs, there'd be 200 or 300 people, and The Boys Next Door would be who people were coming to see. At gigs during the week, it was a much smaller audience."

Rowland: "Gen, Mick and I had a flat on The Esplanade in St Kilda. A couple of buildings along, there was a big apartment house, and the bottom part was glass. In the lobby there was a gold-coloured chair with red leather. Nick, Pierre and this girlfriend of Pierre's (we'll call her 'Mary' - RB), who was quiet and

Catholic and well-read, got very drunk at this party we'd been to after playing. They'd come back to our place, we'd gone to bed, they'd gone off.

"'Mary', in some fit of alcohol-induced insanity, threw a brick through this window to get this chair. So Nick, being the man of honour that he is, thought, 'Well, I'll have to help her, because otherwise she'll get cut', so he helped her get the chair out, and he got cut.

"Somebody saw them, so, clutching this chair, they ran up the road and up our garden path, which lead from the Esplanade down to our flat with bushes on either side and was very dark. The path ended in a 't', our entrance on the left, the back fence in front and a flat to the right. They threw the chair over the back fence, and, trailing blood like little Hansel and Gretel breadcrumbs, came into our flat, and washed their hands in our sink, leaving blood everywhere.

"I woke up to find this policeman shining his torch in my face. At the party, I'd cut my hand on a bread-knife, so there's a little smudge of blood on the sheet. The policeman says, 'Okay, sonny, off to the station', and I was so drunk that when they stood me up I fell back down again and went back to sleep, so they said, 'Oh, we can't be bothered with this one'. They arrested Nick and 'Mary'.

"Nick, being the man of honour that he is, said, 'I did it, she was just watching and telling me not to do it'. So he took the rap, and I think put on a good behaviour bond after his father, who was the head of Adult Education, gave a statement about Nick's good character."

Shortly after the above incident Nick's father, Colin, died.

Shane: "I was soundchecking at Bombay Rock and Nick hadn't shown any emotion, and he came up to me and just kind of . . . let go on me, which was really touching. But the show went on. I admire him for that. He's always been inquisitive about religion, we could talk about that; he had this obsession with it. (It was) Catholicism more than anything. Caulfield Grammar is Christian but not Catholic. He was more interested in the ritual side of it, not the creed or the beliefs. Baptism, confirmation, confession. For someone who's never experienced confession it can be mysterious. I don't think Nick's a driven man, but a *fleeing* man, running from the fear of failure."

Rowland: "I think Nick's eternal problem is that he never got to prove to his father that he was talented, intelligent and articulate in his chosen field. The story in Ian Johnston's *Bad Seed* how his father only saw the band once, at 'Punk Gunk' (New Year's Eve 1977) and Nick rolling in the gutter, and that was a really big thing in Nick's life. When they did 'Boots', and Nick got the single and took it home for his father to listen to and he just laughed. His father was a very intelligent, overbearing, ambitious person who'd gone from being principal of a country school to the head of Adult Education in Victoria, which was an enormous leap. Nick is running away from responsibility; he always said that living in a place where you're completely isolated, going from foreign country to foreign country and living out of a suitcase, being alienated, was an essential part of The Birthday Party and an essential part of his life. That's true to an extent, but you've got to ask yourself why it was so important to him; everybody else followed and went along with it, because it was so important to Nick.

"Nick has amazingly good luck. He probably wouldn't look at it like that, but considering the incredible amount of life-threatening situations he's been in, he's always come out of it unscathed.

"We'd always be in a bar somewhere and there'd be the local Hell's Angels there, The Coffin Makers or something. We'd be sitting there, and these people would come over and sit at our table because we were obviously poofs, and Nick would pretend to talk to them and bait them in such a manner that they weren't really sure whether Nick was being rude to them or not, so they were always a hair's-breadth away from ripping our heads off, so he somehow always got away with it. Although a couple of times he didn't . . ."

Shane: "We caused mayhem just by turning up. We'd support Split Enz and people were throwing full beer glasses at the band.

"I did a pretty good job as a roadie for them. Working alongside other bands and other roadies, you learn stuff, you get better, do a decent light show. They got very professional before they left. The decision to go to England was fairly definite, maybe it was a way of cutting ties with David and I . . . although we got a lot out of the band, when they became The Birthday Party, Dave, Groper and I were really just fans and hangers-on.

"Phill's always been very fastidious, always attuned to the music scene. Phill was the driving force behind it all, and I think some of the other guys . . . particularly in the aftermath of the band going to England . . . well, it was pretty nasty. It wasn't out of character for them, let me say that. Phill, for personal reasons more than anything else, was always going to be a casualty. He was a scapegoat."

Ross: "People in the audience were taking Tuinal – I mean, everyone in the audience was as extreme as the band. We were 19, 20. We held Nick in the highest regard and none of us was shockable because we were there to see extremity. Their audiences genuinely enjoyed what the band were doing, Nick never really appreciated that. You'd go up to the front of the stage, and meet the same 15 people, and you'd end up smashing glasses over each other's heads all night long."

Ross isn't talking in metaphors here. The 'Hee-Haw' EP completely changed the perception of the band in Australia. They were off to England, with unrealistic perceptions of the outside world that only the weird cultural isolation that had characterised Australia for so many decades could produce.

Mick: "We reached the limit of our market long before we were able to leave. We had no intention of making a pop record. People obviously didn't like us much, we tried playing Festival Hall and they didn't like it. The reason we had to leave Australia was because the number of people who liked us wasn't large enough to support us."

The 'Hee-Haw' EP, released by Missing Link in early December 1979, is their most organised and cohesive record, more of a band statement than pandering to Mushroom's whims. The title comes from Nick's "hee-haw" noises at the beginning of 'The Friendcatcher'. The lyrics are totally indecipherable. It is piercing, eruptive music unlike any other Australian band, vastly different in every way. The record, in particular 'The Hair Shirt', presages Birthday Party in its intensity and chaos. Bleak, hovering, malignant, 'Hee-Haw' sounded like it could actually hurt you. The multiplicity of rhythms and constantly shifting patterns create a mood tension and unease that is genuinely disturbing.

The mourning of Rowland's 'Death By Drowning' is reminiscent of Ambrose Bierce's *Occurrence At Owl Creek Bridge*, with its husky panther lope, piercing squalls and dry black humour. In 'The Hair Shirt' the listener is tied to the mast as the ship yaws sickeningly close to a reef with a battle in progress on the foredeck. We see five days in a mutinous crew's life speed up and catch us. It has a more familiar structure, not unlike the sea shanty 'What Shall We Do With The Drunken Sailor'.

There's no hint that this was the band who'd recorded 'Door, Door' the year before, this is a full-on onslaught of sound; experimental noise meshed together in a whirl of sonic indulgence. But it worked – and still does – and it created an impact like no other Australian record had for years. Melbourne's 400 or so scene, plus the scenes in other cities, managed national sales of 2,000 for 'Hee-Haw'.

Rowland: "The words to 'Death By Drowning' are from a French phrase-book. On one page there was a list of English translations of French phrases you might want to say at the beach. I stole the page and stuck it onto a piece of music. I thought some of the phrases were bizarre, like 'death by drowning', that didn't seem to be very holiday-orientated."

Tony: "Rowland's feedback on 'The Friendcatcher' was fascinating to watch! He had every pedal and gizmo he could lay his hands on, including a space-echo, which is a tape-echo machine, but the thing was, Rowland turned every knob up full. The space echo machine, which he didn't know how to work, was turned up full and constantly feeding back, and he was busy stomping on different pedals, so all this dreadful built-up feedback was changing each time he hit another pedal or button. He had no idea what he was doing, but he was getting all this immense feedback.

"He was delighted. It was hysterical to watch him. We were laughing our heads off. There he was, with his guitar, which he wasn't touching, just stomping on pedals, and he'd madly look around to see which pedal he was going to stomp on next.

"The reverb machine had a setting called 'Infinite Reverb' which makes the sound go on forever. They're the only band I've ever heard of who could use it because it creates total noise; the more sound put into it, the more noise builds up; it's totally unusable as rule, but they found a way to use it."

Rowland claims he did know roughly what he was doing, as he'd been playing the song live for about two months, although he concedes that anyone watching him would have come to the same conclusion as Tony.

Rowland: "(I was) . . . um, using the studio technology which was new to me, to make it all much bigger."

Tony: "Another song, we put a microphone on one of the

telephones in the studio offices, and got Nick to sing into another telephone, so he was singing into a telephone upstairs and it was miked up in the studio, which was hysterical. It's a terrible screechy little noise, we combined it with a normal vocal track, it's great."

By January 1980 their set would include: 'Waving My Arms', 'The Hat's On Wrong', 'Riddle House', 'The Friendcatcher', 'Guilt Parade', 'Scatterbrain' and 'Faint Heart'. They also performed songs like 'Let's Talk About Art', 'Cracked Portrait', 'Bones For Borneo', 'Safe House' and 'The Running Goat', all of which remain unreleased and, except for live tapes, unrecorded.

Keith: "There wasn't much more they could do in Australia. No major record company was interested in them. I'd had some interest from Ralph Records in San Francisco. They'd heard 'Hee-Haw' and said they'd be interested in releasing an album if there was more material, which gave us the impetus to go back into the studios after 'Hee-Haw' was finished. It was initially going to be an American release, and this album being released in Australia was met with some resistance from the band. It wasn't a great deal of resistance, and I said, 'Look, we've got these tracks, we've got to do something with them'."

Just before the last single was released, they came up with a new name. They wanted to tie in with the new single, something threatening, Dadaesque in intent. They chose The Birthday Party, partly because they'd seen the film of Pinter's play. It was an unassuming, everyday phrase, chosen to confuse and confront and it tied in with the last single, 'The Riddle House'/'Happy Birthday' released by Missing Link in February 1980. Despite their name, the band never held birthday parties for each other.

Keith: "I was curious to see how many noses they'd get up in England; many people weren't happy with the name change. Copies of this single were given away at their last gig at the Ballroom. The time and place of their departure was part of the poster advertising their final gigs."

'Happy Birthday' was written by Nick and Rowland, which was a first. It's like a children's birthday party out of control as puberty sets in at once, hormones and energy flying about in cartwheels with fireworks going off in all directions, breaking up and waving about hysterically.

Mick: "The 'Hee-Haw' recordings are fairly misguided. The second side of 'Door, Door' is too . . . well, none of the recordings from the 1970s really represent what we were doing. They're these tidy recorded things or perhaps this weird slow style. I've heard live tapes, and I think, 'that's kinda what the group was like' – there's this mixture of stuff that's quite full-on, a lot of fast, strong material."

Listening to The Boys Next Door on record without having seen them live produced a very different impression. Many people liked 'Door, Door', but were confused and disappointed when they caught the band live.

Mick: "I think we were fairly disappointed with 'Door, Door' too. And then 'Hee-Haw', I think Nick and Rowland had been listening to too much Pop Group and Pere Ubu. I didn't have much to do with the recordings in those sessions. I couldn't get involved with what was going on very much because I thought it was too influenced by the latest record you've heard, and by then you're not doing anything original anymore.

"I think we realised that we could take control of a recording and do what we wanted to do with it by the time we'd finished 'Hee-Haw'. We went on in our own direction.

"The first recordings after 'Hee-Haw' were the first recordings where we'd really found our own kind of path. They're fairly closely connected with 'Hee-Haw' . . . 'Friend Catcher' and 'Mr Clarinet', which is all on the CD 'Hee-Haw'. I think we'd found our own ground. That CD kinda represents what we were doing at that time, that's kinda what the group was like. We were mixing some songs, like 'Mr Clarinet', up until the night before we left in February 1980."

The peculiar bassline in 'Mr Clarinet' came about because Tracy didn't show up when the song was rehearsed, so the rest of the band went ahead, learning and recording it without him, leaving Tracy to overdub his bass later.

Rowland: "It was very hard to know what Tracy thought about anything. He was always getting completely drunk out of his brain even back then. He had an ulcer by the time he was 18. He just drank and drank and drank. I don't know if he was an alcoholic or not, but he drank an enormous amount."

Paul: "I always thought Tracy always seemed so stable, but yeah, he did drink, he was drunk all the time. The person who underwent the most enormous change was Tracy."

Helena: "The Boys Next Door were the centre of a cultural scene which existed only in Melbourne. And at the airport there were the parents and there was crying, there was a slew of girlfriends . . . it was a big emotional moment.

"Our boys were on their own. Getting them on the plane took every dollar we had. Keith and I were so sick we couldn't speak. We'd flung them out into a void and we felt bad."

II

Over The Top
(London, March 1980)

. . . Not another unappealing, risible Antipodean band? They'll sink like a brick in a trifle. Uncommercial, forgettable, unsavoury . . .

Mick: "It was a case of what was practical. There's only a couple of places you can go from Melbourne: LA, New York or London, if you want to move in somewhere and establish yourself in a centre of the music industry where there's record companies, big scenes, press and all that shit. We weren't in a position to reside in America, we wouldn't have got visas. Also, London was still very much the centre of attention, the focus of 'something'.

"In 1980 we were stuck in London. We spent months in the most . . . really just horrible circumstances."

They lived in a hotel near Gloucester Road until they could find somewhere better. They did the touristy things – visiting the Royal Academy of Art and flea markets. Within the first few days in London, Tracy had his big ghetto blaster nicked, and another member of the party had money stolen.

Nancy Pew: "It must have been a bit of a shock to the system. They were in their early twenties, and they had things happen to them quite early on."

Keith Glass: "The band arrived in London with a fairly modest amount of money from Missing Link – enough to live on for about a week . . . I'd never taken a cent in management fees, ever, which was part of the plan to get the band over there. They had some money from their gigs. They did a lot of shows just before they left, some of which they made good money on, but some of which we got screwed on. There was a night where an owner deducted about 400 people off the door take, I think, at the Seaview Hotel, but so it goes."

Nick even went on a short trip to Paris two weeks after arriving, but money soon ran out.

Keith: "After three weeks they were living in a one room flat in Earls Court, and they couldn't get anything going. I'd already been over before they got there, but I couldn't get anything set up with anybody, but we had to go anyway. No-one wanted to know about Australian punk groups, even though The Saints had made some inroads. At the time anything Australian was, 'Huh, you gotta be kidding, you're a bunch of Fosters-swilling hoons'."

From their first days in London the band were a gang, a bubble, ex-pats who didn't fit, even back home. London radically changed the band's perspective of themselves. They all managed to find jobs of varying descriptions, with varying degrees of success.

Rowland: "I worked for a day in a factory, but I quit. I got a job washing dishes, and I worked for a whole week. I got paid, and as I was walking home I got mugged. I decided that I just wasn't meant to have a job, and never went back."

Genevieve McGuckin, Anita Lane and Katy Beale ('the girlfriends') were also in London, and they contributed significantly to the band, influencing attitudes and perspectives.

Phill: "The girls paid for themselves to get to England. Katy Beale was there within a few weeks, Genevieve and Anita were there very soon after. It was too cramped, so we had to find another place to live; we had to have a central household, a focus.

"Mick and Katy moved into a bedsit, the rest of us in the flat in Earls Court, then in May we moved into Maxwell Road, in Fulham. The living conditions probably weren't as nice as Mick and Katy's bedsit. They worked for the Lyons food chain that year.

"There was always someone sitting up late at night working songs out with unplugged electric guitars, Nick singing with Rowland. That's how some of those kooky bass lines like 'King Ink' came about – that's Nick on Rowland's unplugged electric guitar. Tracy put it together afterwards. The same with 'Nick The Stripper', and the funny little insect dance that went along with it was something really stupid we came up with one night. I always interpreted 'Nick The Stripper' as the spectacle of the person being on the stage."

London's music press was in its 'Post-Joy Division' phase. English punk had promised so much, but had been subjected to a great deal of media dissection and misinformation. The concept that music could be utilised as pseudo-political but socially valid opposition to the established practices of popular music companies and the rock 'n' roll industry had little or no general support, although it made good copy. Music journalists described punk as a vast, thickheaded, stagnant, soap-operatic score; like an atrocious musical with more form than substance, not as a focus for dissatisfaction and social interaction. The Boys Next Door/Birthday Party still had a close affinity with punk ideals.

While The Gang Of Four were making political pop with what sounded like a Brechtian approach, The Birthday Party were naughty schoolboys who'd hopped the fence to pinch apples . . . only to discover that the apples were wormy, and they couldn't get out.

Popular music was experiencing an identity crisis. England had been declared 'post-punk' since 1978. There weren't that many punks around when punk was happening, so many of those who had missed out (who were the right age to be punks) adopted punk as a uniform. The original punks had returned to jobs, council flats, mums, nightclubs, wives and babies, soaps and the daily drear.

Those who would ordinarily have been more interested in mainstream rock 'n' roll found themselves drawn to new wave bands who'd jumped aboard the UK punk wagon: The Jam, The Cure, The Damned, The Clash, Siouxsie and The Banshees. The music weeklies had rejected The Pop Group as 'clichéd', despite their innovative, radical approach. The Gang Of Four were out of favour – last year's thing, no matter how popular they were. The Clash and The Damned struggled into snakeskins left by The Rolling Stones and Mott The Hoople. Siouxsie and The Banshees were hauling out of a premature slump. Public Image, the great postpunk hope, had released their brilliant 'Metal Box' but were in the USA. Joy Division's popularity mushroomed but in May 1980 singer Ian Curtis died, and the band found themselves objects of deep reverence. The scene was open to the dramatically new. Also in May, Keith arrived.

Keith: "I spent four weeks going to every record company in London trying to get somebody interested in the band. I got up every day and hoofed it. I got to Maxwell Road, Fulham and they were looking forward to me sorting something out. I felt that we'd got this far, we had to try. We sent stuff to all the London music press. We found it very difficult to get reviews, to get even a glimmer of interest from anybody. So when the 'Mr Clarinet' single came out, it had a London address. Nick did the cover, and it was distributed by Rough Trade.

"I then got a call that the people I was renting the shop premises from in Melbourne had given us a week's notice to get out, so I had to fly back to Australia, because that would have been the end of my business if I couldn't relocate quickly. So I had to say to the band, 'I'm sorry, I've got to go'."

They'd climbed a mountain to get stuck on a plateau.

Phill: "When we got to England, we thought we were up against it. Then we saw bands like Echo and The Bunnymen, Siouxsie and The Banshees, Simple Minds, The Psychedelic Furs – and we realised that we weren't at all, because we could play so much better than they could. These bands didn't have the Australian pub scene to teeth on; we'd learnt how to be a really good live band. We'd been in situations where we'd have to play three 45-minute sets in one night."

Keith: "The Cramps really turned them around. They didn't ape The Cramps; they took an aspect and mixed it up."

Phill: "We were rehearsing the Doors' '5 To 1', and I didn't know how the drumming went because I'd never listened to that particular Doors album. I could play any song from 'LA Woman', 'Touch Me', I was a Doors fan – but I didn't know that tune.

"Music was hard to come by. Other stuff I was listening to was soul music. James Brown, his really 'out there' stuff like 'Hell'; Sam and Dave and Wilson Pickett, which from a drumming point of view has a lot of good stuff.

"Public Image's 'Metal Box' was great. We had a few records and a cheap crappy stereo, but we didn't have a tape deck to take with us on the road, or to listen to our own stuff, or to put ideas onto. Very minimal. I had a good record collection in Australia, but not in England. We were exposed to a lot of stuff on the radio, and we used to listen to stuff in record stores, but in the end we stopped listening to other people and started listening to ourselves."

The Birthday Party were trying to break into a closely-knit market, reinventing their music, direction and purpose all at once in unaccustomed poverty and cramped quarters. They didn't have record company backing and they were from Australia, which didn't count in their favour. It was almost impossible for an unknown band to get a gig in London; the band was expected to pay for the privilege. However, The Birthday Party weren't entirely without friends.

Keith: "After I left in June, the band started meeting people like The Pop Group, and met another group whose equipment they used to mount a few gigs. John Peel started playing their records, and once Peel jumped on the band, people began to look up, but that took months to establish."

They also met Jim Thirlwell, from Melbourne, who was setting up his own label, Self Immolation, under the wing of Some Bizzare Records. Jim was a well-known remixer and performer, and he and The Birthday Party shared many aims and attitudes.

Phill: "Mick looked up Jim Thirlwell almost as soon as we got to London. Jim had just released his first Foetus single, and was starting to create the mythic Foetus band. It had to be either 4AD or Factory. Factory were interested early on. Daniel Miller used to give us gigs with DAF, which were very important to us early on.

"We fed John Peel records. I used to go to the BBC every day for a while with records and stuff. He had been given a copy of 'Door, Door' by a friend of ours, Vicky, and he'd played a track from it on his weekly show. I got the 'Hee-Haw' EP to him and he played it, and then some more. Then, after one or two gigs in London, he gave us a session. That's our meteoric rise to success."

Keith: "4AD got interested enough to put out the second single, 'The Friendcatcher'. Rather than working with them in London, I was working to get the band back to Australia to play over Christmas and the New Year period. They were still living in poverty, not making any money as a band."

Used to playing three or four times a week to crowds from 30 to 200, many of whom were friends, The Birthday Party were not in the habit of having to scratch around to get a gig. The first gig was at the Rock Garden on June 29, and their second at the Moonlight Club on July 10. They managed to find about two gigs a month for August and September.

The inactivity caused the band's individual personalities to shift unpleasantly. In an uneasy climate, differences that in Melbourne could have been glossed over became big problems in London. The band had always preferred a sort of osmotic form of communication, and the first real rifts in the band came about primarily because what worked in Melbourne didn't work as well in London. In circumstances of general poverty and apparent stagnation, with few friends to visit in London, no-one handled the situation well.

Rowland: "The Birthday Party was a situation where if you showed weakness, you were opening yourself up as a general scapegoat for everybody else. I was the only person in the band who wouldn't ever show any emotional weakness, and, not so much Phill, but virtually everybody else had this front of being tough to some extent. Mick Harvey's was this sort of 'no-non-sense', 'don't fuck with me' sort of thing; Nick was like, 'I am the King'; and Tracy was inscrutable . . .

"I don't think any of the band's friendships were ever the same after going to London and living in each other's pockets, because everyone in the band was too intense to live with, and we all got on each other's nerves so much.

"I had malnutrition. I used to lie on the couch every day, I felt like I was about 80, I could hardly walk and Nick told me I'd never looked better in my entire life. I went to this doctor who diagnosed malnutrition and recommended I have three big meals a day, and I said, 'I've got no money, can't you give me vitamins or something?', and he replied, 'Well, I'd be rather interested to see what happens if I don't'. When I went back to Australia, the first thing a hairdresser friend said was, 'Your hair's falling out!', and he was horrified. I remember going to rehearsal and playing the songs at half the speed as everyone else because I was so weak. When Keith came over, he treated us like we were like cry-babies or something."

In Australia they'd cheerfully cultivated an abhorrence of neat, crafted, orderly music and professional presentation. Their lives took on a weird mesh mostly compos(t)ed of punk's dis-obedient dishevelment and their own savage satire of the shallow obedience that the new rock rebels in London made so much of. They were the boys-next-door who took this rebel shit seriously, like it was real.

An independent band today is a band the majors can't be bothered to groom into a chart success. The Birthday Party had to do all the ground work themselves.

Missing Link Records released 'Mr Clarinet'/'Happy Birthday' in July 1980. Phill gave John Peel a copy, and he began to play it on his BBC radio show. Peel saw the band when he could; he was at their first important gig in London, in March 1981, when they supported Colin Newman (ex-Wire) and Department S, both at that time important minor players on the London scene. Peel praised 'Mr Clarinet' and The Birthday Party often. Interest in them was still unremarked, but building.

Joy Division were another Peel favourite but The Birthday Party were their spiritual opposite. Where Joy Division put across a mood of emotional contemplation, almost after the fashion of the Romantic poets, The Birthday Party exuded a sharp, knowing sarcasm, and an expansion of the soul.

'Mr Clarinet', with its nastily loopy carnival tune, received a couple of cautiously optimistic reviews and the band began to get a few more gigs, The Rock Garden in particular allowing them to play sporadically. They had nothing to lose, so they allowed their irritations and imagination more rein. The Birthday Party were as outside the London scene as you could get. Total aliens.

In early September, they recorded their first John Peel Session for the BBC. Artists at these sessions record and mix four songs in eight hours; a 'sample only' type of production. It was broadcast on September 10, and on that night more potential fans heard The Birthday Party than at all their six or so gigs put together.

Naturally enough, they'd selected the songs to represent their current live set and their current direction. Nick's 'Yard', with its vast spaces, harrowing moans and inexplicable lyrics was captivating. 'Figure Of Fun', the oldest of the four, was performed by a much tighter machine than The Boys Next Door. 'Cry' was imperative, urgent, as if all the band's previous work had come together for the first time; the lazy rolling bass, fuzzing slightly and smelling bewilderingly of ozone; Nick's hysterical intensity; the fusillade of drums, musket balls battering a tin roof, slotting neatly in and out of the bass lines to create an intense, implicitly savage thunder. 'King Ink's majestic, threatening bass rumble swaggered like a Norse god across the airwaves into England's homes. This song was The Birthday Party's manifesto. Clear, precise, dominant, 'King Ink' caused many more ears to turn toward the band. What the song was about was irrelevant; it was what people thought the song was about that was important.

Rowland: "We were in this flat that belonged to a friend, and we started writing 'King Ink'. I think Nick had a couple of lines for it already, and we had to have the lyrics in a day or something. So we started pulling all these books from the shelves, poetry or whatever, finding all these good lines and rephrasing them so they fitted into the rhythm of the song. 'Zoo-Music Girl' was written around the same time, but we rehearsed it in Australia."

The Peel songs were all new, and had a quality which the band had not explored in Australia. A brooding, tense, hysterically violent feeling permeated their new set like an unexplained stench at a wedding. From September onwards more people in London and even a few music press critics began to pay attention to the band. A week after their first Peel Session, they played at the Hope and Anchor Hotel.

Andrew Browne: "The Birthday Party now appeared to be fairly freeform in the construction of their songs, but then they would reproduce that over a series of concerts, so their music wasn't formed from the traditional concept of jamming or jazz. I think they were intelligently taking influences from a lot of different places and really pouring them into The Birthday Party and making something totally new, and that's what good creative activity is about."

John Peel played the band's music regularly over several months, and more people became aware of them, that they were from Australia, and were radically outside the bounds of the independent music scene. At one Moonlight Club gig, some members of The Pop Group jammed with The Birthday Party. Despite The Pop Group's influence on them, it is difficult to imagine what similarities the two bands would have had on the same stage.

Ivo Watts-Russell, who owned independent record label 4AD, became interested in them at about the same time as John Peel and suggested they release a single on his label. 'The Friendcatcher' EP, taken from the Tony Cohen sessions, was released a year after it had been recorded. Ivo also arranged for a couple of their old tracks to be remixed by Adrian Sherwood, but these never surfaced.

Phill: "Ivo did do quite a good job, but he could have maybe done a better job. Ivo might have felt hamstrung since Keith owned the material."

After 'The Friendcatcher' received frequent airplay on John Peel's programme in October, far more people began to check them out and before long they had the beginnings of a following. The older songs in their set were 'Safehouse', 'Hair Shirt', 'Guilt Parade' and 'Let's Talk About Art' but there were several that crossed over: 'Catman', 'Mr Clarinet', 'The Friendcatcher', occasionally 'Riddlehouse' and 'Happy Birthday'. Their new songs were 'Figure Of Fun', 'King Ink', 'Cry' and 'Yard'. A slavering, hungry song, Gene Vincent's 'Catman' seems an insidious precursor to Nick's later 'woman killing' songs (such as 'Six Inch Gold Blade'), a nasty, gritty chunk of alienated psychosis. Some thought they were funny on stage; some thought they were useless. The crowds were mostly quiet. "It was like playing to a spilled half packet of frozen peas," remarked Tracy.

The Birthday Party were cautiously sniffed; the music press noting, like dutiful students, John Peel's interest and the 4AD single. In October, their first interview concentrated on how to define them from their records. A couple more equally uncertain interviews were published.

Mark M: "'The Friendcatcher' . . . An overwhelming, well-paced row, an impossibly long destructive moment, from which a song of regret defines itself from second to second, gulped at by this noise and is finally engulfed. The lyrics seem like an emotional shorthand. Live, Rowland and Mick would hit their guitars until the feedback and howling leakage came out like a demon."

'The Friendcatcher' EP reached the top five in the independent singles chart in *New Musical Express*, but, same chart, same week in *Sounds*, it was 31. Thanks in no small part to John Peel, 'The Friendcatcher' was number 3 in the English 'alternative' charts by the time they returned to Australia.

Mick: "They'd just finished slagging off The Saints when we arrived; they'd said 'Fosters and kangaroos' as usual and then we turned up and I think they started getting confused. They started wondering if there was something going on, and opened up to the idea that there might be good groups in Australia, which made a very big difference to everybody that came over after us. The Triffids, The Moodists, The Go-Betweens. We got treated well because of The Saints, we'd turned up and were what we were and they took us seriously because they couldn't slag off another Australian group for the same reason."

Phill: "We'd rehearse in Battersea. Tracy borrowed Kevin's bass; he ran the rehearsal studio. We played with some funny bands to get into the scene; people didn't know what we were going to sound like or what we'd be like."

Late 1980 saw them add a handful of older songs into the set: 'Let's Talk About Art', 'Waving My Arms', 'Guilt Parade', 'Hair Shirt' and their new 'Yard'. They were playing 45 minute sets in London, not as long or varied as they would at home.

Keith Glass had spent a lot of money on the band, but with his improved licensing deal with Seven Records (an appendage of Australian TV station Channel 7), he could release a compilation album to coincide with a return-to-Australia tour, which would generate more interest in the band; maybe even some money.

Keith: "I had a choice not to put the album out, but the label needed money to go on; it needed product to be out there to maintain some sort of profile, both for the band and the label. I thought the band's arguments why the album couldn't come out were totally stupid, so there was plenty of correspondence that went on between the band and myself.

"I said, 'We've recorded these tracks, we need to get some return, what do we do: not put them out?' Singles and EPs you don't get any return on, they're not permanent fixtures, they disappear. So I put the album out, which, as an album, held together fairly well, I thought."

Negotiations began after Keith returned to Australia in June; Ralph wouldn't release the compilation. Nick suggested several cover designs and the title of 'Drunk On The Pope's Blood' (again). Most of the songs had been released, and the two unreleased tracks they considered bad recordings. If Seven had been more successful in distributing and promoting it, their profile would have been significantly elevated.

Many of those who bought the record were hearing The Birthday Party for the first time. The band were enigmatic, frozen awkwardly in transition between the full bore of the live band and the experiments made in the studio. 'Hats On Wrong', for example, was very different live. The soft beginning and the loud, raucous change wasn't recorded properly, so a good deal of the impact, and the humour, is lost. 'The Guilt Parade' is a sly, insidious, twisting tune freshened with blasts of the bizarre, with a wicked, parodic sneer.

Around this time Rowland was experiencing difficulty in having his songs accepted, partly because Nick was asserting his role as *the* singer. Both songwriters were writing poles apart from each other, and since the most immediate crowd response came from Nick's songs, the band felt more comfortable playing his songs than Rowland's. Nick was now toying with some ideas for short plays; not to be performed, just read.

On stage, Nick was increasingly the archetypal wild front man who also wrote the songs, sang and did the interviews. Although the band might be interviewed, Nick would be quoted more often than anyone else, but there was always much more to them; everyone in The Birthday Party was essential, irreplaceable.

In November 1980, the band returned to Melbourne. They'd developed and benefited greatly from their months in London. They were now an international act, and well aware of the distinction.

Back home the Australian 'alternative' scene had shifted emphasis and expanded at a rate of knots. In tandem, Midnight Oil, Cold Chisel and The Angels were making significantly deeper inroads into the Australian mainstream. The Saints and Radio Birdman had left a mark on these bands as well; hard rock characterised the late Seventies and early Eighties.

Inevitably, the alternative scene dismissed the hard rock revolution as old-hat. AD/DC's 'Back in Black' was the hoon favourite; The Models' first album wasn't. Alternative releases tended to be pop-based. Mushroom's Split Enz had a monster smash with 'True Colours'. Graeme Revell took his SPK to London. Chris Bailey toured his new Saints in late 1980. Just when the audience began to get interested in new sounds and new directions, the pioneers weren't around, or weren't FM-friendly.

The Birthday Party became more popular and gained more acceptance within this expanded scene. The compilation enabled people who hadn't bought the imported London singles or 'Hee-Haw' to hear what the fuss was about. 'Alternative fashion' was more widespread, trendsetters aped English fashions and accents, but The Birthday Party were probably unaware of this change. Regarded as the atonal band with the pansy effrontery to change their name, confusing everyone, they were a new flavour of the month. The band that everyone had enthusiastically booed and thrown glasses at last year were now important. They'd made the UK inkies.

Keith: "Because we'd managed to hype things up a bit, when

the band came back things exploded. They were very cynical about it, they had every right to be, but I was thinking, 'Great! At last!' "

Many were impressed by the transformation, and attitudes towards them changed dramatically. To The Birthday Party, it was a complete about-face.

Ross Waterman: "Nick has altered the way that I relate to the world and my own environment. I do get fanatical about things that I see as being very important in their own time. There is greatness, always greatness in your own time, but when you can't recognise that greatness when it's just across the road . . .

"Nick was so glaringly brilliant, the first time I saw him perform there was no notion in my mind that he had any major influences. In 1981, these smartarse dickheads were saying he was doing Captain Beefheart, which was stupid. Couldn't they believe that an Australian could produce something of such quality without being heavily derivative of some international style?"

Probably not. The truth was that the band were a hodge-podge of styles and reference points, from The Stooges to soundtracks to Alex Harvey to The (early) Cramps to The Velvet Underground to Roxy Music to The Lounge Lizards, to The Gang Of Four, Fifties' rock 'n' roll, to James Brown circa 'Hell', mixed to their own recipe.

The 1980 Beefheart song 'Ashtray Heart' from 'Shiny Beast' has a similarity in tone and structure to some of The Birthday Party's songs, particularly Nick's vocal delivery. While newer songs like 'Cry', 'Zoo-Music Girl' and 'King Ink' bear a surface similarity to the Captain's abrasive, sensitive blues, they're not identifiable as an *adopted* style. There's no shared lyrical concerns, and they depict a more out-of-control world of emotional seasickness than the bleakest Beefheart. The humour is different, the Captain's is a familiar, bittersweet thing; their's is sardonic, leering, absurdist, panicky.

If the influence existed superficially, it existed alongside a slew of other, more disparate elements. By November 1980, their mutation was becoming more apparent, forcing themselves into a shape the Captain could never have developed.

During their return tour of Sydney in November, Tracy and Nick got tattooed.

Nancy: "The first tattoo, I wasn't upset. But tattoos are forever, and that worries me. And then I thought, 'It's his body to do with what he wants'."

Phill: "Nick drew his skull and crossbones on a piece of paper and handed it to the tattooist. Tracy got his first tattoo in Kings Cross in Sydney with Nick, of a sinking ship, a classic sailor tatt."

Nancy: "Tracy was dead keen on trying everything in this world. Tracy had this enormous curiosity about experiencing and knowing how things felt."

Their personalities *were* their public faces, and they made few apologies and fewer explanations. On stage, both appeared like all performers do, larger than life. Nick and Rowland are close on six foot or taller, which made their physicality quite intimidating on stage and off. In the minds of many, they appeared to be huge, awesome, expanded. At first glance, Nick seems unaware of the effect he causes, but he enjoys playing with reactions, emphasising his presence to an amusing and extreme degree. To a certain extent, this trait was shared by the band.

Phill: "People often missed the humour. It was a very funny band. We were often funny on stage, and people would often misinterpret that as us being arrogant, or too fuckin' serious for our own good, and a lot of the time we'd be pissing ourselves with laughter."

Dave Graney: "When I came to Melbourne in 1980, The Boys Next Door were overseas, but their shadow was huge in Melbourne. In their absence they grew bigger than they were when they were there. They'd grown by exiting into the world, leaving the precious inner-city music scene behind. Their future was to either stay around Melbourne and split up, or do something dramatic.

"There was this scene of people in St Kilda who were basically suburban people that existed in a world that was totally imported. Imported music and books, and fantasies of some urban lifestyle, things from everywhere, a Gothic kind of look. It only existed in a pressurised little inner-city kind of place, especially in St Kilda which was full of cheap rented rooms.

"Outside that area, you'd get beaten up. They'd created an exit to another dimension, where the world really happened in a theatrical way, like London with all its music papers and their contextual view of the world rather than drab Ozrock.

"So these people who worshipped The Birthday Party could

see this as a place and a way that they could live, too, and they were connected to other more happening, glamorous places than the suburbs of Australia, like Berlin and London.

"In their absence The Birthday Party's audience grew 10–20 fold. Melbourne was a horrible place. I'd lived in Adelaide and it was horrible, too, but it was very exciting to be around people who were so dramatic and full of their own epic dramas. People have to have conviction about what they're doing, and The Birthday Party had it in spades.

"At The Crystal Ballroom they'd show videos of The Boys Next Door even though video was a new thing then . . . on *Countdown* doing 'Boots', there was a clip for 'Boy Hero', 'The Hair Shirt' on this strange set, 'Shivers' live."

The band had no idea these were being aired in Melbourne in their absence. The 'Boots' and 'Boy Hero' videos were refused airplay by TV stations; *Countdown* forced the band to mime rather than play their clip. ABC shot some live footage at The Crystal Ballroom. The band never realised their earlier work was held in such high regard; they'd moved on dramatically in their absence. Had the audience?

Keith: "The album came out, the band came back, the crowds were 100% bigger, so they could play places they'd never played, as well as their normal places which were their strength, where they went totally through the roof. The shows were great, the band had improved so much and had moved in this other direction. They were able to soak up influences pretty fast and utilise them."

The week before they returned to Australia, Mick did an interview with *RAM*'s Clinton Walker. Couldn't the interview have waited a couple of weeks? Clinton's interest certainly reflected a new level of interest . . .

Mick Harvey tended to pull the wayward elements of the band together for a common purpose. To Clinton, he represented the band as a cohesive unit. Their new attitude, and mostly new set, turned some away but others were captivated by their new, invigorating and uncompromising music. With Mick on drums, they performed a legendary set of Stooges songs as a four-piece.

Rowland: "We were doing 'Prayers On Fire', and were asked to play a benefit for Laurie Richards because the Crystal Ballroom was going broke. Although Laurie had given us lots of gigs, he had also, we felt, treated us like shit. Considering that we guaranteed him an audience and played there every week for a year and made him a lot of money, he used to pay us really badly, and his attitude was, 'I've given you your big break, I made you'. So our immediate reaction was, 'Fuck you!', and then we thought, 'Let's go and play something ridiculous and stupid', and Phill said, 'No, I'm not going to do it, there's a principle involved here and I refuse to play'. So we said, 'Fine, we'll play without you'.

"We decided to do Stooges songs, so five minutes before the set I was showing Tracy how they all went, and we got up and did forty-five minutes of Stooges songs: 'I Wanna Be Your Dog', 'Funhouse', 'Loose', '1969', perhaps others. It was a great set. I remember getting off stage and my guitar was covered in blood. I'd been playing so hard my fingers were cut. People were coming up to us saying, 'Gee, your new songs are really great' . . ."

They missed the joke again . . . The Stooges were a legendary bunch of alienated, drug-fuelled Detroit hedonists with a lust for music and experience. Bands like Radio Birdman and The Saints had already incorporated The Stooges' love of feedback and wah-wah into their sound. They now added 'Loose' to their set, and though their version doesn't capture the lazy threat of the original, it runs away with itself like a drunken dragster.

The line for their first Crystal Ballroom show since returning to Melbourne had stretched around the block. This was unheard of, and the band distrusted the throng on sight. Instead of bringing out the band's extrovert sense of play, writers focused unerringly on what they didn't understand: The Birthday Party's intolerance for lacklustre creative endeavour. They'd grown up reacting against things in order to develop what they were. London had been boring, and their songs railed in the face of facelessness.

Ironically, they were paid much more for being the same as they were in 1979. To be hailed as conquering heroes on their return from an indifferent London was absurd. No-one had even heard their new songs yet. The change in their popular perception seemed perverse, and they regarded their new and unexpected popularity with deep cynicism. This was the sort of reaction they'd craved from London, not dreary old Melbourne.

They were more forthright, more palpable. Prior to leaving Melbourne they didn't feel they had much cause to force themselves on their audience. Now, they did.

Rowland: "We came back to Australia in 1980, and independently Nick and I both decided through a process of discovery that nobody was doing what we thought a rock gig should be, which was basically a *riot*; something that was teetering on the edge of complete chaos. Not necessarily musically but physically.

"The band always operated on a level of what you see was what you got. It was virtually the only decision we ever made; that people couldn't understand what we were doing because it wasn't obvious enough, and we decided that the best way to rectify this was to go out there and hit them in the face with big symbols marked 'Exhibit A' and 'Exhibit B', which involved larger than life clichés, which were so absurdly ridiculous. On one level we were playing the part seriously, on another it was like a deadpan role. Yes, I think we had read Flannery O'Connor at this point. In a way it was like a direct extension of the Australian sense of humour, like shitstirring, and sarcasm, irony. People eventually thought that we'd become *reduced* to symbols, and we were taken literally.

"We didn't think they'd respond the way they did. But the Australian sense of humour doesn't translate well, because people take it literally. We'd say how superb Genesis were, and they'd be mystified because they hadn't perceived that it was a joke."

Topless, with his skinny torso, stick-like arms and skull and crossbones tattoo, Nick seemed desperate for a response. Addressing the crowd, he'd clutch them, tease them, or rub his sweaty body all over them. Nick demanded the audience's individual, personal attention in ways which broached previously accepted stage practices. This was the last tour on which Nick played saxophone, realising it detracted from the spectacle.

It was on this Australian tour that The Birthday Party *became* a major modern musical influence. The band were tighter, more spendthrift with their time on stage; the crowd was no longer mostly acquaintances or intimates. Thriving on provoking some distinctive, often adverse, reaction from the crowd, it was evident that they were happier with their creation.

Much much larger than life, they were increasingly perceived as wallowing in the destruction of the self. They created responses that hadn't been seen on an Australian stage since The Beatles, dragging their audience out of themselves and into the dark, as if a vortex was on stage, sucking in everything and everyone, making *everything* The Birthday Party. Band and crowd shook, shivered and merged.

Everyone had their own niche, their own role. Musically, Rowland's 'guitar with a nervous breakdown' took the 'shitty noise guitar' to the most preposterous, outlandish limits. Spraying out raucous sirens, human sounds in deep fog, spattering over the heads of the taken-aback crowd, he splintered the band's rhythms. Tracy's rusty, oil-encrusted bass machine was intensifying, far more intrusive on stage than their records admit. Phill was still out there, his soul, country and jazz drumming, sticking against the wall of squall which they created on stage. Mick's rhythm guitar synced in with Tracy and Phill, who provided a solid, racing heartbeat backbone against Nick's mocking, tragic, comic and engaging vocals.

Dave: "They'd totally reinvented themselves. Their last few records had been very good, and there was a lot of expectation. When we saw them, they'd moved on; there was always a lag between their records, and what they were doing. Nick was trying to sing in this old man's voice, like a growl, like Captain Beefheart, and his voice didn't naturally have that . . . but he kept trying to do it. I think they were writing the songs as they were playing them, so they were very exciting to see. I must've seen them about five times while they were recording 'Prayers On Fire'."

Ross and Andrew: "The people familiar with them naturally expected The Birthday Party to be developing because they were seen as the top band. Nick was creating a much more guttural sound to his singing; he'd changed his voice. Hearing 'Prayers' for the first time . . . 'Jesus, it's incredible the difference and how good it sounds . . .', like Nick was straining to be really gruff. I remember being struck by 'A Dead Song', that hysterical quality . . . this was a dramatic transformation, a perfectly natural progression of demonstrativeness and abrasion in their structure and impact. If you only hear the records, you won't get it because they were primarily a live act in terms of delivery and emphasis."

Creative turnover had always been high with Nick. When he got home to his old piano, it was easier to write. 'Ho-Ho' was a more reflective song. 'Zoo-Music Girl' (apparently about Anita) and 'A Dead Song' were written in London, and 'Ho-Ho', 'Capers' and 'Just You And Me' in Melbourne, where they were rehearsed at friend's houses.

Tracy Pew's 'The Plague' was recorded but not released, and turned up on the later compilations, 'Best And Rarest' and 'Drunk On The Pope's Blood'. With the air of a ballad and some lovely piano, it could have been quite a contender had they taken time to work on it. Nick's vocals are neither loud enough nor delivered with enough conviction, but the rhythm is solid and Rowland's feedback is wonderful. Could Tracy sing? Intriguingly, Nancy mentions several unfinished songs among his papers.

Phill: "'Zoo-Music Girl' was written in London, but we came up with the music in rehearsal in Australia. I came up with the drum pattern, Tracy locked a bassline into it, and Nick started singing 'Zoo-Music Girl' over the top. I came up with the drum part that drove the rest of the song. Where I come from, I am entitled to a slice of the song, as is Tracy. It was never considered a writing part. Many bands view it like this, but money was never much of an issue with The Birthday Party."

Rowland: "I wrote the bass-line and suggested the hi-hat breaks. A lot of Birthday Party songs were based on a bass-line, where I'd direct them as to what I wanted them to play and what sort of mood it should be. More to the point, Nick's songs were often skeletal and fleshed out by the band.

"For example, Mick and I 'wrote' the guitar riff and chord changes in 'Mr Clarinet'. 'Zoo-Music Girl', 'Junkyard' and 'Hamlet' weren't written the way I'd normally write; I was trying to write music specifically for The Birthday Party."

Whoever kept a song flowing was helping to write the song; the composition of songs was a band effort, all parties throwing in material to bring the song to fruition. Whoever actually came up with the initial music or the extended stretch of music got the music credit as they were the directors of that song. Since Rowland's bass line leads this song, along with Phill's tremendous rhythm, it would seem that a great deal of confusion, not to mention bad blood, could be drawn here. Should Tracy have got a credit?

By Phill's account, yes. Rowland's account contradicts this. But without Tracy's unique interpretive skill with the bass, without his heavy monster sound, 'Zoo-Music Girl' wouldn't have sounded like the head-on, invincible supertanker it is. Should Tracy have been given an equal fifth share of the music of all their songs?

Nick's songs were recognised as the most successful; prior to recording 'Prayers', things had been more evenly matched. Anita Lane had considerable influence on Nick's writing. Many of his songs were inspired by a line or an expression from her writing, or something she said. Her credits on 'Prayers' don't mention that she provided Nick with essential inspiration.

Phill: "The 'Prayers On Fire' sessions were really inspired, our sound had taken us into a solid direction. That tour was good; everything was building nicely for us. When we got back to England we were really peaking."

The Birthday Party, with reasonable UK press but few sales, were recording what they described as 'Drunk On The Pope's Blood' in AAV's Studio Two. Split Enz, who received consistently disastrous reviews from London's music press, but had begun to sell there, and were phenomenally huge in Australia, were recording their follow-up album in Studio One.

Tony: "We'd start in the afternoon and record into the early hours. Split Enz had every piece of equipment in Australia and we had nothing. I'm very proud that we got a good album without flash equipment. I recall dropping a brick on a Fender Rhodes just to get a sound. Their producer was perhaps a bit paranoid, he kept saying that their knobs had all been changed overnight, but we never went into their studio.

"Tracy had discovered these expensive bottles of champagne from Mr Gudinski for Split Enz. All the way along the corridor down to Studio Two was the wrappings and the corks. He'd taste this $80 bottle of French champagne and say, 'Uurgh, this is horrible . . . but I'll have to drink it anyway', leaving the empty bottle in Studio Two."

Keith: "Because they'd had an incubation period in London 'Prayers On Fire' was a strong album. They'd thought about it. We were trying to get better sound, so we went to AAV to record most of it."

Mick: "Since we changed our name in 1980, we thought it was a good idea to change our name all the time. When we were doing 'Prayers On Fire', we were thinking about kicking Phill out or changing the group somehow."

Rowland agrees, explaining "there was a long period of time when Phill had trouble coming up with beats". When directed to play in a particular manner by Rowland, Phill would "normalise" them because what he was being directed to do wasn't 'schooled'.

Mick: "We'd talk with Tim Finn from Split Enz, and Nick would say things like 'we're changing the band's name'. Tim knew we'd changed our name, and he'd say, 'Oh, don't do it, man. God, it'd be commercial suicide'. Jesus Christ. Get a sense of humour, take a risk. We were quite serious about changing the name to throw everyone into confusion, 'cause we like that sort of thing."

Phill: "Mick is the most consummate musician in the band. Everyone thinks the solo on 'Nick The Stripper' is Rowland, but it's Mick, the playing is too dexterous to be Rowland. Mick came to the fore during 'Prayers On Fire'; by 'Junkyard' he was in the driving seat."

Tony: "They'd become a band. They weren't a ramshackle outfit, they were a tight assault band. They played better together; the rhythm section was thunderous. There was definitely more of a rift with Phill. He was getting shunted more to the background, whereas in the earlier days of recording he had quite an input."

Phill: "The first two years in England I was so fuckin' in the band, and we were so fuckin' in with each other that there were no real problems. It was only during the last Australian tour that there were problems, and it was all spiralling out of control."

Rowland explains that Nick, Mick and himself had difficulty getting Phill to play precisely what they wanted him to with their newer songs, although until they were rehearsing in London they didn't have any problems. Rehearsing of 'King Ink', Rowland asked Nick to play the snare drum because Phill's sense of rhythm wasn't allowing him to hit it 'wrong', as Rowland wanted. According to Rowland, Phill wasn't on the same wavelength as the rest of the band; he had no intuitive understanding, in the same way that the others did, of what the band was about.

The Birthday Party were like a truckload of drunken Aussie larrikins poking fun at the self-importance of the industry they'd infiltrated. Their attitude was solid and inflexible.

Keith: "Not many people understood their pranksterish nature. Nick's cover for 'Prayers On Fire' was done in our living-room with my little daughter's paint set!"

The childish skull with wavy arms appears sinister yet silly; the initial impression is contradictory, a cross between death and a wobbly octopus. The execution is childish, clumsy in its simplicity. It is an accurate portrayal of the band, reinforcing the image they were growing into. By the time the music press woke up to their intrinsic Aussie pisstake, they'd moved on to more dynamic and wider concerns. Pranksterism wasn't the only driving force behind their art; as corny as it sounds, their life had become art. Once this was acknowledged by the press, the intrinsic nature of that art was void and a new art-form was unintentionally created.

Mick: "One of the best series of gigs were the three nights we did at the Tivoli Hotel in Adelaide in January 1981, when Hunters and Collectors were our road crew (with the huge, dark-red Hieronymous Bosch 'Hell' reproduction hovering above the stage).

"The first night was really good, and we thought, 'Oh, we gotta do two more here', and the second night was even better. It was a really great show.

"The build-up to the next night . . . 'Tomorrow's going to be disastrous because the last two nights were so good'. We were sitting there all day thinking, 'It's going to be a disaster'; it had such a build-up beforehand that the third night was actually better again. That was when Nick first started painting his chest."

Rowland: "At the first Tivoli gig, Nick and I walked in holding hands and all these people were going, 'Look at those *fucking* Melbourne fags', which was another thing to annoy people, part of the whole faggish rock tradition, of the whole 'junkyard-rock schtick'; y'know, Jagger/Richards, Lennon/McCartney, like when Nick would lean on me while I was playing on stage . . . which the Jesus and Mary Chain later adopted."

Robert L: "Nick painted a skull and crossbones, like his tattoo, on his chest with water soluble paint. As he sweated, the paint would run and blur. He wrote 'HELL', 'SHERIE', 'HEAVEN' on different nights in red, the skull and crossbones in black. He was pushing to see how far he could go, and the band fed off the crowd response and fed more back, becoming an escalating spiral of energy and lack of restraint.

"The crowd danced frenziedly, the opposite of London. Nick resembled a debauched, half-naked ringmaster; and the audience, a group of Pavlovian dogs with the blinkers off. On the first night at the Fantasia, Nick wrapped his mike cord around Tracy, and dragged him across the stage.

"Rowland had developed a more aggressive stance on stage; he'd pace the stage with increasing abandon as if his legs were disconnected and loaded with caffeine. The crowd were increasingly enthusiastic. 'The Hair Shirt', with it's punctualised rhythm and mayhemic gallop, like a merry-go-round on a tilt, rotated the crowd into wild dancing and giddy abandon every night.

"Everyone loved them for having made any sort of impact in London. That they went on to expand it all over the next year cemented their success in the minds of the Australian scene."

Paul Slater: "Nick was jumping around singing 'Nick The Stripper', half-naked with 'Hell' on his chest; I thought, Who *are* these tedious pricks? They looked wanky as hell, but when I got up close, the sound was different and they looked completely different. Close up, they had a much more obnoxious, intense and earthy feel to them. Nick had a skull with arms on it painted on his chest – the cover of the 'Nick The Stripper' 12″, was taken at The Tivoli on one of these nights. Nick hugged a woman at the front, smearing her with paint, but she didn't seem to notice.

Goya: "Fantasy abandoned by reason produces impossible monsters. United with her she is the mother of the arts and the origin of their marvels."

Brian Masters, author of *The Shrine Of Jeffrey Dehmer*: ". . . the fantasies did not march with reason, they collided with her. They ultimately became more real, more cherished, more important than reality itself."

Fantasy is about maintaining the stability of the present via a relationship with a reality more vivid than the here-and-now.

The Birthday Party stumbled and strode alternately through such a morass of hypocrisy at an increasingly breakneck pace. The monster they created nearly devoured them. They represented disorder, revealing the hidden strings by which a puppet-like populace jerk and die.

"King Ink' was their first song to propel the fantasy of the band into the fantasist's world, prompting some observers to be drawn into a confusing arena where the roles of fantasist and fantasised-object were blurred and criss-crossed. 'King Ink' became more important during 1981; an enunciator of their intent. That perverse delight in setting up the crowd's expectations only to turn them on their head had been a part of them for so long that it was a major part of their driving force.

The video clip for 'Nick The Stripper' is indicative of their 'art bizarre' approach. Filmed by Paul Goldman and John Hillcoat on borrowed equipment, it recalls a Fellini debauch.

Phill: "On tour, you're playing three or four nights a week, at 11.00 in the evening, you go on, kick butt for an hour, and come off. You can get so totally 'up' and adrenalised that it takes time to come back 'down' so you can go to bed. When you switch that situation off, when it gets to 11pm, and *Nightline* is on BBC 2, you're in the pub, you're at someone else's place or party or you're at a gig; you're subscribing to that lifestyle. At 11.30, you want the lights to go on; when they don't, they've got to go 'on' in some other respect. I'm sure that's how a lot of musicians get into the circuit of partying, hanging out or doing drugs, because at 11.30 they want to strap on a guitar and go."

Rowland: "Particularly in a high-energy band like The Birthday Party, you come offstage totally wired, and there's nothing to do, so you either lose yourself in oblivion or indulge in whatever's about that you can get."

If The Birthday Party sensed that the crowd were out there expecting them to do a stark stone crazy show, they'd react against that and do a crap, ugly or tedious show, making the point, 'We do what we do because we like it, not because you want us to do it'.

Ross: "80% saw their gigs totally out of context, and had no way of slotting it into what came before. So they made statements based on that, and Nick and the band blamed the audience."

Another 'bon-voyage' gig at the Crystal Ballroom on February 21, 1981, became a talking point for weeks.

Rowland: "We were doing 'Loose' and Nick called this guy from the audience onto the stage and gave him the mike, and this guy sang 'Loose' very well, better than Nick was doing it. Tracy hadn't seen any of this happen, and walked up behind the guy and pushed him as hard as he could with his boot in the small of the guy's back, so he went flying into the audience and landed on his head."

Here are some excerpts from the man's letter to the band, typed the next day . . .

Michael: ". . . I hit the floor hard, and landed on my head. As a result, I spent the next half to three quarters of an hour in a daze, occasionally verging on semi-consciousness. Most of the time I was seeing double. There were moments when I couldn't see much at all . . . If I had just invaded the stage and snatched the microphone off Nick, then I would've deserved to be kicked off. But the truth is that Nick invited me onto the stage, to sing . . . maybe Tracy did it because he was drunk . . . he really made an idiot of himself, but the worst part is that it reflects on you all.

"I really wish it hadn't happened . . . it's left me slightly angry . . . but more puzzled than anything . . . please don't think this has put me off the band at all . . . you're still one of the best bands going anywhere in the world."

Rowland: "Mick and I were *most* upset, and Nick was pretty worried too. Michael is right, it *did* reflect badly on the band. It was really horrible and mortifying, because everyone had been tainted."

Tracy was still drunk by the end of the night, and Rowland didn't see Tracy the next day so he doesn't know what his reaction was, he was probably equally upset; he would have known he'd made a foolish mistake. Rowland knew there was no point bringing it up later because he knew he'd get no satisfactory response.

Although it reflects badly on Tracy, it's easy to see how he could have made such a mistake. It also points to the band's lack of clear communication. It's amazing that no-one was killed at their gigs. Michael remarks: "Many of the people attending your gigs . . . behave like heavy metal fans."

Paul Goldman: "The level of anger about the band really got out of hand; I remember being told that they were just pretentious, stupid idiots, that they did everything purely for shock value, and the band had no real integrity. I've never experienced a similar hatred and intensity of anger directed towards any other band."

They returned to London.

Rowland: "As Nick and I were getting on the plane, Keith said to us, 'You're getting out of Melbourne at just the right time. Everyone hates your fucking guts'."

The Birthday Party were unknown enough in England to be a new band. The London press delight in discovering a new group, especially a new trend with its attendant uniform. The English are into wearing the right uniform: Mods, Teds, Punks, whatever. But pouncing on a new band can stifle it's creative power; the band can respond to expectations, entering into a self-destructive dialogue.

The Birthday Party had been performing for over six years, and weren't about to be crushed by media attention. They'd already rejected the disdain of the Australian media with a haughty glance. Remaining isolated in London, creation was still their primary objective. How the crowd responded to them was a secondary motivation, and the press took a back seat. Crowd response to them was always organic and diverse.

Back in London, Tracy extended his aggressive appearance – he dyed his moustache black, and wore a string vest and motorcycle boots, in addition to the cowboy hats, jeans, t-shirts and lumberjack shirt cut-offs. These clichés melded into a confusing image; was he a gayboy on the prowl, a genuinely perverted sexual fiend, a brawny Aussie, homesick for the lowest possible traits of his countrymen, or baiting the rest of the band?

Tracy's movements on stage became increasingly repellent to behold; his dildo-crotch thrusts competed with Nick's equally ridiculous over-the-top tough guy bluster. Think of him squirming in tight lewd leathers or fucked-up jeans, dirty, sweaty, hair like greasy weeds, hollering the anthemic sexual braggadoccio, 'Release The Bats'.

Nick would tease and bait the crowd by addressing it in extravagant, mock sincerity, making fun of their expectations. On stage, an intimate expression of sincerity is a falsehood, especially if the audience aren't sure how sincere you are. The crowds quickly realised The Birthday Party were much more than a pub band. Anything could happen, and many were carried away by this unexpected feeling of freedom.

"Express yourself, say something, say anything, express thyself, express thyself, say something loudly"; 'King Ink' struck at crowds like a bullying ringmaster's whip, challenging them to further excess. People in crowds are strange creatures. Properly wound up, they'll do anything, follow anyone. The "express yourself" line slipped in and out of the audience's collective laps, reflecting on how easily we can be led to a specific end.

The "express yourself" line granted permission for part of their audience to go berserk, and when someone's repeatedly screaming this at you at a gig, when you're under the influence of hormones, alcohol and one or more drugs, it's a sound piece of advice. We all get carried away in the heat of the moment, like children at weddings.

Gigging around London started on March 10. A suspicious English capital gradually warmed to them.

Phill: "I think we were perceived by the press as a band you had to take very seriously, so people weren't seeing the innate humour, or that some things were tongue in cheek. They took everything pretty much at face value, because they were trying to understand us and looking for something very complex, and we weren't trying to present anything that complex. I'd get good write-ups in the music papers 'cause I was combining rock with jazz, swing and big band styles, and that was perceived as being fairly inventive. People would come up and ask me about my playing."

Rowland: "One of the most appalling things about the band was our total inability to cope with other people's sensitivities or feelings. I'd show the group a song and there'd be complete silence, and perhaps Nick would say something like, 'Mick, do you remember that 3-note thing you were playing on the piano last July?' I've shown them something I've put all this work into, and nothing would be said.

"In England when we were finishing off 'Junkyard', the writer Barney Hoskyns was in the studio with us. He was elected by Nick, Mick and Tracy to come out to tell me that this song was unsuitable, armed with a bunch of reasons why. I think it was the only time I got any kind of reason why something I wrote was unsuitable.

"It didn't happen often, because, unlike Mick, I wrote complete songs, so after a while I realised that unless I had something that Nick could relate to lyrically, there was no point in showing them to him, because he felt so uncomfortable singing other people's words.

"Once you gave the band a song, it was taken completely out of your control: that was a problem – I was forever trying to retain control of these songs I'd written; I should have realised that wasn't where the strengths of the band lay."

On this second visit to London they became more isolated. Nick lived in Chiswick with Ollie Olsen and Anita, Phill had a flat which everyone stayed in from time to time, Mick with Jim Thirlwell, Rowland and Genevieve with John Murphy and others. Jim and Mick appreciated the important musical genres, such as Sixties pseudo-classical/jazz spy soundtracks, and the tension-ridden themes to spaghetti westerns.

Nick, early 1979.

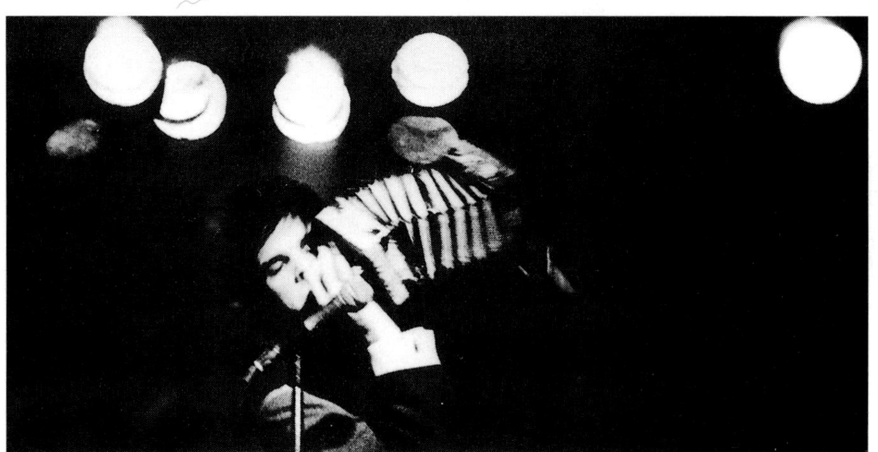

Nick plays 'Safehouse' at The Crystal Ballroom, mid 1979.

Live at The Crystal Ballroom, mid 1979.
Left to Right: Mick, Tracy, Nick, Phill, Rowland. Nick in 'cocktail-shaker' pose influenced by Simon Bonney of Crime & The City Solution.

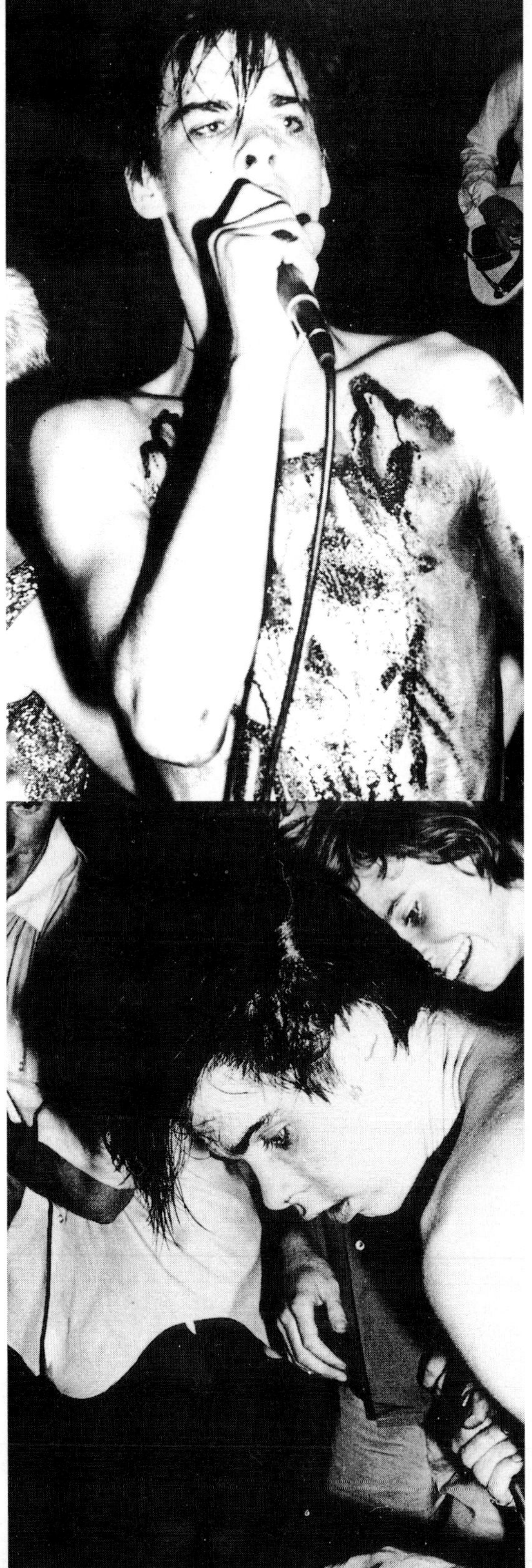

Nick live at The Tivoli Hotel,
Adelaide, January 1981.

Tracy

Phill

The Birthday Party at Vauxhall Bridge, London, April 1981.

Mick

Rowland

Dear Phil, 12·2·83

just a few lines to say hi! and everything's fine with us and we all hope everything's fine and dandy with you – keep whackin' them skins, ~~fuck~~ FACE ~~[illegible]~~.

yrs. Tracy + Nick

Phil Calvert
31 McKinnon Rd
McKinnon.
MELB. AUSTRALIA

Postcard from the Delinquent Twins.

Nick Cave onstage during the second to last Birthday Party gig at the Seaview Ballroom, St. Kilda, Victoria.

Left to Right: Anita Lane, Rowland Howard, Kate Jarrett, Nick Cave and Tracy Pew at The Jungle, Berlin, late 1982.

Backstage in Germany in 1982, just before Phill left.

Nick reading from *And The Ass Saw The Angel* at Id's, Melbourne, March 1988.

Mick Harvey and Nick Cave at The Club, November 1985, during the first Australian tour by Nick Cave and The Bad Seeds.

Nick Cave and The Bad Seeds performing 'The Carny' at The Metro, Melbourne, July 1990.

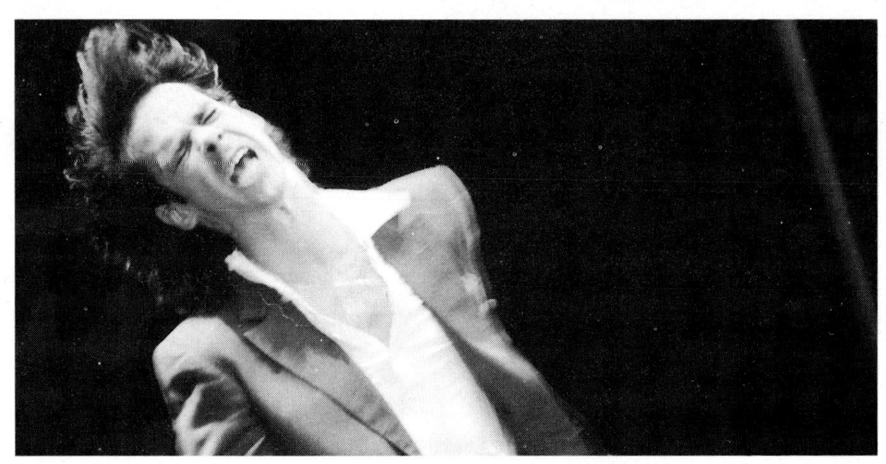

This Page: Nick onstage, Melbourne Showgrounds, February 1996.
Centre: With Blixa Bargeld performing 'Stagger Lee'.
Opposite: Nick with Kylie Minogue.

Mick: "I met Jim Thirlwell at Boys Next Door gigs in 1978. He left in early 1979. Jim and I lived in the same flat in London during 1981/82 where we listened to records together and shared influences for our 'Dirty Jazz' compositions.

"That first Lounge Lizards record matched us perfectly. It's brilliant, and it coincided with a lot of our influences, old film soundtracks from the Fifties and stuff. I think that's evident on a lot of The Birthday Party songs – there's a kind of 'dirty jazz' undercurrent which was turned on its head. Especially some of the songs I wrote the music to . . . 'Big Jesus Trash Can' and 'Six Inch Gold Blade'. Not all of the songs I wrote were influenced by that; I'd come up with other things.

"'Release The Bats' is a bit like that, but it sounds more like rock 'n' roll than its 'dirty jazz' basis. You could play it as a blues song, as a rock song, as a jazz song; it depends how it's treated."

Ross: "Their songs had a free-form feel to them, kinda broken-up jazz, in the construction of the songs as well as the initial impact. They'd reproduce that feel over several concerts, so they weren't jamming. They were intelligently taking influences from different places and making something new."

Mick: "Y'know what used to be said, that we used and incorporated clichés and stuff; well, we used deliberate clichés, and in the context of what we were doing, they were like a joke; or sometimes, by accident, they'd be made really effective."

Mick and Jim tried out ideas on each other, and much of Mick's music began to take on a garbage-jazz feel to it, a cross between bebop and The Stooges. They enjoyed experimenting, putting these sounds through a funhouse mirror, mutated and vaguely decayed. In deconstructing a confining order the whole was reassessed; Jim and Mick springboarded their music forward.

Mick began to come up with very bent, twisted rock 'n' roll, more so once the band had rehearsed it; the strained silences of 'Pleasure Heads' recall early Morricone, and 'Release The Bats' has a stride, hillbilly element, with Rowland's guitar slicing pervertedly through it.

'Nick The Stripper' backed with 'Blundertown' and 'Kathy's Kisses' was released in April 1981 on Missing Link in Australia and 4AD in England.

Mark: "Phill and Tracy announced themselves as a dangerous

rhythm section. Offset marvellously by Rowland's trailing, unpleasant guitar – he fucks up another nice little melody – Nick wrote the music, but Rowland corrupted it. There's a bluesish tilt in there, and the brass sets it on it's side."

'Nick The Stripper' describes an unpleasant, unavoidable situation, its rhythm adding accents with indifferent lollop. The drifting guitar is like so much countryside zipping past, like a Polaroid memory. Nick's vocals become gradually more insistent, his voice increasingly full of self-loathing and disgust. Over the top, bizarre, intense; the thunder of giant hooves, Nick obnoxiously screeching 'insect! insect!'.

Mark: "Rowland's 'Blundertown', is one of his most fully realised songs. There's great musical interplay between Phill and Tracy here, quite comical; the guitar is fantastic, and also amusing. A black drama, Rowland's guitar makes funny little turns, shoves in undertones of unpleasantness. Rowland backing Nick up towards the end – the effect is very powerful.

"'Kathy's Kisses' is all wonky and hysterical, laden with broken jazz metaphors; the piano working exquisitely with the drums. It's funny, but often taken at face value. The line 'She kisses me more and more and more!' suggests that Nick is terrified of her kisses yet helpless to prevent them coming!"

In April 1981, a short tour around England was followed by more gigs around London, and they recorded their second John Peel session on April 21. Radically different from their first, this was the aural equivalent of a towering skyscraper collapsing onto the streets below.

They performed Nick's 'Release The Bats', but not as uptempo as the later single. They'd been doing the song live for a while, it was a more or less throwaway joke on themselves. Nick's hawks and swoops amuse and startle; his Iggy Stooge-style grunts and whoops were a vocal extravagance which was simply '*not done*'. Whetting the listener's appetite for more, this session helped the single sell.

'Rollin' Around In That Stuff' (renamed 'Rowland Around . . .' when Rowland was out of the room) is a humorous, up-tempo scattering of drums and guitar – a passionate sex song. As the couple roll around on the floor obsessed with each other, there's a tension about their activity which makes the situation wrong; the couple are 'Junk on the floor', predating the complex heroin-excess concepts running through 'Junkyard'. Drugs, long a part of their background, are used as a device to confuse and intrigue the listener, to provoke response.

Nick's 'Pleasure Heads Must Burn' was a forceful highlight of their set, like a drag racer at maximum revs skidding down the track. Their future direction: *more so*. John Peel commented it was "a wonder they didn't need to rebuild the studio" after they'd finished recording. 'Loose' stated their mutinous intent and ended their shows in the most ridiculously over-the-top way possible. The guitars hammer at each other like electromagnets bleeding cities dry, Nick's prominent Iggy grunts and Rowland's white heat feedback rips through indiscriminately.

Back in London, they flailed 'Loose' at their more sizeable crowds as a 'leave 'em wanting more' encore. During the course of this year, they began to interfere with the desires of the crowd at the end of a gig, playing songs designed to bore or annoy the crowd. They also played a game . . . who could remain on stage making noise the longest after the set had finished. This resulted in sets ending in walls of feedback from Rowland, indiscriminate howls from Nick, and finally, because Nick *always* won, the mindnumbing '*thud*' as he dropped the microphone on to the stage.

The band's media profile went up a notch.

Ralf S, medical student: "Their clothes seemed defensively normal. Jeans, lumberjack shirts, t-shirts, suit jackets. They had a knowing, amused-by-it-all air; their prank was being taken seriously.

"Nick's hair grew longer, messier; he looked like some obscene urchin with a habit of writing filth on backstreet walls. Rowland's was equally as wretched, he looked more intense and harrowed as he paced the stage; one expected the guitar to change into an axe or a sword, Rowland to flail the crowd with it. Tracy's aberrant ex-pat style was knowingly noxious; his degenerate appearance confirmed for the unwary that here was a band as appealing as a blowfly on an insufferably hot day. Mick and Phill's apparent innocuousness reiterated the extremes; something is not right. They were not a band to tread in."

Some nights the band would be seriously pissed off about something, and their greasy, mucky rock 'n' roll would spatter about the hall; sometimes they'd be in great good humour, and the night became one of jest, their more comic aspects brought to light.

Nick, ever emphatic, always upped the ante, poking fun at his performance, or perhaps the reaction of the crowd. They were all well aware of the performer's dilemma – to improve, you have to better yourself. If you reach a peak, how do you top that? Nick was more visible than the rest, and that pressure fell mostly on his skinny shoulders.

Phill: "People would come up to me afterwards and say, 'How do you work your changes? How do you know that this is the bit where you go to the other chord? You're playing on one chord for ages, on one riff, and then there's one key change! How do you know when to change, it's never in the same place twice?!' Easy. It's cued by the vocals. Or when Tracy looks at me; 'Yeah, we'll do it now'. Or Mick'd play a figure and that would be the slide down to the change."

They never played 'Dull Day', 'Just You And Me', 'Ho-Ho', 'Capers', 'Blundertown' and 'Kathy's Kisses' live. They'd set another challenge – the significant discrepancy between 'Prayers' and their set. Same band, different impact. Rowland relates how, after rehearsing 'Release The Bats', Phill said; 'Hey guys, I've got this great idea. Let's record a Beatles song'. Absurd? Rowland and Nick were flabbergasted. Certainly 'the Fabbos' were light-years from The Birthday Party. But Phill meant the scuzzy insanity of the white album's 'Helter Skelter', not some McCartney whimsy. After hearing George Martin's (made for Lennon) 60 minute edit of 'Helter', Phill's idea doesn't sound so absurd. Indeed, it makes far more sense than their jokey cover of Nancy and Lee's 'Jackson', The Loved One's 'Sad Dark Eyes' or The Doors '5 to 1'. But when did rock 'n' roll make sense? 'Release The Bats' and 'Blast Off' were recorded in late April. In London, they'd play to around 350 or so.

Phill. "The drum sound in 'Release The Bats' and a lot of the overdubbed parts, cymbal sounds and so on, are doubled with me playing bits of corrugated iron. We screened Rowland's amp with corrugated iron and put contact mikes on the corrugated iron on 'Blast Off!'."

More London gigs in May were followed by a brief tour of the sticks by hired car. The rented truck carrying their PA had its tyres slashed after a gig at Leeds. By mid-June they were supporting Bauhaus on a short tour of England. Bauhaus took five lights – one each, plus two for their singer, Peter Murphy. This basic technique worked to great effect. The support bands couldn't use these lights, but since they couldn't play in total darkness, they played with the house lights on. The Birthday Party were still an unknown quantity, playing to either enthusiasm or bemusement. Bauhaus were pleasant enough to The Birthday Party, but Nick, Tracy and Rowland found them artistically loathsome.

How would Bauhaus feel, walking onto a stage to a shuffling crowd, following Nick's condescending, parting shot: "Bauhaus are on next. Do stick around, they're really quite good", daring Bauhaus to disagree or disprove him. Few bands would enjoy playing with the house lights on. There was no outright animosity between the bands, though Bauhaus' fey spy-horror Bowieisms did arouse a certain contempt.

Phill: "At the Lyceum Ballroom in The Strand, Tracy turned up with his second tattoo: a cobra wrapped around a mongoose, each trying to kill the other, by Dennis Cockell in Finchley Road.

"The last gig, at the Cambridge Corn Exchange, was something to remember. There's an English tradition that the main band cream pies the support band on the last gig. A vaudevillian tradition? That didn't fit in with where we come from, although we'd got on well with Bauhaus.

"The other band, Vic Godard and The Subway Sect, weren't playing, so we went on to play in daylight, so it didn't feel right. It was an okay crowd, but the place had a noise meter, and with the light it all sort've dampened us. We came off spewing, spitting chips; 'Okay, how are we gonna get 'em back?' We had Johnny Waller from *Sounds* with us and we're going, 'Peter Murphy, what a tosser' and so on, and one of their roadies overheard us.

"We were saying, 'We'll get him, we'll pull his pants off on stage during their set'; but we decided that was a bit too heavy, but the roadie had split and warned them, so when Bauhaus were on, they thought we were going to pull Peter's pants down during their set.

"Peter saw us from the stage trying to get on stage, and the roadies trying to hold us back, but we'd all been appointed to our places: arm, arm, leg, leg.

"Johnny Waller's a short stocky guy, and goes hurtling on stage in this major rugby tackle. Peter Murphy hits the deck, we're all holding him down, Tracy runs in with a big black felt pen. Peter was fighting like hell; he was wearing these black leggings like tights and no top, and he thought his daks were coming off and he'd be left on stage starkers. Tracy drew this great big dick on his chest, and we all ran off.

"Peter stood up, looked down, and cracked up laughing. At the end, we all got up and did 'Fever', Nick and Pete swapping verses."

'Prayers On Fire' was released in July 1981 on Missing Link, Thermidor and 4AD.

Wendy Munro: "They started to be described as 'chaotic', but unless you'd seen them live, chaotic is not the word; revelatory's more like it. The strength and force of 'Prayers', its seamless quality, Nick's change in vocal style, and the continuation and unity of themes made it seem like the most brilliant 'rock' record ever."

'Prayers' has a multitude of writers, and the tumult of world views – each unique and creative – represents a bizarre inner landscape which takes several hearings to digest. It's a landmark, their first classic album. The tight, thunderous opening of 'Zoo-Music Girl', with its brazen trumpet, heralds their arrival with its intensely sexual lyrics, utterly relentless pursuit of a rhythm, and Nick's frantic and obsessive lyrics and delivery.

Nick's image, to "murder her dress nightly", is a simile for sex, and clearly marks the beginning of a period where he merges desire and hate, forcing self-examination. Rowland's ripping, clawing noise rolls around the rampant jungle beat set up by the bass and Phill's urgent, abrasive drums.

Rowland dominates 'Cry' with brutal interruptions and his wonderful feedback breaks mix with punching, repetitive guitar lines. Nick performs emotively: desperate, bordering on nervous collapse, gradually building the tension from something slightly risible to a captivating emotional state, leaving the washed-out listener doubting whether the final words are a demand or a frantic plea.

'Capers' was written by Genevieve McGuckin with Rowland's music. A creepy schoolyard chant, similar to Rowland's little nursery rhyme spoofs, this combined with Genevieve's alliteration creates an enclosed world, with no escape for the emotions. 'Nick The Stripper', with its emphatic and disturbing atmosphere of mayhem, seems to emerge from some dark chrysalis.

Fantastically tense, yowling cougar feedback announces 'Figure

Of Fun', and Nick's yelps and grunts hold sway. The bastard son to 'Nick The Stripper' is about the absurd things expected of a performer. It's made ridiculous when the threads of hokey rock guitar suddenly turn nasty. The unexpected exclamation, "Rock!" is so spoofy it's hilarious.

'King Ink' swaggers in, a wealthy jaded young lord, cocksure. More frantic is Anita's 'A Dead Song'. Tracy's clarinet sets off Mick's guitar and piano marvellously, and Tracy's effortless bass lines slide in and out. The tight breaks and pauses alternate throughout, punctuated by Mick's rippling assaults. Rowland plays only during the last 10 seconds . . . "as I never really liked the song. Nick gave Anita credit a couple of times, but I'm sure that she probably inspired or helped out a lot more than she's credited with."

Anita's contribution to Nick's music will probably be forever underestimated, but Nick's primary ability is to catalyse, and blend random elements into a cogent form. A successful artist appropriates from the immediate environment and makes good art. 'Zoo-Music Girl' is frantic, paying fetishistic attention to the details of the 'girl' the 'singer' is singing about. There is no mention of what the girl herself is like, the focus instead is all on her physicality, her clothes and movements. Although it starts with an admission of failure, that "our life together is a hollow tooth", it ends with the singer helpless to prevent his obsessive nature overruling his common sense. Many dominatrixes will agree that the ultimate fetishist's fantasy is to be killed by the object of their adoration, hence Nick's "Oh! God! Please let me die beneath her fists!"

A Freudian might argue that such an attitude is itself misogynistic, because the obsession with the object of desire rules out any interactive emotional relationship between equals, although the 'object of desire' usually has the option to leave. An interesting inversion of the lyric appeared in one Melbourne underpass; "Nick Cave – Please let me die beneath your fists!".

'Zoo-Music Girl', removed from its context, presents a male point of view which is both tragic and comic. This theme runs through Nick's writing: loss of innocence does not usually result merely in the gathering and utilisation of experience to produce a better life (William Blake's ideal in *Songs of Innocence and Experience*), but in a moral and deterministic chaos, which causes the most bizarre and extreme elements of human behaviour to emerge, with results as amusing as they are tragic.

'Zoo-Music Girl' is clearly 'about' Anita, but the Anita who appears in his lyrics is not the woman he knows. She's a symbol . . . reality has never seemed sufficiently vivid, so Nick tries to improve on it in his writing and general creative endeavour as well as in his much-documented compulsive behaviour.

Nick's 'Yard', the most underrated song on the album, is a lament or form of blues. Certainly the song is laden with grief, and the guitar hangs overhead like a thick curtain. The rhythm is relentless, like traffic driving around an accident. 'Yard' is one of the most emotionally powerful songs on the album, and if it had been placed elsewhere it might perhaps be better appreciated.

'Dull Day' is Rowland's best song here, strongly piano-driven, with the bass and drums at right angles to the piano. The drumming is more complicated, with several variations zipping about, complementing the 'life passes me by' theme.

'Just You And Me' is about repressing desire, which would fit with Nick's later themes. The 'fairground from hell' atmosphere continues, and, as it's the last song on the album, it's an ambivalent and disturbing conclusion.

Nick's religious expression in 'Just You And Me' and 'Prayers On Fire' (the poem on the LP cover) demonstrates an interest in morality and human desire. That modern society still has old religious rules as its moralistic base instead of more practical, and just, deterministic rules, is a niggling thorn to any perceptive person. This may not be Nick's intent, but he does focus on the resulting chaos, and the cause of the chaos is implicit: the loss of innocence and the resultant bewilderment.

People began to come to their shows as a direct result of 'Prayers On Fire', which remained on the independent chart for several months. One English reviewer described it as 'the greatest rock 'n' roll record ever', while another declared 'give praise to the almighty'. Coupled with such over-the-top reviews, their live reputation picked up. Truth be told, however, the nature of their rhythms kept others away, unable to get past the initial thundering, splatty impact.

A schism in the hierarchy of pop/punk was occurring; lines of musical demarcation were reinforced and redefined. The Birthday Party were instrumental, though not alone, in forcing this situation.

Mainland Europe was different; audiences there were new territory. The London press remained mystified, European audiences simply reacted. During 1981, it became increasingly obvious that The Birthday Party were their own creation and always had been, doing what they did naturally, owing little to anyone save The Stooges; and that was more attitude than anything else.

Europe reacted to The Birthday Party as a child does to a new toy: a ready made, alien music with a distinctive, aggressive daring, delivered with a force which left no room for uncertainty. The stagefront crowd were forced to react, Nick pushing himself on them, forcing them back or leaving them no alternative but to carry him. In North America The Birthday Party were an undeniable musical influence on a truckload of bands because the scenes there were in a state of creative flux.

Their mid-'81 set included: 'Nick The Stripper', 'Figure of Fun', 'Yard', 'A Dead Song', 'King Ink', 'Cry', 'Zoo-Music Girl', 'Rowland Around In That Stuff', 'Pleasure Heads Must Burn', 'Release The Bats', 'Loose', 'Happy Birthday', 'The Friend-catcher' and 'Catman'.

September 1981 was their public watershed. After the release of 'Prayers', they discussed managers, and after looking around, they remained happy with Mick representing them, organising tours, and Phill handling the gear. They continued with their present arrangement, hiring tour managers when necessary. Leery of becoming involved in the fickle world of pop, they didn't want to be beefed up to a level of importance, only to collapse like an overworn waterbed as soon as the money ran out and the records didn't sell quickly enough.

With their high turnover of songs, they'd quickly tire of their sets and arrangements of songs. A poor performance was about half as likely as a brilliant or 'average' night, though an average show was always interesting, as parts of their songs were explored in new and unusual ways.

More came to check them out. Many stayed, becoming more familiar with the bands' material and shock effect. By mid-1981, their followers knew how to 'read' the band. Most of this following was in London, where, as in Melbourne, fans would watch to see how the band behaved toward each other, and respond to the way the songs were performed. Their sets could develop in markedly different ways, according to the mood of the band.

Increasingly their gigs were about crowd response and the way they worked with each other. Very situationist. Except they weren't situationists. They were artists first, musicians second. And their art was their life. Everything they did was reflected in an audience, and the band responded back. Always. Nick had been goading the crowds around England for almost 18 months, and by September, he'd become far more physical. He assaulted the front row, and they were begging for it. The spectacle of a rock 'n' roll beast feeding on the Christians of complacency was also drawing in spectators. (The slogan for their advert for 'Release The Bats' was: "Dirtiness Is Next To Anti-Godliness".) The press began to catch on and by the end of the year, after touring Europe and most of England, many more were familiar with them, even becoming predictable in their response, especially in Holland and London.

European audiences were bewildered when the band was nothing like their records, and the band thrived on the joke. If the audience didn't get it, they played brilliant, flat or out of whack, pocketed their pay, got drunk or whatever, and crashed out at the 'hotel', elated or in disarray. Italian audiences went into hyperdrive, and lost control rapidly. When they played to an unfamiliar crowd in the boondocks, literally anything might happen.

The set was switched around nightly according to whim, or experimental urge. They put in untried songs, which could result in a really bad gig or a fabulous one. The degree of passion put into each night's performance was very much a personal matter. They were 'unprofessional' even for a young rock band; if they were too tired to do a show, they admitted as such. No plan, just expression. They went out and did a flat show, and usually apologised to the audience. Despite the apology, the tone was more, "Here we are and we're no good tonight. Tough shit."

Sometimes the sound would be terrible. Sometimes one or more members of the band had over-indulged in one drug or another, which produced either a brilliance or total fiasco. Or one would be trying to give a shining performance, and would be let down by someone who wasn't shining tonight, so the gig would go all over the place as the shambolic structure tried to right itself.

Their continuing empathy with The Stooges had its inspiration mostly in the 1970 album 'Funhouse', a reaction against diplomacy and compromise. Little wonder they covered 'Loose' and 'Funhouse'. It became pointless to perform 'Loose' when it didn't stir the audience but pandered to them. While they delighted in being taken seriously, 'Loose' became an albatross; poking their fingers into forbidden electric sockets out of curiosity was their delight, not coasting on a 'rebel rocker' image. Their music became a disjointed merge of jazz and rock, described as "a sort of parodic, splatty jazz full of hysteria, sadness, exploitation and revenge."

From September 1981 The Birthday Party seemed to shudder on the verge of imminent collapse, both musically and visually. They grew tighter as a result of the constant touring, but weren't achieving what they thought they should be. Where was the money to go with the front page? New songs weren't turning over quickly enough. Ideas didn't pop up as readily. No longer living in each other's pockets except on the road, they no longer thrilled to share musical discoveries. Friendships began to fracture and, depending on who they were living with, strange little cliques would develop.

'Release The Bats' and 'Blast Off' was released by 4AD in August 1981.

Mick: "The only song we realised could do well was 'Release The Bats', and we immediately didn't like it by the time it came out. It seemed too obvious. It was done tongue in cheek, almost a send-up of our own stuff, this kinda ridiculous thundery rockabilly thing. The first time we got from beginning to end in the rehearsal room, everyone completely packed up laughing, it was just so funny.

"It used obvious tricks; key change at the end, all that traditional stuff. But it worked, it was strong, simple and it was very successful and got us a lot of attention.

"We'd become more successful from doing what we want to do, so we felt no desire to compromise what we were doing. The thing I liked with The Birthday Party was when the songs were structured, like they had a relationship to a traditional song however sketchy that might have been initially."

'Release The Bats' became inordinately popular with people who didn't much like them but recognised a burst of raucous adrenalin when they heard it.

Phill: "We were at The Moonlight Club in London, and this young kid comes up to me and says, 'Buy me a pint'. 'Sorry?' 'You know . . . buy me a pint.' 'Well, why?' 'You must be fucking loaded, mate, you're number one in the *NME* charts'. Which meant jackshit, but he expected me to have folds of pounds in my pocket."

Some fans of 'Prayers On Fire' abruptly dropped the band, leaving for artier shores. The Birthday Party were still pushing the envelope, still larrikins. Keeping the audience on-side is important, and not many musicians break this tradition. In place of the few disappearing backs, a larger punkoid audience was waiting. 'Release The Bats' attracted fans who took the raucous rockabilly at face value, and loved it.

Mick: "We had a really bad attitude. It started with The Boys Next Door, quite early, long before it was justified, and continued for most of the time of The Birthday Party. I've noticed it in other groups since . . . when a group has a distinctive style and they hit a kind of purple patch and get popular and so on, they end up in their own world, completely oblivious to what's real around them and what anyone else might think.

"Everything revolves around their own thing and what they're doing. They take their gauge for what anyone else is doing from their own stuff, too. That's the situation The Birthday Party were in for a couple of years. You can become very arrogant. Although I think it's quite productive. It creates an artificial environment where you can take your obsessions further, kinda create a little bubble around yourself. It's quite a good thing as long as you come out the other side.

"We must've thought of ourselves as a rock band, but we felt very separate to the rest of the music world. We didn't feel any connection with the rest of the music industry, and all that competitive stuff. We didn't care about anything. We just did what we did."

The 'Goth' tag was attached to Nick like a bargain basement sticker. When 'Release The Bats' went to the top of the UK independent charts it brought The Birthday Party to the attention of a wider audience, and was even mentioned on Australia's mega-conservative *Countdown*.

The London press tend to focus on their own experience, thus giving the impression that they're the centre of the world. In 1982 a London nightclub called The Batcave opened.

The 'great British music hall tradition' had created a barrier between entertainers and audience paralleled with the class-conscious social shape of England. Coming from 'the classless society' of Melbourne, The Birthday Party represented a threatening, perplexing enigma which required a solution so that entertainment could be entertainment once again. Some newer bands cited The Birthday Party as an influence. They seemed to be into the amateur dramatics, rather than the substance.

The arty entertainers will always bc part of poprock, boisterously claiming to be teen riot idols, but their faces fade so quickly. This inspired Nick's letter to the *NME*, 'HMS Britain 1982', which was reproduced in his book *King Ink*.

Throughout 1981 they'd used the Rough Trade booking agency for their English gigs, but Mick took over around September, organising an American tour. He continued to book their gigs everywhere apart from Australasia.

Phill: "In 1981–1982 in England, Mick and I ran the whole thing. Mick booked the tour through Rough Trade and their booking agent, and I would do the gear, the trucking, the transportation; PA's, hire backline. That became mixed duty, although in Australia the gear and that kind of stuff was still my thing."

There were live audio tapes for sale in London's Camden markets which were like polaroids, no negative . . . it ain't going to happen again.

Phill: "We caught the ferry to Holland and we drove as fast as we could to get to The Melkweg (The Milky Way) in Amsterdam, fuckin' killing ourselves to get there.

"There's this guy doing kinda beat jazz poetry on the dancefloor as we're setting up behind him. They've got a small jazz drumkit, a guy doing this beat poetry, a flautist and a percussionist. They're Dutch, but the poetry's in English. This guy's singing kinda free-form, ad-lib beat-type poetry. One of the things he sings is, 'I am the king, I am the king, I *am* the king, I am the king of the junkyard'; and, 'Junk sculpture turning back to junk, back to junk, back to junk, back to junk'.

Rowland: " 'I am the junk sculpture made in Japan', I believe was the line."

Phill: "The original version of 'Junkyard' was only played a few times; it was jazzier and faster."

Mick: "The violence? It was what it was, an expression of frustration or whatever. If it became manifest in physical violence it was rarely from our side. Occasionally it did through being very drunk or whatever, but generally it wasn't us who were creating the violence, it was people's interpretation of how to react, and sometimes they got out of hand, sometimes they didn't reflect the kind of positive destruction that we were advocating.

"In the live environment, it's like a mob situation, so you take a big risk if you go out there and do something very violent. Most of the heavy metal groups are so soft and non-threatening, it's just stylisation, very neat and tidy; everyone knows they can go so far with pulling dirty looks, and they know that's the end of it.

"(The violence) became an element that people came to expect or we got advertised as or whatever and some people'd come along to deliberately use what was going on or misuse or abuse what was actually going on. It was counterproductive for us, it made it difficult for us to keep doing what we were trying to do. You get some real psychotics down the front too; you can't really be sure what they're going to do."

Phill: "We did a very good show at Brixton Town Hall, with a great audience who were really going off, and this guy in the audience was going mental, dancing off his head. During 'Release The Bats', where Nick did the little whacks on the snare drum, Bingo hopped on stage, grabbed the drumstick out of Nick's hand, put it between his teeth and broke it in his mouth with his hands."

Bingo also bit through Nick's microphone lead – imagine the effect of being on the receiving end – and imagine the risk of biting through a thick live mike lead!

Phill: "We got talking to him backstage, and he turned out to be a really well-balanced guy who was into making sure that he had a really good time. His father was in the army, and he'd been in the Marines, but had bought his way out. He would go to every gig, so if we were playing in Coventry, he'd be there. He'd catch the train or hitch to get there. He did this all over Europe, and when there was room he'd be on the tour bus, or he'd be with us on the train. He'd check into the hotel and sometimes we'd let him crash. He was totally, totally into the band and what we were doing for a lot of the right reasons. He later became a really good friend to me . . . he's a hell of a guy."

Bingo's response to the confrontational nature of the band was to challenge the band right back, particularly Nick. He used several ways to bait the band on stage, threatening their poise and power, without attempting to wound or maim. That wasn't the point; this was a duel between forces. He'd grab Nick's legs, letting go only when Nick said 'Please'. It was a game of one-upmanship, similar to the way the band fed off each other whilst they were on stage.

The Birthday Party wantonly poked fun at the gross self-coiting rock-thing, mimicking and mocking its conventional rebellion by attempting honest self-expression, designed neither to be understood nor consumed. Professionally irresponsible? Considering that The Birthday Party always said they weren't professional, that they considered the idea of tailoring art to meet consumer's needs to be disgusting, they make a lot of sense.

From September 23 The Birthday Party toured America, using New York as a base. Keith and Helena Glass also arrived.

Keith: "Tracy got to New York and went to a 'Western' shop and bought the biggest black cowboy hat they had. I paid for (the tour) . . . it took years to explain that the reason they weren't getting any royalties was that I was still paying off their (first) American tour! Because I didn't know I was being charged for it in the first place, I thought it was only fair that I recouped it. If I'd agreed to pay for it in the first place we probably could've come to some arrangement, but I didn't know until I got the bill."

Their first gig was at a previously hip and cutting edge disco, The Underground, in Union Square.

Phill: "Nick ended up in a very strange situation; kinda like a folk hero. People wanted Nick to be a legend; Nick wanted to be himself, but no-one was seeing the bits he wanted them to see, everyone was trying to glorify him. This began when the violence started in England, around August/September 1981, which was triggered by the *NME*'s New York article. The *NME* was like an electrode in the nervous system of the body of music; *NME* would say something and everyone would twitch: 'Yes, that's how it is'.

"That first gig was at Union Square (Subway), there was no-one there to see us, Mick was jet-lagged and pissed. I've never seen Mick that messed up before or since."

Rowland: "Mick was screaming drunk; before we went on, he was face-down across two chairs above a pool of vomit that was mostly pure gin, and I had to strap Mick's guitar on for him. I think we were thrown off because Mick was playing appalling white noise; in between songs, he was abusing the audience until the song started, saying, 'You stupid cunts, you fuckin' bastards', really slowly."

The owners soon realised they had booked an unsavoury band who were rapidly driving away their customers.

Phill: "The management shut us down after three songs. It was a middle-aged disco, but the news spread over the club scene in New York that we'd been too wild for a club to handle."

Keith: "I'd arranged for 'Prayers' to come out through Thermidor. We never got any money from that release, but we had some presence there. Helena and I got to New York (from Australia), we walked in, saw all this disco lighting and thought it was a pretty weird place; 40-ish guys in three-piece suits dancing with their secretaries, and about eight fans there; four of them from Chicago.

"This was 'New Wave Band Night'. Nick wore a pair of gold lame trousers which someone had made for him which promptly split. The guy who was running the place came up and pulled the plug. 'It's not gonna work. Here's your money. See ya later'.

"Barney Hoskyns, the journalist from the *NME*, had been paralytically drunk and was asleep, woke up and asked what happened. 'Oh, band thrown off stage? Okay, I'll write that.' It was on the front of *NME* the next week."

Rowland: "The Ritz had a clause in their contract saying we couldn't advertise any gigs prior to their gig, so we were billed as 'The Birthday Boys', and only one woman came to the Manhattan Chase Lounge gig. We didn't know about this until we got there. The management said, 'we're really sorry, we can't give you any money so we'll put you on next week.' They rescheduled the gig a few days later, after The Ritz gig.

"We were all in the hotel room, and Nick and Tracy were horsing around and knocked something over, and Phill immediately rushed over and picked it up. This culminated in Nick and Tracy capering around the room knocking everything over, leaving a trail of destruction, and Phill racing around tidying up behind them. He was so concerned that we might invoke the wrath of the hotel. Something that might've been 15 seconds of chaos ended up being 15 minutes, because they were so entertained by Phill's horror.

"At the Ritz, they honestly thought we were going to start a riot, which is why they threw us off. As far as we were concerned it was just another rock gig, and as far as they were concerned it was another riot like they'd had a few months previously with PiL."

Keith: "Public Image had taunted the crowd some weeks earlier at the Ritz, so the Ritz were kinda nervous, partly because of the type of band The Birthday Party were, and partly because they'd heard the story from Union Square. They had about six security guys around the stage, and when the first microphone stand hit the ground they said, 'You've got 15 minutes to get out of here, and if you're not out by then you don't get paid.' So . . . instant legend in New York."

Phill: "We went on, the curtain went up, and they had a line of bouncers across the front of the stage because they thought there was going to be trouble. The minimal audience really reacted to that. Nick reacted to the bouncers more than the audience, and after about four songs they pulled the plug. They paid us just to get out."

Rowland: "We went on and came off in about 10 minutes . . . I was confused when we were pulled off; they confiscated our beer, and we were being escorted out by five bouncers, and when I asked why they needed so many people to escort us, they replied; 'to protect their patrons'."

Mick: "I was told the crowd kicked the management's door in and did a whole lot of stuff. The management dragged us upstairs and locked us in our band room and said, 'stay there, don't make any trouble', so I didn't see what went on. They decided we were going to be outrageous. We were playing a really good concert, but I suppose that was pretty outrageous for them. It was 1981, and there was about 450 people there, a potential riot."

Rowland: "New York was important for us because we thought New York was a place that had seen everything, yet we were considered to be beyond the pale. That changed us, we realised that we could have a serious effect on things, that people found the band threatening, which made us realise the capacity of the band."

Phill: "Barney's article was a real turning point, it triggered a lot of the reaction to the band in England. The confrontational thing was something we developed and the band were working towards, but that article was a linchpin thing. After America, everyone thought we were this wild, dangerous band.

"Once we got out of New York, the other gigs on that tour were fantastic."

The 9.30 Club in Washington was followed by Philadelphia and Boston. Malaria! supported them in Washington, Phill recalls them wearing "funny hats and big baggy clothes at the soundcheck, but gorgeous glamourous costumes on stage."

Rowland: "We were on stage in Boston, mucking around, playing what we thought was cocktail-lounge-type music, such was our inability to distinguish musical styles. We were in rehearsal in England one day and Tracy was the only person at the muck-around who'd played anything repetitive. So we asked Tracy if he remembered how the bass line went, and he started playing something which was probably how he remembered it being, but which I think was completely different, which didn't matter as it had the same purpose and intent.

"Because a lot of the songs originated from bass-lines in the first place, it was only fair to give the music credit for 'She's Hit' to Tracy because the bass-lines were usually the first things that our songs were built on.

"Tracy had an ambivalent role in the band; he was important because he didn't let Nick get too serious. Although Tracy loved music, I think he was in the band because it was what his friends were doing, he didn't seem too serious about the quality of his playing, whether he was drunk on stage or anything. The more I talk about Tracy, the more I realise I didn't know him at all."

Keith: "We were in this black bar in Washington, D.C., and I went over to the juke box and it had all this great soul stuff on it, so I put some of it on. Tracy got up and said, 'What the fuck's this shit? Get this black shit off!', or something like that, and I'm thinking, 'Oh, no, we're going to get killed.'

"That Washington gig was really hairy. There were middle-class/upper-class punks down in this ghetto-area punk venue; lots of nerdy guys. I remember Nick pulling one real nerd across the crowd by his skinny tie, and the guy turning blue."

Helena: "Wasn't it Tracy? From the stage, he grabbed this boy's tie and broke his glasses and he slammed the guy into this pillar. Keith and I said to each other, 'We're running away.' We did not want to be dealing with the police in Washington."

Phill: "At our first gigs in England the audiences were really cold, so we tried to excite reaction, we wanted people to get into it, we were playing with just how far we had to push the English to make them get into it. The English audiences were spurred on by the *NME* thing and the press response in general, believing that what they read was the way we were.

"They'd been through the punk thing, the art-'new-wave' things, which was more about appreciation than participation. We were coming from Melbourne, playing the hot, sweaty deal; and we wanted the hot, sweaty deal back, but the English crowd weren't giving it.

"When we got back to England from New York, the crowd was expecting an onslaught. None of it was conscious, it was purely a development thing. I don't know if everyone realised it at the time, but I recall stating to the press that 'this band will be be bigger, and much more relevant, when it's all over'.

"That to me was the important thing – it wasn't like we knew what we were doing and no-one would understand it because we were so fucking clever. I thought that what we did, and why we did it would only make sense in time."

Phill had the misfortune to be in a band whose individual members projected an attitude very different from his own. Given Rowland's comment that the band would be quite cruel to anyone who didn't defend themselves, Phill was a natural scapegoat. In any other band no-one would be quite so singled out. The baiting game the band played on Phill was the same game they played on their audience.

Rowland: "We were at the Iroquois Hotel in New York. Phill had done something petty, inoffensive and unimportant which had angered everybody, because we felt it was a display of how little understanding he had for what we were doing, and we all took great exception. Nick and myself were sitting in our room drinking and fuming over this ridiculous offence that Phill had committed, and we decided to punish him.

"We got Mick to ring him up and say, 'Phill, get down here right now!' Phill said, 'Okay, Mick!', slammed down the phone and came racing down. As he entered the room, a bucket of water fell directly on his head, and sat on his head like a hat, covering his entire head. Phill stood there in the doorway and said, with no anger in his voice at all, 'I know you'll be sorry about this in the morning when you're sober', and walked out . . . which only infuriated us all the more. He'd treated us like naughty children."

Lydia Lunch is as effective a catalyst with other musicians as she is a solo artist. Well-known for her involvement with a number of New York's 'No Wave' bands, Lydia had set up a tour with 13:13, a friend introduced her to 'Prayers', and she was in New York at the same time as The Birthday Party.

Rowland: "At the Chase Park Lounge, there were these football jocks who were having a splendid time, throwing themselves around and drinking beer, and . . . there was Lydia. It was one of the few times when I've met someone whose work I genuinely admire and had some respect for, where they were uncool enough to be enthusiastic about meeting us.

"I'd been wanting to cover 'Some Velvet Morning', so I asked her that night, and she said yes."

Lydia was pleased to find them "so friendly" compared with the stiff and snobby New York scene.

'Some Velvet Morning' is a Sixties song by Lee Hazelwood and Nancy Sinatra about heroin addiction, an aching bittersweet lament on the loss of sexual appetite; a perfect vehicle for Rowland and Lydia's distinctive voices. They backed the single with their, 'I Fell In Love With A Ghost'. Mick, Genevieve and Barry Adamson were later asked to play on the record in London, using Phill's kit.

After their last New York gig at The Peppermint Lounge, they went to Chicago.

Phill: "We were down on the door receipts. Wax Trax in Chicago came up with this gig at Tuts. We flew there, played, and flew back to London the next night."

Rowland: "At Tuts, somebody threw money onto the stage. Nick said, 'Don't throw money, throw drugs', and this little plastic bottle came up, and somebody pocketed them. When we were on the plane back to England me, Nick and Tracy decided that it was essential that we should take all of these speckled, multicoloured tablets, and I think we had three each."

Phill: "During the flight Nick got extremely out of it, he couldn't work his body very well. At the airport I got all the gear together onto the luggage trolleys. Nick was floundering by this stage, he wasn't having a good time at all; he couldn't walk. 'Okay, I'll put you on my trolley, you hold the side, I'll walk it like you're helping me push it. Keep your head up and look straight ahead and we'll get through'. The customs officials pulled everything apart and got us all together. They let me go, they let Nick go . . ."

Rowland: "I vaguely remember going through customs and Nick being asleep on the customs desk. Tracy, Nick and myself were all so unco-operative and unconscious that they strip-searched Mick. I vaguely remember getting home, having negotiated my way very carefully, rang the doorbell, and sat down on my suitcase and fell asleep. I woke up three days later . . ."

Genevieve McGuckin: "Here am I sitting in our new bedsit and looking forward to seeing Rowland. He arrives at the door, and I went down six flights of stairs to let him in, because he couldn't manage to open the door. I was greeted by this creature that had nothing to do with Rowland, who was talking to the lady in the pink dress and who believed himself to be at a party! I was thinking, 'What the fuck is going on? Where has my boyfriend gone? Somebody's superimposed a new personality onto Rowland!'

"Rowland wasn't compos mentis enough to tell me what had happened, although I gathered that some substance had been consumed. He looked quite pale, and I didn't know what to do with him in the bedsit, because he believed he was at a party, dancing and talking with this woman.

"He said he was hungry, so I decided to take him out to dinner at a nearby Indian restaurant; maybe if I put some food in him he'll stop being so strange. He was acting like he was at a party, and was alternately very funny and very abusive to the waiters, and at one stage he had his head in his curry. The manager asked us to leave, and Rowland picked up his meal and threw it at the wall, narrowly missing me. They wanted us out so much that I didn't have to pay.

"Rowland's nice blue suit was dripping with curry, I had curry in my hair and Rowland was still talking to the lady in the pink dress at the party, I was screaming at him and pulling at him, really furious. I dragged him home and he fell asleep on the floor, I couldn't get him into bed and by then I had no wish to. I rang someone up and I was told the story. I had no idea how he managed to get to the doorstep because we'd just moved; I'd moved everything in while he was away.

"He kept getting up in the night, going to the sink and pouring things, opening cupboards and drawers, moving things around with no idea what he was doing and talking to people who weren't there.

"Twelve hours sleep had no effect. I was tearing my hair out trying to stop him from injuring himself; I wanted to run away and leave him there but I thought if I did he'd probably jump out of the window. Then Nick came over because Anita had thrown him out, so I had two of them! They were managing to communicate very well, they were having a great time! Rowland lasted for three days in that state."

Rowland: "Presumably Nick and Tracy had the same reaction."

From September attention began to concentrate on Nick and Rowland. The centre of a whirlpool of mystic innuendo, Rowland and Nick had wilfully played on the two rock guys (guys or gays?) schtick for years: in the 'Nick The Stripper' clip, Rowland chases and kisses Nick. Rumour and counter-rumour flowed and the intense attention had a tendency to warp perception. The band came to loathe the fawning, backstabbing English press, its presence an interference. Nick developed a derisory contempt for the press, regarding it as a sort of conceited parasitic moneychanger.

The impression that Nick and Rowland were the prime movers in the band was a misrepresentation; important, yes, but really only two fifths. Nick wrote many of the band's songs, but he was in no way the band's primary instigator. Although he attracted more focus during 1982, he was never their leader.

Developing a song was a band effort. Mick had an increasingly intuitive grasp of how to patch a song together, particularly those by Nick. Mick was also invaluable in managing their bookings along with Phill who organised the equipment, rental, roadies and hotels, and lugged the gear in and out. Phill's personality may not have been in keeping with the rest of the band's self-image, but the only other person capable of (or who could be bothered with) handling mundane chores would have been Mick, and that might have been too much work.

Phill: "I often came up with the drum line. There were songs which were worked on which never came to fruition which were jams where you got parts together and maybe used one part in something else later. An early song of Nick's ended up being 'King Ink', with the rhythm slowed down.

"Rehearsal of new songs was a barbed-wire street, unless it was being dictated by someone with a firm idea of what they wanted. The same thing with the arrangements. I'm positive I helped arrange some of the songs, although I don't receive credit for it. Things like 'Why don't we put this bit here' and 'What about we finish like this' or 'I'll do this and then you can do that' tend to float around from all directions in rehearsal. Tracy was the same. We didn't need to argue about who did what because we wanted ourselves to be the primary creative force in what we did.

"Rowland stopped measuring up to Nick or Nick and Mick's ability to write songs. Rowland could write with Nick, and Nick could write with Mick, but Rowland couldn't formulate a whole song on his own once we got to London in the second year. I'm not saying he withered and died, nor am I saying that he can't write. The other guys overtook him, and he either held back, or decided it wasn't worth submitting anything unless he felt it was brilliant."

Rowland: "Since I joined The Boys Next Door, Nick and I had always written songs that were basically skeletal ideas that were turned into a whole song by the band. Not just anyone could do this; Nick and I had a very strong idea of what should happen with the song."

Rowland couldn't be replaced, his sound was too distinctive. Without Tracy's intuitive grasp, the band would not have fired as well. Tracy's slimy roiling rhythms could not be underestimated; without the sheer strolling-god thunder of his bass, their songs simply would not work. Tracy often acted as a buffer in more serious squabbles without actually becoming involved in the squabble itself. Mick often took this stance as well. For the London weeklies to focus on Nick and Rowland was understandable, but they misunderstood the band.

During 1981, London was experiencing a lack of musical novelty and excitement. Nothing fresh and interesting was around, no credible bandwagons, and the usual blaggers were hyping everything under the faint sun. Although the London music press were now trying to pigeonhole them, The Birthday Party carried on, heads-down. Mainstream acceptability? They couldn't care less about that, more intent on following their adventure and see where it all led, how far they could push the envelope.

Nick talked to Lydia Lunch about his 10 plays. They were too extreme, not right for the band. He'd put them aside, but Lydia suggested they find time to write some more, which they did in London. The result was 50 one-act plays with themes like 'speedway', 'filth', 'gun play'.

Nick's plays were based around characters who lived a sleazy, trashy life, struggling amongst moral and physical garbage. The idea, I think, was to present a one-dimensional world to provoke a response from people who lived in their own, separate, one-dimensional world. They served the same purpose for Nick as the 'Junkyard' LP, but Nick's desire to produce them as plays waned, although they were mentioned in interviews for some time. Each play ideally took about three minutes to perform. In a way, they were the ultimate revenge on an endlessly demanding audience.

Some of them appear in Nick's book *King Ink*, others appeared in the American magazine *Forced Exposure* in 1986. The comic *As Fix E 8* was published with Lydia and Nick's assistance in 1993. Others have been published elsewhere, and bootleg copies exist.

The Birthday Party played more gigs in London while Rowland worked with Lydia in the studio. There was a brief tour of Europe: Berlin, The Netherlands, Switzerland, Italy, Germany, London. Too poor to fly, they drove. The Birthday Party wouldn't have felt they were a band unless they were performing. Presenting themselves in as many countries as possible was a wise decision; their music didn't attract commercial radio.

Rowland: "The Birthday Party had very few groupies because we scared the shit out of people; nobody would come backstage to see us, except in Australia. If we met girls, it was because we sought them out."

They organised the tour through Rough Trade, who set them up with a promoter in each country and an English driver and a British Rail workman's bus-cum-site office, "a box on wheels". Many of Rough Trade's bands didn't like touring, so they were delighted to find these maniacs from Australia who liked to play.

Winter. The bus was draughty. The bus couldn't go above the speed limit, and leaked petrol into the back. By the time they got to Zurich it was late, and everyone was all but vomiting with the stench. The promoter dragged the limp band to a restaurant and fed them huge steaks which they still remember as the best they'd ever eaten.

Their next five gigs were in Italy, starting on November 11. For this European tour the band had been billed as 'London's hardest band' – 'hard' meaning tough or violent. Some gigs were just shy of an all-out riot, with chairs, glasses and bottles being hurled about.

Rowland: "We arrived in Italy late because the van broke down, so we took a train. We were picked up at the station and taken to the hotel in Rimini. Because we were three hours late, the schedule went out of the window. Instead of going to a hotel in Florence, playing a gig and going back to the hotel, we stayed in Rimini every day. The promoter picked us up in the afternoon, hours after he'd said with two cars and we drove like maniacs, usually down the middle of two lanes of traffic, arriving at the venue hours late and go on with no sound-check. We were told we were going to play just outside major cities like Florence, but we actually played at places miles outside the cities.

"The first venue had provided amps and drums, but no drumsticks, so Phill got a broom-handle and broke it in half and his hands got split. It was a disco, and the stage and steps were all metal. On stage, Nick would come up to me and put his arm around me, and I'd get a big shock off the P.A. There were these Italians leaning into the front of the stage, and one of them had wire-frame glasses. Nick put his finger between the guy's eyes and touched the frames, and these big blue sparks went flashing everywhere and this guy shoots back into the audience, and all the Italians were standing there looking quite alarmed.

"We played at a Communist festival in a big circus tent, and they thought we were fascists because one of us was wearing a black shirt or something, and threw chairs at the stage. The promoter had hired all his nephews as our roadies, so we had a small horde of about 12 roadies. One of them was leaping around the stage like a salmon, deflecting flying chairs and so on with his head like a soccer player.

"Nick had met this girl, Layla, who didn't speak any English, who'd been with us for the last three days. At the end of the tour the promoter handed us an incredibly arbitrary amount of money, and said, 'Nice to work with you, see you later!'

"We said, 'What the fuck is this?', and it became obvious he had no interest in paying us what we were owed, so Layla threw a firecracker at him. It was about a finger's length, not very big. We heard later that he'd told people we'd kidnapped him, tied him up, and pelted him with fireworks in a shed for an entire day."

Phill: "Rowland had good presence on stage. People perceived that Rowland was doing more because of where he was standing than what he really was. I'm not trying to bag Rowland here, I have praise and criticism for everybody in the band, including myself. Nick's hard to compete with for the limelight. People gobbed, threw cigarettes, they'd burn Nick with cigarettes, he had lots of scars from cigarettes."

Mick: "I was probably the only one who wasn't drunk most of the time or on drugs. I was usually sober, so I was in a more psychotic state than them because I could see what was going on. I think I started getting nervous before concerts in 1985, because they were getting quite big, so I started getting regular stage nerves. It's good to get a bit tense before you go on, it's important to get worried that everything is set up properly, that there's not going to be some huge fuck-up in the first 10 minutes. The rest of the band never seemed to be concerned about anything, and that also used to make me nervous. I never knew whether they were going to get back in time. They'd go off to do some nefarious activity. Very often they only got back a couple of minutes before the gig.

"Before that I used to be psychotic before I'd go on, I couldn't talk to anyone for about half an hour before we played. It was quite dangerous going on stage, there were quite a few incidents that happened that were disturbing, frightening things.

There were gigs where we had to be very aware of the danger, there were some very violent situations, audiences really raring to go, y'know, going crazy. There'd be dangerous stuff flying at our heads sometimes. We had to be on the ball; you had to duck at the right time or you'd be in trouble.

"The violent thing was in the audience, and sometimes the violence coming off the stage at the audience would contribute to this atmosphere. Even the way Nick was behaving was kinda . . . it was like going out to . . . it was kinda dangerous. A Birthday Party gig comprised a very volatile mixture of people, the subsequent potential for physical conditions to occur was very high. I think I got tense before we went on because I never knew what was going to happen, or whether someone was going to get seriously hurt. On many nights there was serious risk of electrocution, which in itself was frightening. Once in Italy these huge flames were bursting in front of the microphone if we went near it.

"At another gig in Italy, I think these punks up the front were gobbing at Tracy or something, and he went up and threw his boot at them. But then they decided we were fascists and it was a communist-run gig . . . and there were chairs flying up on stage and everyone trying to get up onto the stage to beat us up. The group could be explosive at the wrong time.

"During certain phases Nick or Tracy would do things that I

thought were really fuckin' stupid. Like if Nick started being violent or get so out of it so he couldn't sing. I didn't find that very interesting. I knew it was part of the group and there were times when that was good in its own way, but generally it wasn't what I was up there trying to do. I was trying to play the songs well, make them as exciting as possible, rather than let Nick indulge himself being out of it, crawling over the monitors for half an hour.

"The tension before the gig was from wanting everything to go alright, and having so many instances at every second gig of something disastrous happening or something dangerous or where the gig would get fucked up, or we'd play a really rotten concert. I think all of us wanted to play good concerts and play the songs and create excitement from that, and not have all that shit that was surrounding us, things that'd take over the gig.

"Tracy knew he'd fuck up when he'd get drunk and fall flat on his back, that it wasn't helping us play the music well. It might've looked good if the general atmosphere was chaotic anyway; but on the whole it didn't help us continue playing the songs."

At a gig in Cologne they met Christof Dreher's Die Haut, who supported. Die Haut found much in common with the extravagant Birthday Party. Recording their first EP, Nick hung out with them, contributing "noise" to one song. Die Haut's open attitude and creativity impressed The Birthday Party. Lydia suggested she support them with a pick-up band in London on November 26 and Manchester on the 27th. The band planned to record the London gig for a live EP. With the intention of producing a joint project, Lydia approached Murray Mitchell and Steve Severin.

Phill: "At London's Venue, Tracy got his Swiss Army knife and wrapped it up in some socks, and gaffed it inside his leather pants leg, so it stretched way down, just short of the knee. You know how he'd arch his back and grind his hips while he was playing? He strutted right up to the front of the stage. I noticed these two girls in front of Tracy, one of them frantically tapping her mate on the shoulder, her eyes wide, saying something like, 'Oi, oi, quick, look at this!' They both had this expression on their faces like, 'Aaargh!, the monster in his pants!'"

Rowland: "Tracy wasn't this 'happy-go-lucky' person by any means. On tour he would often deliberately isolate himself from us and just . . . go on a bender, not participating in anything with the rest of the band and be solitary and really, um, depressed."

Mick: "Nick had attempted to climb the P.A. stack a couple of times and failed, really embarrassingly. He couldn't even get a foothold to get off the ground, he was falling over backwards, and went up to the front row and was hitting people. We were playing 'She's Hit', I think, and we were playing, waiting for Nick to come in and then crash, bang. I looked around and Tracy's fallen flat on his back, spread-eagled, bass in the air, and everyone at the side of the stage . . . they couldn't even watch, it was just so embarrassing. This gig was in front of 1,000 people, the London Polytechnic (December 11), and here I am, I'm connected with these people, and it's really embarrassing."

Not surprisingly, Rowland remembers the Polytechnic gig differently to Mick.

Rowland: "It was our first big headlining date, we'd brought Malaria! over from Berlin to support us, it was a big rock industry do, with all these publishers and so on to further our career. We weren't making any money from it but it was this important date following on from the Hoskyns piece. Nick and Tracy got so stoned and drunk; the rider was finished before the soundcheck. Tracy was falling flat on his face during songs with a resounding 'boom'. Mick and I were standing looking at each other across the stage, not playing, but looking at Nick and Tracy and wondering what on earth we were doing on stage in the first place.

"Nick would attempt to scale the P.A. and fall flat on his back. Then Nick had this huge fight with someone in the audience between songs, and he was hitting them on the head with the microphone. The mike had all this reverb on it so the sound was much larger and went on for much longer, this huge noise echoing through the hall. People in the audience were literally standing there with their heads in their hands, really embarrassed.

"I was the first offstage because I was so fuckin' horrified; I was unfortunate enough to be completely sober. I was sitting backstage and this figure came up, literally covered in blood, and I thought, 'Oh, my God, I'm dead'. He walked over to me, stuck out his hand and said, 'Fuckin' great gig, mate!' That was how I met Bingo.

"That was the start of The Birthday Party *as junkies*, which snowballed pretty quickly."

* * *

Talent scouts and company representatives were at the London Poly. It wasn't the best of occasions to witness The Birthday Party as they fell about their set, trying to make everything fit together. This display convinced many that there was no way this unruly, wayward, raucous mob would ever be a hit or a prestigious catch, despite their fulsome publicity.

When any of them fucked up, any other member who happened to take offence would feel free to lambast the offender. Rowland recalls one night in Sydney when Nick, in his thrashing around on stage, broke a mike lead so that the jack got caught in his guitar, causing Rowland to walk offstage for 10 minutes or so to untangle it. Coming offstage, Rowland recalls screaming at Nick, 'You fuckin' idiot!' The band were angry because it transformed them into some sort of freakshow, and detracted from the primary aim of their music being recognised as significant.

Phill: "The record company people never knew what to make of us. They were probably looking for a more coherent version of what we were. People knew John Peel would commute a long way to London to do his show and to see us. He's a barometer of what's going on, so the company people would think, 'Peel's playing this band, Peel's going to see them, there's potential for this to be huge'. Even though they may not've understood it, they'd go along to see it. No major record company ever considered signing The Birthday Party that I can recall.

"'Release The Bats' was 1,000 sales away from becoming a realistic top 40 single in England. If it had gone the extra distance it would have put us in the same echelon as Echo and The Bunnymen or Joy Division."

Wendy, Ralf, Robert L: "*You are wicked – You will burn in Hell* . . . So growls Nick, preaching in frustration at the brainless part of the audience who try to create attention for themselves by attempting to induce Nick to violence – preferably enacted upon them . . . Tiring of this, Nick dashes across the stage, throwing his body into another contorted primitive dance and another song, a mass of guttural growling, screaming and howling, reaching from the depths of his twisted, exhausted skinny body. Half-man, half unearthly creature, the band look on with a sense of ironical familiarity.

"They look like raucous caricatures. The unrestrained noise, the heaving and rhythmic beatings of the band's evocative and expressive music is perfectly offset by their incongruous appearance.

"Nick's aura of maleficence, his gangling thin animal body crowned by a dark shock of wild dishevelled hair framing a grotesque-looking face from which stare piercing eyes which silence with a glance. A superb, unsurpassable focal point, he is at once bizzare and comical.

"Coupled with Nick's ever-presence is Rowland's gaunt stick figure, seemingly indifferent to the chaos which reigns around him, content with maintaining an air of enigmatic silence and that ever-present hint of amusement caused by the behaviour of chunks of the crowd on his lips. Sullen, a man with black eyes blazing, he is not to be trifled with.

"Tracy Pew completes the unholy triangle. In his rancid, macho-gay cowboy outfit he quickly affronts our senses with his obnoxious, repellently sexual mannerisms. However repugnant he may be, he's nonetheless charismatic, just as Phill and Mick are in their own way. 'The others' unassumingly and quietly perform their duties within the band, adding to the huge dripping shashlik which is rubbed on our faces, hands and body.

"Phill's drumming is, if you can tear your eyes away from the maximum pantomime in front of him, a marvellous display. He adapts to the wayward chaos of the others around him, still playing with an intricate blueprint of rhythm. Strong but not self-consciously tense, he lends greater flexibility to their sound.

"They're far more immediate and aggressive than their records, their sound leaps out at us. Being open to the pitfalls and limitations of live work doesn't dampen or hinder the sound, but adds an excessive edge which raises it far above their records.

"Their lyrics and music grow to monstrous, twisted and tortured proportions of violence, menace and claustrophobia in a live situation. Hardly confining the inflamed passions of the brainless minority, the very personal nature of these reactions prompts many to perceive themselves in a manner they'd never considered.

"They manipulate and handle the crowd impressively. A glare, a few well-chosen belittlements act as a silencer or a further incitement to a more frenzied response . . . at times Nick dives relentlessly into the assembled crowd with no regard for self, life, or limb.

"Nick forces himself to a state of extremity, physically and mentally, enacting and evoking extreme emotional responses. Hugely entertaining, a spectacle of genius and unrelenting intensity.

"The crowd are ever receptive, baying for blood, and Nick plunges into them. "*Dead! Dead! Dead!*", his finger points accusingly, ready to pounce, eyes blazing hostility against the antagonism of some fool, Nick is watched almost exclusively by the crowd. Paroxysms of movement create a scene that is at once an exaggeration, a ludicrous absurd self-parody. A ritual of angry manic intensity is backed by the almost primitive chaotic noise of instruments competing discordantly and romanced by the blasphemous sound of Nick's voice."

Creatively on a roll, they'd changed radically during the year, and were now struggling for positions of dominance; a potentially self-destructive thing for a band which had no leader. Nick was more figurehead or wayward captain than *leader*. 'The Birthday Party' had a life of its own, an appetite, and a fussy palate.

They recorded their third Peel session on December 2. The songs were: 'Bully Bones', 'Six Inch Gold Blade', 'Big-Jesus-Trash-Can' and 'She's Hit'. For this session, they were going pedal to the metal past the point of no return.

'She's Hit' is the key song of the session, as Nick's development as a writer continued. This cut-up narrative, sung in a slow, emotive and reflective manner, marked an axis in their progression, a precursor to the next album. Imagine the audience's response to Nick's line "Anyone who'd wear their hair like thaaaat", indicating some poor boob in the audience. Given Nick's outrageous hairstyle, which appeared to have more to do with Dada than punk, the line gestures towards the responses Nick himself no doubt received from 'straight' people as he walked down the street. 'The vinyl is so cool/But the paperwork is cruel', encapsulates the situation Nick found himself in – the sometimes rude and ignorant comments made by the music press.

The earlier line about '40 hack reporters'; comments on the dishonest way in which human tragedy is reported; the figure of '40' comes from the Biblical tale of Noah and the rain of '40 days and 40 nights', implying a terrible revenge is due these clumsy and slipshod journos. Or is it the 40 Thieves?

Rowland's 'Bully Bones' has a wonderful guitar break and a powerful ending. Played fairly regularly in their set, it was considered 'old' by the time they got back to Australia.

'Big-Jesus-Trash-Can' was also important, despite stumbling along raggedly here. 'Big-Jesus' and 'Six Inch Gold Blade' indicate the direction they'd go in next. 'Big-Jesus' nods in the direction of 'junk' as a concept and a comment, and is probably the most elliptical of Nick's songs lyrically.

Despite little national English radio airplay, an atmosphere of expectation grew, anticipating the band's tumultuous return, with Nick being torn limb from limb by the adoring throng. Their new and improved crowd would be well-prepared for their return.

Rowland: "If we were doing this as a career we wouldn't have put so much energy into it, we wouldn't have left ourselves so open to being damaged.

"Rock music was considered to be the lowest form of art, and we were determined to prove that you could be an incredibly aggressive rock group and yet be intelligent. To be intelligent you didn't have to rub people's noses in it or express that intelligence all the time. It was important in rock music to know when to be dumb. You were being 'rockist' if you admitted to playing rock music at that time in England.

"Guitars were really passé, so we used them to full effect. Nick and I took that cliché from Jagger and Richards, Iggy Pop and James Williamson; we presented ourselves as a cliché because it's an incredibly powerful cliché. You only notice a cliché if it's done badly; if it's done well, it's a very powerful piece of imagery. We weren't as interested in being innovative, we were far more interested in affecting people on an emotional level rather than in a cerebral way."

III

The Slow Death Of The Impossible Monsters

ON THEIR SECOND RETURN TO AUSTRALIA in December 1981, The Birthday Party were breaking new ground musically. Their success could be measured only in notoriety and attendance, not 'units'. As their mad adventure picked up steam, the Australian press treated them like pariahs and, quixotically, local boys made good. They weren't punk, and they weren't a safe forgettable 'indie' band either. Melbourne's national scandal and racing weekly, *The Truth*, ran a bemused story on The Birthday Party in their first issue for 1982 which tried to *explain* the band.

Phill: "When we had good gigs in England, and things spontaneously happened, things got crazier than you expected them to for no apparent reason, that just made those gigs that much more special. That's the peaking experience, and I think that happens when people are cutting into new areas of music. I mean, we were re-exploring a lot of old ground, but in a different sort of way."

Take the title 'Drunk On The Pope's Blood'. The phrase introduces doubt and unease into basic concepts, and because the amplification is non-specific, the intention of the phrase is uncertain. It's an impossible statement. Is it a lie? If so, why? There is no answer to this, except that the band delighted in creating a moral and emotional discomfort. Duchamp's famous urinal 'Fountain' springs to mind. Their experiment rose from the table with a life of its own.

The Birthday Party never really discussed their ideals with each other. No doubt they discovered more about each other from their interviews. Cultural nomads, The Birthday Party were a conundrum poking rude fun at the predetermined pop/rock structure. Nick and Rowland's extravagant hairstyles inhibited any conventional reading of them. Tracy's Ocker gay thug made the whole schmeer look more outlandish and improbable. Was it a joke? The term 'punk', as in the *Truth* headline 'Jail Stops Punk's Party' seemed woefully inadequate.

Rowland: "We started to exaggerate our own natural inclinations into cartoon versions of ourselves around the first trip to America. It was natural for Nick and I to have exaggerated versions of the way our hair had always been."

Haircuts were very important to punk; badges of allegiance, entrance to the scene. The Birthday Party presented a transmogrification of this revered ritualistic pantomime, defining themselves explicitly as . . . themselves. By the end of 1981, the joke was becoming a little laboured, fatigue was in the air.

This very close-knit gang were broke, shared their love of music and had fun together. Although there were disagreements, they were a close-knit entity. Being broke isn't an excuse for theft unless you're hungry or need shelter, but the band felt so alienated that Tracy's theft of things like a ghetto blaster before they first left Australia would've seemed appropriate, given the situation. The band took what was within reach, relative to their needs.

Rowland: "Tracy stole so many things that it wouldn't occur to me to say, 'No, he didn't steal the ghetto blaster'. When we were doing 'Junkyard', Tracy was so drunk one night that he sat there in his chair saying, 'I am the producer' over and over for two hours. When the cask of wine was empty about dawn, Tracy left, walked straight out of the studio doors, and stole the car that was sitting in front of him as he walked out, and drove home. It was extraordinary to me, but nothing unusual for Tracy when he was drunk.

"The National Theatre is in St Kilda . . . In 1979, Gen and I and Nick met this ballet dancer who invited us to a party at the National Theatre. We showed up with Caitlin and Tracy. The party was five other people. They were very artistic and got a bit worried after a while because we weren't as genteel as they thought. Caitlin, Tracy's girlfriend, went for a look around and she found this sewing machine, and said, 'Tracy, steal me that sewing machine', and Tracy did.

"The police found Tracy after a while, so he went to the station and they said, 'Come back on this date', and he didn't. The police issued a warrant for Tracy's arrest, which they didn't do anything about it until February 1982. Tracy wasn't always drunk by any means, nor was he roaming the street with a mask and a crowbar. A friend of mine, independent from the band, lived in the same house as Tracy for over two months and mentioned that Tracy was quiet, read a lot, went out occasionally, and was quite gentlemanly."

Too busy with immediate things like touring, interviews, sleep, travel, practice, finding homes and partying, the band had no time to take stock. Recording in Melbourne was constantly interrupted by gigs through December and by a national tour in January.

Phill: "After the Sydney Trade Union Club gig in January 1982, there was talk that the band had gone as far as we could with what we were trying to do, so maybe it was time to split up. It was said again but wasn't mentioned much once we were back in England because then the emphasis had shifted towards work and fulfilling obligations."

Rowland: "We had discussions about splitting up quite a lot. I felt that what the band was doing was at odds with what I wanted to do, but I always realised that that was untrue, that it was at odds with *some* of what I wanted to do.

"We were all taking that for granted, thinking that what you *can't* do is better than what you *can* do. I always realised that the band was such a great band and there was nobody else doing anything remotely in that area to touch us that it was always worth continuing with."

At a cross-roads, they should have streamlined it all. Unable to do this, events developed out of the band's control to such a degree that any major change wouldn't have been effective. If it weren't for the powerful ties of friendship, culture and above all family back in Australia, there's no doubt that the band wouldn't have returned. The Melbourne scene, although 'home', was no longer their creative base. Their scene had been themselves against the world for years.

It was difficult for the Melbourne scene to accept that they had been left behind. The band liked the attention, but not the faddishness, the inane hipness, of their popularity. The immediate applause as they walked on stage – weren't they Melbourne's pariahs? The lepers from St Kilda? Was their plague now an acceptable rock biz shtick? Where to from here?

Musically, they began to resemble an extremely bad heavy

metal group. They'd do a shambolic set one night, a threatening 'in your face' set another night, and a disastrous, disorganised set the next. One gig could be a potent mixture of any of the above. Surviving tapes are all significantly different. They were a fantastic Tom & Jerry: Dionysean, savage, sexual, perverse, unpredictable.

Mick, Nick and Rowland toyed with a change of line-up. Phill was considered an annoyance by Nick and Mick, and there'd been occasions where Phill couldn't play the sort of thing they needed quickly enough in rehearsal to capitalise on the mood, so the band would wait while Mick showed him how. Phill wasn't the only member of the band to hinder progress in rehearsal. Tracy caused problems when he simply got too drunk, yet he was under no threat of expulsion. No-one suggested that Nick be kicked out either.

Rowland: "The problem was one of understanding, attitude and being able to keep up with the pace of change. Phill became superseded. He had no natural understanding of what we were doing."

This problem became more obvious during the hectic months in Australia. 'Junkyard' represented a challenge for them to present themselves at a peak. Their concerts had gone about as far as it was possible to go without serious injury, so where could their gigs take them now? Especially since they didn't have that many songs in hand to execute a rapid change.

Mick, Nick and Rowland began recording a song with The Go-Betweens' Robert Forster and Lindy Morrison during a break in the 'Junkyard' sessions, but didn't have time to finish it or record a flipside. 'After The Fireworks', by The Tuff Monks, was released in March 1982, with a B-side called 'After, After The Fireworks' . . . the instrumental track backwards. Keith would've felt justified in releasing it to recoup some of the money he'd sunk into 'Junkyard'.

Collaboration was fun but implied a restlessness on the part of the band. Nick and Mick felt it was time to throw everything into the air again and take a risk; Rowland would've welcomed a change in the balance of power. Thriving best on absurdity, risk and instability, they ran the risk of touring themselves into a rut.

Rowland: "Being in a room with no windows is dull because nothing changes; you're stuck in this room with these other people who are also getting irritable."

Phill: "We threw the regular equipment out the door. We all used really shitty equipment, like Tony's weird studio drum kit, using cracked cymbals with contact mikes on them, and other stuff to get metallic sounds."

Tony Cohen: "There was less experimentation with each successive record. 'Junkyard' was all in their heads, particularly Mick; he knew exactly what instruments were going to be used. We were forcing things to work more in the early days; later, Mick knew what would work because he'd learnt how to best use the recording process. Amazing man to work with. An implosion was imminent. Nick and Mick were becoming like, uh, 'the Nick and Mick show'; everything else was secondary, like Rowland's stuff wasn't treated with such priority. The seeds were already sown for The Bad Seeds I guess."

Rowland: "I was writing complete songs and Nick expressed a wariness of singing my lyrics . . . 'it's like driving a friend's car'. I didn't bother to show him any songs unless I thought they were thematically suited. I realised during 'Junkyard' that it wasn't necessary for me to write songs to have a large impact on the band. I always preferred my playing in other people's songs rather than my own and often added crucial riffs and so on to Nick's songs."

In January, Nick said the band had gone as far as it could go.

Tony: "That seemed pretty obvious to me, too. The drug consumption and the burnout factor in the studio was absolutely intense, it was hitting the edge, it was as far as you could go and live. It worked as an album, but as far as I was concerned, the mixes could've been so much better."

Keith Glass: "'Junkyard' was a big strain, I think they were a little under-rehearsed for it, and Tony had this idea of recording it so that it sounded like the inside of a tin can. It's a bit of a waste when you go to the best studio in Australia to record it. Oh, it's a great album, but it broke the label, y'know. It cost 45 grand, which is like 120 grand today. It came out and sold 1,000 copies in Australia.

"I'd sold the shop, and I was pretty burned out from everything. I'd bought a house with the money from the sale of my shop, and the advance for 'Junkyard' from England was about £5,000. We wanted to cover as many territories as possible, so I did other licensing deals which I've still never seen a cent from, because I'd done them through a third party and had no control over them. 'Junkyard' came out in Germany and four other countries and I've never been paid for it and neither have the band. 4AD have always been good. But I couldn't maintain that sort of profile. I tried to get the label distributed in America; I had The Birthday Party, The Laughing Clowns, The Go-Betweens, The Dynamic Hepnotics and I thought that gave me a strong impetus to get a label going with somebody here who'd say, 'Here's a year's operating capital for you to get the label up and running.' I couldn't get one backer, yet people were setting up labels in Sydney which had a lot less going for them; the Sydney labels said, 'Melbourne's Gudinski's town, if he's not interested, we're not.'

"People asked me, 'Why did you go to the big labels?', but there were simply no alternatives, there was no 'alternative' distribution worth a damn. If the records came out and the companies couldn't sell them, which became apparent almost straight away, you were stuffed. The best seller I had was The Dead Kennedys. I couldn't continue to run my label, so I let it peter out, and went back to independent distribution deals when possible."

So did the band owe Keith money?

Keith: "I doubt it very much. I think I've got it all back by stealth and opportunism, by putting out things like 'It's Still Living' – which the band also objected to, which sold very well. I managed to get it back and make maybe a small profit on everything. I don't think that anyone believes I've made a fortune, I think everything's equalled it's way out . . .

"I was a bad manager, anyway, because I wasn't able to go and hype the record companies, saying, 'Hey, this is a great band!' Nick would taunt me by saying, 'We'll do this and we'll do that'. If I was a normal manager, I'd be horrified. But I'd go, 'Yeah, okay. Do it'. I went along with their most outrageous ideas, like using Ed Roth to do the cover of 'Junkyard'."

Tony: "On 'Junkyard' it was clear that Nick and Mick were at the top of the heap and Tracy was like a moon orbiting a planet. Rowland was out on his own, and Phill was out in the backwaters somewhere, almost forgotten. He didn't have much input. When he did it was mainly laughed down, quite cruelly in a way . . . he was laughed out of the studio."

Phill: "'Hamlet' was a new song, and no-one liked what I was playing for it, and Mick said 'I've got an idea', and it was patched together with Mick and Tracy. 'Hamlet' got a lot better later on."

Tony: "Mick played drums on 'Hamlet' and 'Dead Joe'. Phill just couldn't get it, so Mick just threw him off the kit, sat down and played it. It was pretty bad for Phill, but that was when they were realising they didn't need Phill anymore. He was fitting in less and less I guess . . ."

Phill: "It was very much the way it was, that that was what was called for to do the thing we needed in the studio. For example, there was a stage with The Rolling Stones, in their middle period, where Jimmy Miller produced, and Jimmy played drums on a few tracks, possibly 'cause Charlie wasn't in the room, no one was suggesting that Charlie was on the way out.

"Nobody, certainly not myself, was thinking, 'Shit, there's a power shift going on here!' I was thinking like with 'Just You and Me', 'Shit, there's no way I'll make the drums sound like that, but if Mick plays them, they will sound like that'. You can hear half the drumming on that track is really slick and the other half's fractured; that's the way we cut it. There's no way someone schooled in drumming can play unschooled."

Tony: "We worked through the night on 'Junkyard', and by the end we were totally knackered, we were geriatrics. We all looked like corpses; when they left, we were all speaking like zombies. The drugs and the hours we were working, recording after doing gigs, it was insane.

"The band had just started the first rhythm track to 'Big-Jesus', which was going fantastically. Their friends were in there, these weird-looking punks, and this fellow with a clip-board said, 'You'd better stop them, there's too many people here'. 'Well, I'm not stopping this take', which is the one on the record. He wanted me to stop them recording, and tell them to get rid of their friends, which I didn't do.

"When they finished, they came in and got up so close to this guy that the fear on his face was uncanny. The band, all their punk-looking friends intimidated him into leaving.

"The studio had just had a new Harrison mixing desk put in, with a long leather armrest. At 11am, Tracy had started on his second wine-cask. I came back from the toilet and noticed that the entire length of the armrest had been slashed into little ribbons. Tracy had been having a go with his spurs, which he wore then. He was swinging his wine cask back and forth, and said to me, 'Yeah? Whadareyagonnadoaboudid?' 'Nothing! Nothing, Tracy!' "

Keith: "That was a new mixing console they'd just put in, worth about $200,000. Tracy cut up the leather armrests with his spurs. The studio wasn't doing a lot of rock groups at the time, but a lot of film work. They were appalled, they'd never had this sort of thing happen before, and Roger Savage hauled me over the coals something rotten about it, said they were going to charge me for it, but never did. I felt rotten, absolutely terrible about it.

"Tracy was a lovely guy when he was sober, I don't hold any grudges against him. There were a few other incidents; he had a Rickenbacker bass which disappeared, I had to buy him a new bass. So I said, 'You're going to have to pay for this out of the band's fees', so I deducted the cost of the bass over three instalments. One time he needed the money, and came over to my house to have an argument about it. He was pretty aggressive about it, he wanted to smash my head in, basically. But Tracy was actually a great guy. When he went to prison none of the band came down to the courthouse, but I went and stood up and said something to the judge about him, and Tracy said, 'Keith, thanks for coming', which was really touching."

Paul Goldman: "Keith did give me money to film the band but it didn't cover all the expenses; I had to hire equipment to shoot with, and I was in a lot of debt."

Rowland: "That money that Keith gave you was our money. Keith was just doing stuff with it and he'd never ask us."

Paul: "But I didn't know that, and in retrospect, it's good that he did."

Rowland: "But he acted in such an inconsistent and cavalier fashion . . ."

Paul: "But he said it was his money!"

Rowland: "Yeah, but we owed it to him. Keith paid for my Fender Jaguar in 1979, and every gig we did after that I gave him $20. When we came back to Australia in late 1980 we were on a wage of about $50 a week, and Keith took $30 of my $50 a week, and then Tracy sold his bass because he knew he could just borrow one, so Keith bought him a new one because the borrowed ones sounded like shit."

Paul: "All I know is that whenever I was desperate for money, if I sat on Keith, he'd give it to me, but it's ridiculous to think that $1,000 would be enough to pay for three cameras and lighting and film stock. That's why we've never done anything more with it, it's expensive."

Phill: "I think the drug thing in The Birthday Party is made too much of. Although there was drug use, it was reasonable. There wasn't what I'd call heavy drug use; we're talking maybe one shot a night of heroin and maybe three lines of speed to keep you awake. No-one was sitting around, nodding off and drugged out of their minds; we were making a record.

"Speed was part of day to day life, y'know, what it would take to get the job done. Most of the time the drugs were after gigs or between things, nothing to do with the shows; it was something to get creative on. Nick always drank more than he did drugs, and more for performance, the drugs were for relaxation for all of us.

"'Junkyard' is something I'm very happy with, very proud of. The stuff on it that I didn't have a handle on, well, that was a turning point for everybody. People in the band went, 'Phill's not copping it, man, he doesn't know why or where we're doing what we're doing musically', and so on."

There was also tension between Rowland and Nick . . .

Tony: "Rowland's stuff . . . Nick wouldn't want to have anything to do with, as long as Nick sang it, of course. This had been going on since 'Prayers', when I got Rowland's vocals of his song 'Ho-Ho' onto the album. Nick sang 'Ho-Ho' as well, but I said we should use Rowland's version for the album, but from then on Nick said, 'I'm the singer and no-one else sings but me', so that was the end of that.

"It was much worse with 'Junkyard'. I think it was more Nick's strength of character that made Rowland give in, you just couldn't argue with Nick. Nick'd say, 'This is how it is and that's that', he was very good at standing over anybody, although I suppose Nick was a bit in awe of what goes on in the studio . . . he didn't understand how it operated. Nick would try and turn things up full at the studio board and he'd ruin the effect, it wouldn't work, so he'd always leave this side of it to me."

Phill: "All those times were very happy ones; we were working hard and having a lot of fun."

Tony was effectively the band's producer, in the widest possible sense of the term, contributing as creatively as anyone else. Tony added to The Birthday Party in a way that probably no producer of the time could have done.

Tony: "Nick was fascinated by my little figures that I'd draw, occasionally they'd be quite demonic . . . they were the original idea for the cover of 'Junkyard', but . . ."

Keith: "I had a mate, Dave Hodgson, who's a screen printer and comic-book writer, and he said, 'I've found all these screen print designs of Ed Roth's 'Sixties stuff', and I said, 'Great, I love all that!' So, unauthorised, we printed up t-shirts, I put them in the window and sold them mail-order. I remember putting them out for sale and Bruce Milne going, 'Oh, these aren't of the time', and I was going, 'I know, but they're great, they're fantastic!'

"Not many people bought the t-shirts, but I remember Nick getting interested, and I think he had some of Ed's dragster models as a kid. About the middle of recording the album, Nick said, 'Wouldn't it be great if we could get Ed Roth to do the cover?', and I said, 'Let's do it! I'm going to Los Angeles in a couple of weeks, I'll check out where Ed's at.' So I got onto Ed Roth, and said, 'I'm from Australia, I want to talk to you about doing an album cover for this band I record and manage'.

"Ed said, 'Oh, yeah, I get ya, okay.' 'Look, I'm in town for a couple of days, why don't I come and see you this Sunday?' 'Oh, that's bad, I have to go to church. But, maybe Sunday afternoon?' 'Great'; it was the only time I had.

"I showed up at his house and we talked for about two hours before we started doing anything about the album cover. I said, 'I love all your Sixties stuff, 'The only good cop is a dead cop' and all that.' 'Oh, no no no no, that was a bad influence on kids'. I thought he may've had some problems with his children; he'd recanted his early life. In his book, *Rat Fink*, he's rewritten his whole history, making himself out to be this kooky fun-loving-beatnik. He said, 'I've got a question for you. Are they morally sound?' I did an internal double-take, and said, 'Yes!'

"He said, 'Now what's your idea?' 'Well, this monster in a trash-mobile, with the big tongue . . .' 'Yeah, yeah', and he started to get right into it . . . 'We can have this and we can have that'; my ideas were the Cadillac tail-fins and the Edsel grille; he started getting more technical, 'We'll have the rocker arms from the '47 Oldsmobile, and Rat Fink underneath, firing a machine-gun'. For the next hour we mapped out the whole thing.

"Two weeks later he sent me a rough which looked really good, which I showed the band. Ed rang me up, 'I want US $2,500 for the painting', which was a lot then, so I gulped and agreed. I sent the rough back to him because I had to approve it and he wanted to get a friend of his to airbrush it; to me the way it turned out was too chintzy and plastic in relation to his Sixties stuff; it's too smooth. We were looking for rough-edged stuff; Ed and I were on a different wavelength.

"The painting came back and the band were overseas and had no opportunity to see it, so we put it out. Ed wanted me to send him a copy of the album, so I sent the cover, but I daren't send the album, because I knew what was going to happen. He kept writing, 'Hey, love the cover, when do I get to hear the record?' Finally some English journalist sent him a copy of the record when he did an interview with Ed, and he said, 'That Birthday Party band, that's the worst band I've ever heard in my life, that's disgusting!' in this article. In Ed's book, he trashes me completely, it's great!"

The album cover certainly continues the band's savage/silly, absurdist humour. Ed's cartoon painting hardly incites sexual violence, but serves to robustly thumb the band's nose at their ridiculously extreme image, reflecting the same: a cartoon rock-monster. It upped the ante and prepared the world for the worst. The Birthday Party had no intention of providing what the audience clamoured for; their most trusted counsel was among themselves and their immediate clique.

Tony: "I came close to capturing The Birthday Party's sound but I never really got it, I don't think. Perhaps on 'Junkyard' I got some of it. I think it was captured most with 'The Bad Seed' EP. With 'Junkyard' we were trying to get it all down live. But Nick would be doing another vocal bit here, and something else had to be added there, and another fiddly bit. As soon as you start adding the fiddly bits, you lose the feel of the band playing live."

Phill: "We'd always have a lot of fun messing around in the studio. Tony was always an instrumental force in this, you'd say to him, 'we want it to sound like this', and he'd take it way past what you could ever imagine, even more than what you wanted, and you'd be thrilled. He was always good at getting sounds.

"We were mixing 'She's Hit'; Mick played the overdubbed percussion stuff on that by the way, which I played live. We'd done two mixes already, and then spent four hours on a third mix. It had been a fairly long day, we'd been going since 11am, it was now 1am, we said, 'okay, kill it, enough'. Everyone was knackered, so we left.

"We came back in the next morning to start a new session, Tony's still there, rolling up mike leads and stuff, really fazed, smoking a cigarette and tired as hell. 'Well, that's it. I got it'. I said, 'What?' He'd stayed there from when we'd left and he'd been mixing solidly since then until 9am, just doing 'She's Hit'.

"He played it to us and we went, 'Fuck!' We'd done a 'this is how the song goes' mix, but Tony turned it into this huge aural experience, just remixed it because he wasn't happy with it, and done a fucking amazing job.

"In the real world, the world of money, you'd do a rough mix, a reference mix, and the producer and engineer would then mix it, just calling the band in every now and again to ask them questions. I used to spend a lot of time with my hands on the mixing console, mixing with Tony, running the cuts through the faders and switches and stuff like that, because I could never bear not to be there."

In January 1982, The Birthday Party played what became known as the Skeleton Race Tour or The Violent Australian Tour.

Phill: "Tracy was making these wanking gestures along the neck of the bass as he was playing, and got up to the front of the stage, pumping and grinding away, and he'd gaffed a tube of KY lubricant on the head stock of his bass, and he started squirting the stuff into the audience. Tracy was always cracking us up, like one night wearing *all* of his belts, y'know those big wrestler belts he had.

"Although we had a sense of cabaret early on, The Birthday Party had it as well. We tried to heighten that, we were always interested in people who could do the lights in a theatrical way rather than a rock 'n' roll way. We were also very much into what we did being of a theatre-ish kind of nature. The dialogue and rapport between us and the audience; and Nick's Brechtian approach to theatre, which is that he brings the audience into the performance rather than it being just a full-on presentation. In Brechtian theatre, you acknowledge the audience rather than presenting a fantasy or make-believe piece. Like a Shakespearean aside, but much more than that."

Tony: "Recording them at The Ballroom on New Year's Eve

1981, I had this little rentavan with a four-track and some equipment out on the footpath. Nick was in there with me, trying to have a hit of speed before he went on stage. The band were on stage going, 'Nick, Nick, where the fuck are you!', and he was desperately trying to have his hit. He had blood pouring down both arms when he raced out on the stage. Then some drunks came along and were rocking the van while I was inside recording the band, hanging onto the 4-track and everything else."

Rowland: "When we played Brisbane in January, there was an uproar there because Lindsay Kemp had finally been allowed to perform *Flowers* in Brisbane after first doing it 15 years ago all over the rest of the Western world. At the same time, there was this newspaper article saying that 'while the moral majority are up in arms about Lindsay Kemp's homosexual *Flowers*, the most degenerate, disgusting bunch of drug addict rock stars, Sodom and Gomorras, have crept across our border' and so on, proceeding to defame and libel us in various extreme ways, which was just . . . great. He actually advocated killing us in the article.

"When we played that night there was a policeman at the door, and the police had decreed that 'no punks' were to be allowed into our gig, which certainly meant the audience was rather slim."

Paul Goldman filmed the band at the Astor Theatre, Melbourne, on January 15, 1982.

Wendy Munro: "This cameraman was following them all over the stage and pissing them off because he'd get up very close. Rowland was trying to dodge him with his guitar sticking out like a machine gun doing that staggering lurch of his at the same time. Tracy was standing at the back grinding away with his hips and trying to ignore him, whilst Mick was glaring, really furious.

"During one of the slower songs Nick put his arm around the guy, ostensibly as part of his performance, and dragged both of them down to fall on the floor and over this expensive camera equipment.

"Later, Nick threw himself into the crowd and it looked like he'd never get out, although he was still singing. I couldn't see him for what seemed like a long time, lost in the crowd. The song continued; it was a great exciting gig. That was a rock band; yeah, you bet. Fantastic.

"They did 'Dead Joe' for the encore. At the end the band pissed off leaving Nick alone on stage, looking totally psychotic, howling and screaming the words, then tossing the microphone aside, making this crunching noise as the microphone hit the stage and rolled about."

Phill: "Paul had the cameras packed in foam, and he was hand holding them, the intention being that Nick would throw him offstage into the crowd. One night Paul copped it severely because we all got pissed off that the shooting of the film was getting in the way of us performing the gig. The lights for the films ruined our lights, and the guys kept getting up right in front of us on stage with their fucking cameras. So we're thinking, 'What does this look like to the audience?' . . . 'It looks like shit', Nick worked hard on that gig, I hope it came out well on film.

"Then again we were always pissed at bouncers for interfering; good crew and good bouncers create a situation where everything goes on but no-one gets hurt, but when the bouncers go in and start trashing people or trying to save the singer, that's really bad.

"During the violent Australian tour, the guys who'd feed the mike leads out when Nick was deep in the crowd, would have to run, squatting down, to the front of the stage and gesture to Nick, 'How bad is it?', and then they'd have to make a decision whether to help him out or not, and Nick would either call for help or would just get out himself. Years later I bumped into one of the roadies on that tour, 'Fuck, you guys used to scare me every night!'

"Nick would also work hard when he'd be singing on the foldback wedges, he'd be standing on the horns, and get up high and topple over, backwards onto the stage. He was good at that sort of stuff, he could turn a fall into a dive; he'd be falling backwards, just losing it, and he'd kick up his legs and hit the stage on his back full tilt. He took some pretty tough falls, but it all looked great.

"Nick used to dedicate songs to girls in the crowd; it might be because they brought him a poem or a fluffy toy, it might be because he spoke with them earlier. It added to the rapport the band had with the crowd.

"Nick's knees used to get pretty fucked up. He used to fuck up his hands quite a lot, skin off knuckles and things like that, but mainly he'd bruise his legs and back quite badly. Rowland got accidentally knocked out by Nick's flying mike stand in

Melbourne once, but Nick's performance would cause him injuries. The only people doing something dangerous to themselves were Nick and Tracy; Tracy arching his back, and falling into the bass drum . . . that was always pretty funny."

Rowland: "The Cell Block in Sydney was a great gig, in a cell block which had had all the floors removed so it was this huge stone building very long and tall. Chris Walsh said it looked like Dante's Inferno, because all the lights were red and orange and yellow. Nick went off the stage and got wedged directly between the stage and the audience, with his back to the audience. He was off the ground, and his waist was level with the heads of the crowd. There was a girl with a bunch of keys, just ripping his back to pieces with this fucking bunch of keys. His back bled a lot, it must've hurt like hell. Things like that weren't uncommon. It seems extraordinary now that I should be in any situation where a friend of mine should be having pits gouged into his back with a bunch of keys and not pay an enormous amount of attention to it, but at the time it was just par for the course.

"I also remember Nick cutting the rings off his fingers on occasion with wire cutters because they were so mangled from him pounding his fists on the stage that he'd bent the rings so out of shape that they were restricting the flow of blood to his fingers. It wasn't common, but his rings were always completely bent out of shape. This story demonstrates Nick's complete disregard for his personal self when he was on stage. I quickly learnt that you never, ever lent Nick pieces of clothing if you ever wanted to see them again, because they were either torn from his body, or torn to shreds by his wild gyrations. I lent Nick a jacket to wear when The Boys Next Door were on 'Countdown' doing 'These Boots Were Made For Walking', when Nick's stage performance was relatively tame, and the jacket was not worth having back after one performance of one song."

The Birthday Party played three nights in Adelaide during a monster heat wave which was built up in the days prior to the band's arrival and worsened for the weekend they played.

Robert, Paul Slater, Daryl Champion: "It was 42°C in the early evening . . . Some sort of tremor jerks the spine, rivets the eyes, and the jaw hangs without moving for the entire set. Struck.

"Nick Cave had turned into a werewolf or something, and Rowland looked more like a rat than ever. Tracy was now a cowboy . . . 'What the fuck's happened to him?' I'd thought of Phill as an affable, rational guy, but he becomes a rangy threat on his kit, some sort of . . . beast.

"The place evacuated shortly after they came on. Two-thirds of the crowd, the trendies and the regulars, just upped and fled. A few regulars even came down to the front to see what all the racket was. Staying, they found they actually enjoyed the band.

"Opening with 'King Ink', the album version was no comparison. The lazy stride of some misplaced earthquake had the crowd awed and thrilled. They were in classic form and played well, obviously enthusiastic and fired up.

"The Birthday Party created an undeniably tension-ridden atmosphere for the rest of the night. With the first lines of the song, Nick strode across the stage and, pulling off his boot with one hand, he banged it against the stage and shoved it back on again, all while keeping perfect time and the sense of the song.

"Tracy was the grinding gay cowboy, his pelvis thrusting away for most of the duration of the first two gigs, with his back arched backwards, his head almost hitting the drum kit's mini-stage. He looked like he was constantly fucking the bass. With his cowboy boots, spurs, cowboy hat, gay boy moustache, lumberjack shirt, leather pants and leather jerkin, he was the picture of depravity. Downright disgusting; hypnotically filthy.

"Rowland was lurching about back and forth in his caged-wolf mode, wearing jeans and a lumberjack shirt which would look tough on anyone else except him, puffing endlessly on a cigarette, without ever taking it out of his mouth. He managed to light up several times during the night, but I don't recall ever seeing him light up. I only recall him being endlessly cool, endlessly smoking, great white wreaths spiralling up past his cadaverous face, always looking anxious and intent on his playing as he staggered about the stage. He'd pass for a mannequin learning to walk any day.

"The band were magnificent the first two nights. I remember thinking that Mick Harvey was such a good guitarist, better than Rowland Howard, although he was certainly a lot less prominent on stage, almost invisible.

"Nick was roaming about the stage, dressed in an Ed 'Big Daddy' Roth t-shirt, with the principal statements 'I hate every cop in this town', and 'A good cop is a dead cop!', crummy blue jeans with the knees out and swastika belt buckle, directly addressing the audience, screaming into their faces, demanding some sort of reaction from them. Suburban yobbos gone extremely weird. Astonishing. Full-on intensity.

"They had these professional roadies, and Nick would hurl the mike stand about, leaving it like an open jack-knife on the floor, and some burly bouncer would run across, bent double, to right the fallen stand, rescue the mike itself from the floor, and wind the cord around the stand very 'professionally'. Nick would then scowl like a schoolboy forced to do homework, unwind the cord, fling the stand about and eventually collapse it again, and leave the mike dislocated somewhere else on the stage. The sight of these roadies flying from one end of the stage to the other all the time just added to the outrageous element of mayhem in the process of destroying some sort of order.

"This was when the notion that The Birthday Party were parodying a real rock band came home to me; they were effortlessly upsetting the notion of what a rock band was for. Cave was a great showman. He used to get a strange look in his eye and search his audience. Whenever we had eye contact, I refused to yield to him, and he looked uncomfortable.

"There were a lot of people clamouring to pull Nick off the stage and into the audience. During these two gigs Nick got dragged into the audience a couple of times, usually during 'Six Inch Gold Blade' or 'Junkyard'. Nick was forcing himself physically upon the crowd, almost bullying them to respond, pushing himself against them or diving into them.

"Once he was in the audience no-one knew what to do with him, so they carried him above their heads on their hands, passing him along the top of the crowd in a rough circle all around the audience on upstretched hands, a screaming platter of meat, and eventually dumped back onto the stage.

"A skinhead was also bounced up and down on the top of the crowd by his mates and then thrown on to the stage. I'd never seen this before. Heady stuff. A great deal of camaraderie passed between the band. They were having a lot of fun with the crowd's obviously abandoned response, these gigs were still an adventure. Rowland: 'C'mon, you haven't thrown anything at us yet. Don't you like us?' Silence, then a thick empty glass beer jug was thrown incoherently, thunking onto the stage somewhat anticlimactically. The band cracked up, Rowland enquiring, 'Come on, who's the big brave boy then?'

"Nick had a great time responding to the cheers after each song; he'd bow from his head to his knees or lower, as if he had a hinge in his spine, this hugely exaggerated bow, and sneer 'Thaaaaaanks' in this nasty, nasal whine. A little unsettling and very funny at the same time.

"They encored with 'Loose', exuding a powerful, howling amphetamine rush, raw thrills like nitrosweat spilling out all over the heads of the crowd.

"At the end of each set and encore, Nick would deliberately drop the microphone, producing a shocking 'thud'. As most singers seem to take inordinate care with their mikes, his action seemed all the more . . . reprehensible. The roadies looked very worried when he dropped it, which made me laugh each time.

"It seemed like there was a little game that Rowland, Tracy, and Nick would play, to see who could make the last noise on stage, however pointless or meaningless. Which explains why Nick would often be the last on stage, and drop his mike immediately after Rowland's guitar had stopped feeding back or after Tracy had stopped thumping his bass."

Adelaide's heat wave reached over 43°C for several days; the worst heat wave for 30 years. It didn't make for a brilliant show. By the third night the band couldn't perform because they were so uncomfortable. It was a tired, placid, flat show; everybody had soaked shirts fairly early on, and most of the crowd had soaked trousers by the end."

Rowland: "You write songs and you play music and that is a manner of articulating something that you cannot articulate in any other way, and then people come along and demand that you supply footnotes to what you've done. The point of writing songs is to express something, and you're trying to express it in the best way that you can. If the way in which you choose to express yourself is oblique, that itself says something."

Tony Cocetta, public servant: "We were down the front having a really good night and Nick was being himself, really cool, paying out the crowd, so we just started paying him out, in a nice sort of way, and just took the opportunity. He was just holding the mike stand, leaning across right above me, so I just stuck my fingers up his nostrils, started pulling him out into the crowd, but I didn't want to do any real damage. So I held him there for a few seconds and then let him go back on again. He took it all in his stride, he wasn't shitted off. I'm a bit surprised he played it so cool, took it in the spirit it was intended; do it, get the effect, and once I had that I let him go. I was paying him out earlier, so he knew it wasn't a nasty violent act."

Phill: "The crowd did influence what we did on stage a lot. If the crowd goes, then that lifts the band, but if the crowd's flat, and you can't get 'em up, you start the next song and you feel a bit foolish getting into it so much if your effort isn't creating any action out there."

This interview was conducted with Nick after the third gig in a row in the middle of the heat wave, on January 24, 1982, for a fanzine.

Wendy Munro: "Why do you take such an aggressive stance on stage, is it to achieve some aim or does it just come out that way?"

Nick: "I try to excite people and confuse their normal way of thinking, if they react in an aggressive way to that, so be it. The object of live work is to make the music more visual, not like sitting and listening to a record – it's important to be as physical as possible with the audience."

Wendy: "Have you found that audiences often act to try and impress you rather than the band impressing the audience?"

Nick: "I think the audience has as much right to perform as the band, the band aren't the only people with a licence to impress. There's a certain amount of showing off going on on both sides, and that's quite healthy."

Wendy: "Do you find that you push yourself to extreme physical or mental limits whilst on stage?"

Nick: "There is a trigger point beyond which I lose myself, sometimes around the third song, then all I know is that I'm coming off at the end. I didn't achieve it tonight, but do on successful nights. When that happens though, things can get dangerous, especially when all the usual restraints of self-control are lost."

Wendy: "It seems sometimes that your behaviour on stage is almost a parody of yourself."

Nick: "Yeah, it's very much a self-parody thing. With all the things that have been written about us, we're constantly being bombarded with this image that we're supposed to have, especially in a live situation. The 'parody' thing is to amuse ourselves and make fun of the audience and their expectations.

The hip-grinding thing I do, it's just a sort of fun thing . . . it's not serious. There's a strong element of humour in the aggression thing as well."

Wendy: "Do you think that initial success in England could've been easier had the band adopted that sort of popular horror image like The Cramps?"

Nick: "I wouldn't like to be like The Cramps, although I enjoyed the early version of the band with Bryan Gregory. They've gone down a bit now. Image-wise The Birthday Party can be taken on various levels, whereas that sort of image and a band like The Cramps are just on one level, really one-dimensional. The Birthday Party can be taken as an aggressive force or an intellectual exercise, or something else – it's a multi-dimensional thing."

Wendy: "So you'd like the audience to react physically and emotionally."

Nick: "Yeah, both."

Wendy: "Did you find the English music press trying to push you in that horror image direction?"

Nick: "Yeah, in a lot of articles, definitely."

Wendy: "In a review of 'Prayers On Fire', the band were described as being hippies like Santana, what do you think of that?"

Nick: "I haven't seen that one, the writer sounds like a real cretin. Just because someone is writing about music doesn't mean they have any real intelligence – and that should be a prerequisite for a journalist.

"We're playing some more gigs in America on the West Coast in February, then to New York on the way back to London. America is a great place, the gigs we played were really good and we still got paid even after being chucked off in New York."

Wendy: "How much further can the band go in its current musical direction?"

Nick: "I think musically the band is being suicidal, we're painting ourselves into a corner, and will probably break up soon. That's all we can do. Recording the next album, it'll be sort of a 'suicide' album."

Wendy: "How important are the lyrics to you?"

Nick: "They're very important to me personally, I don't particularly care if the audience understand them or not. They discuss my basic philosophies and the way I see things although in a very indirect way. They're not written as entertainment . . . I don't sit there and think, 'wait till they hear this one'. They're just a personal statement. I just write them, I don't consider how they might sound, it all makes sense to me."

Wendy: "Visually the band appears as a bunch of very different individuals, yet on stage performing, you all click together like pieces of a jigsaw."

Nick: "I think that the band is good in that it's made up of a clash of personalities, we're all very different people. We don't associate with each other away from the band. We all lead very different lives; that's a major part of the group's success.

"You couldn't interview the whole band because it would just finish up as one big argument – we'd all have different answers."

The Radio Birdman influence shouldn't be ignored; Rob Younger said he'd "lose himself" in extreme performances, as Nick says above. Radio Birdman covered 'TV Eye' from The Stooges album, 'Funhouse', from which The Birthday Party took 'Loose' and 'Funhouse'. The Boys Next Door supported the often incredible Birdman on many occasions.

'Drunk On The Pope's Blood' backed with Lydia Lunch performing 'The Agony Is The Ecstasy' was released by 4AD in February, 1982. The songs on this EP are characterised by their dirty collapsibility. If they'd had the money to record their songs before touring with them, and then again a year later, they would've taken on an entirely new identity. 'Drunk . . .' depicts a very vivid picture of the band at a particular peak, about to enter an entirely different maelstrom.

'Pleasure Heads Must Burn' was a thunderous dragster. They'd been playing it for the best part of eight months, and the proliferation of wayward elements had led the band on a path that was incredibly powerful, frantic and messy.

'Zoo-Music Girl' was now far more guttural, and faster. The ending was acute and emphatic, a far cry from the uncertain fade-out on 'Prayers On Fire'. The lack of jarring horns on the stage were made up for in spades by Rowland's seasick guitar. This monstrous song is the one most likely to fall gibbering into a heap, stumbling and lurching all over the place. The other songs in their set have more core control, and it's difficult to hear precisely where the axis starts to fall; it's certainly not the bass, but appears to be a combination of guitar and drums which evoke an anarchic frenzy of demanding lust, which ultimately leads 'Zoo-Music Girl' into a savage collapse.

'King Ink' is utterly godlike, far more majestic, deadly and self-assured than the album. Tracy's bass loop crushes all before it, aided by Phill's drums which casually reach out and stab the listener as the lord of war passes by. It seems filthier and more driven, featuring more of Rowland's fantastic, billowing guitar, great washes and sails of sound that engulf and isolate the crowd.

The real shock is 'Loose' which allows Rowland to unleash horrorshow guitar. His gales and whirls of feedback can only be taken at face value, and they're stunning. Although the pace of the song is too fast for my taste – I find it limits the original power inherent in the song itself – this version is still magnificent. Performed this way the song may as well be their own.

The Birthday Party went to great lengths to capture their sound, and I reckon got about halfway there. On hearing the record for the first time, still blown away by the gigs I'd seen recently, I recall thinking that although the almighty whumph and crunch of the live Birthday Party is implied, it's not fully present. However, they're captured in brilliant form by an innovative recording technique which utilised contact mikes in the crowd.

'Drunk' wasn't intended to be an important statement, but since there's only one live album, it must be regarded as significant. It played up to the expectations the UK press had created, and ensured that the rollercoaster would continue unabated.

The band were feeling the need to break out of the mould. Events prevented them from making a decision. On February 16, 1982, Tracy was arrested for drunk driving in the parking lot of the Seaview Ballroom, where he'd been hanging out with some friends, including Peter Sutcliffe (AKA Pierre), from Melbourne band The Fabulous Marquises, along with Tracy's best mate, Chris Walsh. Chris and Tracy had both developed an important, cataclysmic bass sound and Chris was about to join The Moodists. Stuck with two sold-out shows and no bass player, Chris stood in for Tracy.

A few days later, Tracy, who hadn't told his family about the arrest, was sentenced to six month's jail, although he served only two and a half. Tracy's outstanding warrants for thefts – the sewing machine incident – were taken into account, which didn't help. His parents were upset; they could've provided legal representation had they known.

Rowland: "Tracy's arrest was pretty awful, he was only 19 or so."

It should have been clear to anyone that Tracy wasn't a hardened criminal; wilder than most, true, but many people go through a similar stage in their youth. Tracy didn't even drive the car out of the parking lot.

Fiona Pew: "It was ridiculous. He was sitting behind the wheel, him and Pierre arguing who was going to drive when the police came up. Tracy didn't have a licence, and this was before photo-id licences, so he gave them Pierre's name; they said, 'What's your name?', and he went, 'Aah, Peter Sutcliffe' (also the name of the then notorious Yorkshire Ripper, who'd just been caught amid a torrent of publicity). So then the policeman looked at Pierre and asked, 'What's your name?', and Pierre was probably going, 'Aah, uuh, Tracy Pew'. They weren't exactly tearing down St Kilda Road knocking old ladies over."

The Truth had a field day – a front page picture of Tracy with "I Am The Ripper" as the headline. Nancy, Tracy's mum, received bitter and abusive phone calls from the caring public. Rowland maintains that Keith organised the story, which could well be true since he wanted the band to get as much publicity as possible and he knew someone on the paper.

Paul Goldman: "Keith was infatuated with Nick, and he did think the band were really important, but I think he lost it. He didn't have the organisational capabilities, the band went far beyond his conception of them, and I think he lost control of them, which annoyed him. I also think there was a certain amount of jealousy, because it hadn't happened to him. Keith's a businessman; he didn't start Missing Link to create an archive or the meeting place for the scene, but because he wanted to make money. But you're talking about a record shop owner who supported a band without major label backing who recorded fantastic stuff in decent recording studios. There was only one band from that scene who released records frequently, and what Keith did for The Birthday Party was fantastic."

Rowland: "Keith ran the label by himself, and when we were having our greatest success, Keith was going through this nightmare of a divorce. When we came back the second time, Keith said to us, 'I'm sick to death of you, I'm not your manager, don't come to me for any kind of help, don't ask me to organise anything, I'm just your record label'."

Because of Tracy's incarceration, some gigs in New Zealand and the projected US tour were cancelled. They returned to London to finish 'Junkyard'.

Phill: "I don't think I was starting to go out of the band until after the second Australian return tour. It really started to happen when Barry Adamson/Harry Howard filled in for Tracy, and when Tracy returned. The early part of the year was such a drag because Tracy wasn't there, and that was hard. We just weren't the unit, y'know, we were playing because we had to. We'd never done anything we felt obliged to unless we had no money and we had no choice, and we couldn't keep the wages up so we went on the road."

Tracy's time in jail prevented The Birthday Party from parting with Phill earlier. They were forced to finish recording 'Junkyard' in England and gig to promote the album without Tracy. The situation with Phill continued to rankle; a largely unspoken conflict which contributed to their mood during the dry period in the first half of 1982. Playing what were now old songs became an increasingly bitter pill to swallow for a band which prided itself on rapid and continuous progression.

Barry Adamson was called in to help them finish 'Junkyard' at Matrix studios in London in March. They'd been friends with Barry since early 1981. Initial gigs were set up with Barry to fill in for Tracy, and after one rehearsal, they played the prestigious London Venue.

The second version of 'Dead Joe', with bass by Barry and Mick on drums, was given to London fanzine *Masterbag*, who released it as a flexidisc in May to tie in with 'Junkyard'. At their second gig, at Hammersmith Palais, Bingo performed his new fire breathing act.

Gerry McCaffrey, a fan: "I'd never seen them live in Australia, and I was reading a lot more in the English press than I'd expected to. They had a very high profile. To see The Birthday Party in this context was very exciting; Australia was just nothing at the time. They were supporting The Fall and The Palais was two thirds full just to see the support band. For Australians to be doing something in an international sense was very impressive.

"For this time-frame, the band sounded very unique, a very flowing bass sound set against this chopping staccato guitar; the guitar was very abrasive. Barry didn't move a lot, although Rowland and Mick seemed reasonably animated.

"Nick came across as very aggressive, violent, with bucket-loads of on stage arrogance. His on stage patter got about as welcoming as announcing 'Kewpie Doll' as a new song. I'd seen this sort of thing before, but not as believable or convincing as this.

"I noticed at front of house right, just in front of Mick, that flames were being thrown up, and I had no idea where they were coming from. Mick was looking at the person throwing them and was yelling at him. The flames were probably coming up about four feet or so above the crowd, the stage height being about five foot, so it was quite a respectable blast of flame. Mick probably needed to change his underwear; he looked pretty pissed off. Very extrovert audience behaviour!

"Cave was still singing really aggressively, doubling over oblivious to the flames . . . he was actually crouching over and bent over into that section of the crowd. His hair was so extremely teased up . . . it looked pretty risky to me, and all highly amusing as well."

Mick: "It was a bit of a shock, Bingo breathing fire at us. I went up to do some backing vocals and suddenly there's this great big flame in front of me, and Bingo's down there with a big disposable lighter and a can of kerosene or something . . ."

Their first performance on European TV was on *Riverside*, at Hammersmith Studios, London on March 15.

Mick: "You think, 'Well, we'll go on and be ourselves, and it'll be good exposure', but it never works out that way because the people who work in TV are so fucking stupid. It's all heavily standardised, sanitised and broken down. There can be exceptions, but they're usually accidents, I think.

"No-one had played live on TV for years. They decided that this was going to be a special show, the bands were going to play live. They'd done about 10 shows by the time we came on, but no-one had played live on this new show, they'd all done playback.

"So we arrived with all our stuff, and said, 'We'll play live'. We spent the whole afternoon working on getting a good live sound. We had our sound engineer in the mobile out the back and all this great equipment and we set it all up properly.

"It was the age of video effects . . . and they totally ruined what we'd spent all this time getting right. They took great exception to Nick's pelvic thrusting, so every time he did, they put video effects all over it, little boxes of still photos so you couldn't see Nick's performance . . ."

Rowland: ". . . through the pixillated mosaic, just dreadful."

Mick: "We did a rehearsal, and they said, 'We want you to do three songs'. And they intended to use two. They came up to us after 'She's Hit', and said 'Look, there's a big problem here. The version on the record goes for 5:30 and the version you did went for 6:28 . . . what's going on? It goes for much too long, you've done it completely wrong! It changes. This verse went on much longer'.

"And we're going, 'Look, fuck this, just forget it, forget all that shit, just . . .' Why bother with setting up shots when they were going to put little boxes of still shots all over the screen anyway? It was really absurd, and we were getting more and more pissed off with them which doesn't help.

"They said to Nick that he had to remember not to sing 'fuck' in 'Big-Jesus' which of course he completely forgot; quite genuinely because he always sang it with 'fuck' in it. So on TV they start at the second verse . . .

"We're doing the take and all this smoke starts coming out. You're there all day, no-one says anything about it. You're actually taping the show and out comes the smoke, this stuff is getting in your throat, really terrible. Nick's singing live . . . this is ridiculous, it's getting hard to breathe. We're all playing, not miming, trying hard to play the songs . . . just an incredible situation. Just a total waste of our entire effort. The sound's good, the versions are good, but the visuals are completely fucked. If they'd just turned their bloody three cameras on and shot the thing it would have looked great."

Barry played with the band for about five gigs, between commitments to his primary band Magazine, until April. Rowland's brother Harry then filled in, playing about seven gigs around England. From March to May, the band toured England, doing the sticks, finishing at London's Zig-Zag Club on May 8. There was a couple of weeks break, then the tour rolled on from London to Europe proper. The music press grew accustomed to what the band appeared to be, and treated them in kind. The next six months were not easy. The more known the unknown became, the more the thrilling venture became a puppet-show, enclosed by supposition and presumption.

Rowland: "The big problem for the band was that nobody understood what we were intending to do, and it snowballed and got completely out of control."

The Australian sense of humour just didn't travel. Also, The Birthday Party's actual and perceived situations were quite different.

Mick Harvey: "We didn't get much in the way of royalties from 'Prayers' and 'Junkyard'; Keith had all the money from those records. Australian groups that get to Europe always have the possibility of getting really big, but Australian groups in Australia kinda forget about the possibility, or don't consider it a possibility. That's a big distinction in attitude, you can hear it – there's an edge to the music if the expectation of big money isn't there."

They started to get some royalties around 1988, but it wasn't until 1994 that they eventually got the publishing rights and $6,000 each, and received royalties from the boxed set of Birthday Party CDs. The perceived success of The Birthday Party caused many Australian bands to develop massive inferiority complexes for years, especially in Melbourne. Around the world, comparisons were made with bands who sounded nothing like The Birthday Party.

Gerry: "I caught them again in April in Glasgow with Harry on bass. They did 'Funhouse' as an encore with Mick on drums with Phill looking on from the side."

Phill: "I think I was perceived as a necessary evil in some respects. I think the band knew I could do what I did well, but towards the end I think they wanted to unload me earlier than they did. It was better that Mick take over the drums than someone else being added."

Bingo was invited to come along on the European tour. They still carried the '81's hardest band' tag, so the crowds were out to take up the challenge, issued or not. Although the band were the focal point of the evening's entertainment, to some degree they were incidental to the event itself.

Phill: "There'd be times where Nick'd be gesturing at the audience and they'd grab him and drag him in, but it was part of the deal. Then he'd have to extricate himself, that's where Bingo helped out a lot. The great thing about Bingo was that he became the guy in the audience; when Nick was making his excursions into the crowd, Bingo made sure that Nick was all right."

By the time 'Junkyard' was released, most of the European audience were familiar with the songs. Because of this lack of surprise, the album seemed like a formal acknowledgement of their presence. As they toured after its release, they noticed the change in the audience's response; Mick later commenting, "The next time we toured, they'd seen it all before!"

On subsequent tours some of their audience stayed away because they no longer found them as publicly impulsive. Their touring schedule was heavier in 1982 than in '81; the constant unsettling sense of displacement which is part of touring added to the tension which threatened to split the band. Something had to give.

Tracy returned in May 1982. 'Junkyard' was about to be released, and the promotional exercise of touring and interviews was under way. Tracy returned from what was for him a health farm environment with no alcohol, regular exercise and plenty of sleep into the grisly engine of beckoning idolatry. His return gig at the Clarendon Ballroom in Hammersmith was marred by Nick breaking a toe, which didn't stop him performing the following night. Bingo showed up in a sinister clown costume, like The Joker in Batman.

'Junkyard' was released by Missing Link/4AD in May 1982. Ed Roth's cover perfectly matched The Birthday Party's dirty diesel racket. Nick's writing, teamed with Mick's musical interpretations, was more pointedly cohesive, more grandly, grandiosely, thematic; sharpened and direct.

The experimental rhythms are deliberately at odds with traditional rock beats. Their sense of timing would've caused rebellion in many drummers. The textures of 'Kewpie Doll' and 'Six Inch Gold Blade' are like some nightmare scrunch of Sixties soundtracks, offbeat be-bop, and bilious big band sing-alongs, a clandestine, drunk and raucous meeting in a West Berlin coffee shop between Movie Elvis and Fifties Elvis. These two songs share the thematic description of the fine emotional barrier between love and hate. Love songs often talk of jealousy, but these songs imply explicit violence as a result.

With the song in the first person of the killer, it's deeply shocking. Interestingly, The Birthday Party's themes are reminiscent of the occasionally harrowing, often maudlin concerns of country and western; which, like The Birthday Party, is a polemic musical genre.

'Big-Jesus-Trash-Can' makes the link to B-movie sleaze, to dubious, greasy morals; an odious soundtrack. With its crowd-spattering saxophone, the hokey cry of 'Let's rock' is followed by a series of ridiculous pantomime Fifties/Cramps style riffs twanging along with malice. It's a satirical snort towards the Emperor's New Clothes lifestyle of the rock biz.

With 'Junkyard', instead of leaving the hammer and chisel in the background, The Birthday Party launch themselves, hammer in one hand, chisel in the other, at the listener. One interpretation of 'Junkyard' is a man finding his partner in bed with someone else, and killing to reassert himself; a love song. The subject matter, like a country ballad, hammered ruthlessly at the listener. Perhaps it's how wonderfully powerful he feels when he's with his girl, how important ("Drink to me this heavenly body/Every inch a winning thing") he is. Ironic? With such deadpan irony, it's hard to be sure.

'She's Hit' is almost literary, a measured tale with a blues structure. The actual events in the song are deliberately obscured so the focus is on the killer's emotions, which makes it even more unsettling. A song to put a torch to the imagination. This is the first of many songs for which Nick was criticised for misogynism; 'Six Inch Gold Blade', which appears to describe a rape and murder from the protagonist's point of view, justified by jealousy and infidelity, was another.

If the lyrics describe murder and violence of the most unpleasant kind, much the same can be said for the music. Taken together, the music and the lyrics are a cathartic experience, but hardly one which would encourage anything except perhaps a re-examination of the way one perceives others.

In 'Dead Joe', the insidious, menacing bass thunders relentlessly toward the listener as the drums crash and hammer. As the song speeds up, it finally crashes out in raucous, drunken splendour. Live versions of the song became a race to see who would wear out first, the band or Nick and his vulgar, twisting pelvis.

'Hamlet' is unquestionably one of their masterpieces, turning Shakespeare's classic moral dilemma into a monster. Hamlet now lives in the USA, and he's made up his mind. Nick zeroes in on his moral and emotional corruption in the pursuit of his own goals, punctuated with Lichtensteinish "pows", like a more sinister, visceral Batman. The refrains indicate the dichotomy between love and hate so explicitly that art may never get this close again.

The title track, 'Junkyard', could be about a prostitute who's a heroin addict, but the lyrics are desperately misleading. 'Junk' is used as a metaphor for self-delusion and deception; a bad pun taken to an extreme, reinvigorating the meaning and power in the text of Nick's songs. So, 'junk', 'trash', and 'garbage' all mean the same thing, with a flip-side interpretation of a substance (and a lifestyle) which promotes self-delusion, like rock 'n' roll. Self-delusion can lead to humiliating and degrading circumstances, rather like their own rock 'n' roll Circus Maximus.

Cave was developing a world view based around loss of innocence leading to a spiral of corruption, wherein one can do bad things but not actually be 'bad' in the traditional sense of the term. In minute detail throughout the album, Nick focuses on the wreckage resulting from extremes of moral or ethical corruption.

'Dead Joe' reduces religion to a hollow mocking aside, promising release from tragedy, but incapable of delivering because the very nature of life is tragic. Christ's birth, a traditional time of celebration ("the holly and the nativity"), set against the most appalling personal tragedy ("oh, speak to me, Joe, speak to me, Joe") is reminiscent of both Samuel Beckett and Flannery O'Connor.

'Six Inch Gold Blade' encounters his female partner in bed with another man. The 'singer' has presumably dispatched several of his partner's lovers . . . "'Hands off this one, Hands off!', she cried/Grinning at me from hip to hip". A graphic image of adultery and jealous rage at a peak provides the emotional reason to kill.

'Junkyard' has a fantastic feel to it. For sheer atmosphere, this was the band's most powerful statement to date. The whole Warner Brothers' Tasmanian Devil/rebel underground biker feel of 'Junkyard' again upped the ante for the band before they'd really had a chance to grow out of the mould. Did they have any cards left to play?

Rowland: "Nick provided good copy. It's so much easier to write about people if you give good quotes. But he was abused by the press to such an extent that he became so wary of saying anything that he virtually ceased to say anything in interviews.

"The Birthday Party was about five distinctly different individuals who were all vitally important to the band, and it was anathema to the band that *one* person should be singled out as more important. I don't know about Mick and Tracy, but Nick and I were both incredibly insecure, and any lessening of our positions of power would have been a big deal. At the end, I guess I was losing out in different ways. When these things occur, you react to them in an emotional manner, you don't think about what it will cost me in the long run, you just do it."

Rowland was keen to expand his repertoire.

Rowland: "After we'd done 'Some Velvet Morning', this guy in Germany who ran Rip Off Records contacted Lydia [Lunch] and said, 'Would you do an album for me in the same manner as 'Some Velvet Morning'. The core was Barry Adamson, Genevieve McGuckin, Mick, myself and Lydia. Barry couldn't do it because he was working with Magazine.

"We did a tour of Holland and France; Mick, Lydia and I went to Berlin where we met Gen and Murray Mitchell, and the rest of the band went back to England. We did some recording, and then after about 10 days Phill, Tracy and Nick came to Berlin about three days before the tour continued and hung around. Nick sang on a couple of songs and Tracy played on a couple of songs."

They recorded during June and July. Nick was introduced to Blixa Bargeld and his band, Einsturzende Neubauten, in early June on Dutch TV . He describes the encounter in *Thistles In The Soul*, in *King Ink*.

Rowland: "Neubauten were the only group we'd met who had the same unshakeable sense of themselves, so much so that they may as well have been the only group in the world. They recorded 'Thirsty Animal' at the same studio; they taped contact mikes to Blixa's body and Mufti punched him in time to the beat. They'd got this dog, starved it for a week, covered the floor with raw meat, and put contact mikes all over the dog's stomach, and taped the sound of it eating and it's gastric juices going insane."

Mick: "It was such a big thing. 'Honeymoon In Red' was going to be this group, they'd do all this material together and make an album . . . they had quite a lot of songs. I think it was a problem era for us. Rowland was feeling more and more frustrated by Nick getting most of the attention, and writing more of the songs and he'd been getting further away from being a singer. I think he felt he needed a bridge back to doing his own stuff again, because we didn't like him to sing on The Birthday

Party stuff. We weren't interested in Rowland singing, he hadn't been doing that for a few years by then.

"We were very enthused about the prospect of working with Lydia, but ran into problems when a few of us tried to work with her on these recordings. We discovered that her attitude towards making music didn't come down to the same reasons that we make music. I found her attitude quite offensive, although the other people in The Birthday Party continued to be involved, but I stepped out of the way, I wasn't interested. I think Lydia felt somewhat rejected by us in the end, which to a degree, she was."

Rowland: "The first time Nick met Lydia, there was no common ground between them at all. They really wanted to like each other, but the pieces just didn't mesh. Mick was sort of similar, but not as much as Nick, because Nick is very rarely challenged and Lydia completely challenged him, which lead to some confused communication."

Mick: "We weren't happy (with 'Honeymooon In Red') at all. Me and Nick refused to have our names associated with it, because it got taken away from us. Lydia got Jim Thirlwell to mix it in New York, and anything that has my name on it, I see through to the end, and it wasn't treated at all the way I'd imagined it, the way I'd recorded it with them at the time. As to what eventually came out . . . the songs are radically changed from how they started, nothing to do with the original recordings."

Rowland agrees, commenting that it was taken out of his control and given to someone else without consulting him. Five years later most of the songs were released with a very different feel. The original recordings should be bootlegged properly. More songs were recorded in August, in London. The full list of songs was: 'Come Fall', 'Done Done', 'Some Boys', 'Sew Your Heart', 'One Thousand Lies', 'Dead River', 'Fields of Fire', 'Still Burning', 'From Her To Eternity' and 'Three Kings'.

Barry played some double bass, Nick sang on some tracks, Mick played drums, piano and sax, Rowland played all guitars and "bad vocals" except on 'Some Boys' where he played sax and piano, Lydia sang on most tracks, and Tracy also played bass.

Rowland: "Although I was writing less it would be very wrong to suggest that The Birthday Party did not represent my ideas. I felt it was my job to push Nick in the opposite direction to Mick's; Mick's direction being more logical, mine more intuitive."

'Honeymoon' effectively suggested a way to solve their current paucity of material whilst retaining the band as a working vehicle.

Phill: "People say that 'There was all this internal tension'. There was a bit of that in the end, but we were making music. A lot of internal tension was caused by too many musical issues; when the music was going right and when everybody was into it, the tension didn't matter. If someone seems to be drifting away from you or you seem to be not getting the input you need from them, if you let it go and don't say anything, it's going to get worse. I feel that to a degree that's what happened towards the end of the band."

It's remarkable that Phill stayed with them for so long – a more realistic man would've quit in disgust long ago, but Phill genuinely loved the music and the band themselves.

A photograph accompanying an interview in *Masterbag* at this time reveals much about the band's sense of itself. They're standing in an abandoned church and Tracy is suffused in light from behind, the cowboy saint, his hat like a halo. Phill is framed in an archway – the article discussed his departure. Mick and Rowland are seated on either side that reads 'Surprising Where You Find God', and Nick stands behind the sign, looking up, in the classic 'Waiting for God' pose; saint or sinner? It's a parody of expectations. Later in the year, Nick pointedly wore a white t-shirt with the name 'Jesus', responding to audiences which seemed increasingly willing to regard him as a Christ-like sacrifice. They weren't making fun of religion but recognising its inevitability, at the same time proclaiming their chosen path.

Lydia joined The Birthday Party as they toured Europe in late June and early July 1982, calling the tour 'The Last Day of the Rest of Your Life'. Rowland and Lydia performed a 15-minute piece before The Birthday Party came on. Rowland reflects that Die Haut, their support, thought The Birthday Party were hillbillies. The hillbillies were touring with just their guitars, using Die Haut's equipment to save money.

Phill: "Die Haut were good guys; we always had good rapport with them."

Lydia also did guest vocals on some songs, from 'Honeymoon' and either 'Loose' or 'Funhouse'. The Honeymoon songs they did with Lydia were 'From Her To Eternity' and/or '99 Ways'. Nick later used 'From Her To Eternity' for his song and album of the same name. On the ferry to Europe, Nick, Lydia and Rowland were deciding what Lydia should be doing, since they hadn't actually planned anything. Rowland explains that the song referred to as 'Dead In The Head' was untitled, and (perhaps Nick) suggested 'From *Here* To Eternity', and Rowland suggested 'From *Her* To Eternity' as a joke. Nick believes *he* came up with the title, and, according to a recent interview, so does Lydia!

Phill: "Mick usually wrote the sets. How it went was dependent on so many factors on any given night . . . any kind of conscious tilt in direction would have been lead by Nick. Nick and Mick led the band on stage. From Mick's side position on stage, with his guitar, he would often conduct; he'd go over and talk in Tracy's ear, or come over in front of the drum kit and indicate, 'We're on! we're on!', and it's the sort of contact you need on stage. Mick would even jostle Nick, and Nick got into that.

"There was a lot of jostling on stage; Tracy would have a bit with Nick, and Mick would often go over to Nick and lean into him and push him across the stage and stuff like that. If we had any staging between the drums and the floor of the stage, Nick would often stand right in front of the riser, or he'd come right around the side and stand next to me on the riser, pick up a stick and bang a couple of cymbals.

"That all added to everything and it always felt good because of the feeling of inclusion within the band. It also felt good because then the focus was on the drummer, because to most of the audience you're just a head or just arms because the kit's in the way. Nick was always good like that, occasionally he'd go, 'Tracy Pew, ladies and gentlemen'. That would be like, y'know, Vegas, but very tongue in cheek.

"Tracy had a beast of a sound, but he had a good touch and good feeling for his bass, so he rarely broke strings. Tracy was very laconic and loping in style, rather than furiously thrashing away."

Rowland: "The 'This Is the Last Day of the Rest of Your Life' tour had the unofficial title of 'The Blood on the End of My

Boot'. When we played in Cologne, we were advertised as 'the most violent band in Europe'. So when we walked into the venue, the promoters were pleading with our tour manager not to let us beat them up. Which is just absurd – they were scared of *me*!

"This was a bizarre occasion. The promoters casually mentioned in passing that this gig had originally been for a Hell's Angels band, and they'd cancelled them to put us on, but the Hell's Angels had refused to acknowledge the cancellation.

"So there'd be stuff happening like the guy with an iron bar under his jacket in the crowd. Another guy was grabbing Nick around the legs, he kept trying to undo his shoelaces, trying to pull him into the audience, and Nick's response was to lash out with his boot, and smashed the nose of this unfortunate girl who happened to be standing next to this guy, which was really fucking horrible.

"It wasn't Nick's fault, I guess, but I felt really bad, really angry because just by staying on stage I was condoning it. Mick and I went up to her between songs to apologise, and so did Nick, but there was nothing we could do about it then."

Mick: "I saw the guy get up on stage, he walked past me; I didn't think anything of it because it was quite normal. I knew Tracy was back there, the guy didn't seem to have any evil intent and I kept playing. Next thing I heard the bass stopping, I turned and Tracy was clobbering him over the head. There was a pool of urine on stage after that."

A photo shows Tracy apparently lost in the music, noticing the wet splashing on his boot. Turning, he sees the German with his dick out, and, abandoning the song, strides over and pushes the guy backwards, and thumps him. Presumably the German managed to tuck his dick in.

Rowland: "Intensity is not necessarily violence. The way we presented ourselves to the audience was a direct challenge to the audience to *behave* in some manner, to *do* something, and to *respond* with some kind of intensity instead of just standing there and clapping politely and saying, 'Oh, yes, that was very nice'. But in doing so, we didn't realise that we had . . ."

Robert: ". . . thrown down the gauntlet."

Rowland: "Yeah. There were bound to be people who would interpret what we were doing as a physical challenge rather than something more . . . intellectual . . .

"Steve Sutherland from *Melody Maker*, was with us. We were in this hotel being interviewed, and this vast uncomfortable silence had fallen after Nick said that the next record we were going to make would be the most depressing record you'd ever heard in your life, and Tracy said, 'Well, thanks for telling me', and had walked out. So there was this big silence, and Nick said, 'Oh, I think I've got blood on the end of my boot'.

"At one hotel, Nick wanted to put his clothes out to be cleaned. I said, 'It's a hotel, Nick, they'll dry-clean them'. Nick said, 'No, they won't', and he put all his clothes out; t-shirts, jeans. They did, of course, and we had to pay this bill of like £150. Nick grabbed his jeans, which had this neat crease down the legs, and was stamping on them and rubbing them to get the neatness out."

Phill: "We'd played this show in Eindhoven (early June 1982). It had been a really, really good show, and I was very tired. When you're the drummer you pack up all your stuff. It had pretty much come to pass that I was loading all the gear out as well. Mick would help a little, but certainly Rowland and Nick wouldn't.

"I was loading with the van driver, grabbing guitars and stuff, and I just cracked the shits, y'know, said, 'Nick, you're fuckin' useless, you never do bloody anything, give us a hand with the gear'. And Nick said, 'Fuck off, you're the drummer, you go fuckin' pack the van'. I said, 'No, fuck you', and I pushed him, and he had a go back at me. Nick's one of these people who will always win a fight, because physical strength doesn't come into it, he's totally driven by his forthrightness of mind. In a situation like that, he's like someone on angel dust, he has the strength of 10 men.

"So now he has me around the neck and he's holding me up against the wall, and I'm going, 'Nope, not backing down'. I think Mick or maybe a girl, Lydia or Anita intervened. Nick didn't help pack the van, but some of the other guys did. I lost, but I made a couple of gains."

The lifestyle had lost some of its innate adventure. Their creativity as a band was becoming more strained than usual. As they toured, they introduced other songs, such as 'Sad Dark Eyes', into their repertoire to vary the set that they'd been doing for nearly a year now. 'The Friendcatcher' reappeared after a year's absence. 'Kiss Me Black', and even 'Nick The Stripper' found their way into the encores.

Neither Nick nor Rowland had presented any appropriate new songs for the band; they'd reached a very grey area and hadn't been able to rehearse what songs they did have. Phill's drumming was too well-taught, so they stuck to songs which Phill could play to the band's satisfaction. This interfered with their preference, or perhaps their need, for a high turnover of creative activity.

Nick had been writing other material since October '81, but he wasn't satisfied with it, and didn't bring it to the band. Although the need for change had been apparent to the band from late '81, the band felt helpless and undecided. By mid '82, the London audiences' familiarity bred an increasingly blasé attitude. More people knew what to expect from The Birthday Party. Except Bingo, perhaps . . .

Phill: "Towards the end, Bingo used to dress up like a devil. He'd have these tights on and he'd make this outfit with capes and everything. His big thing was breathing fire from the audience, and he'd get bones and things and cover them with kerosene or lighter fluid, and throw them on stage whilst they were burning."

The special relationship which had built up amongst the group's initial followers diminished, replaced by a hellish treadmill of expectation. Nick became the crowd's Christ-like figment of desire – his clothes would be clawed at; he'd try to perform while under attack from punches, kicks and hair-pulling. Clearly, unless they redressed the balance rapidly the imbalance would split the band for good. There were mixed feelings about a permanent split, the consensus being that there was still much potential for the band.

Prior to going to the Netherlands, Mick approached Phill to tell him of the band's decision to go to Berlin without him, effectively sacking him. Phill agreed it was for the best for several reasons, but agreed to play out their booked dates.

Phill: "We went to Holland especially for the VPRO show. We tried to make things really chaotic, because TV can make things look staid; you can look stagnant and lacklustre even if you're cooking."

Mick: "We'd done two songs for the Dutch TV people. One was going to be shown one week, the other the next week. They showed 'Junkyard' with Tracy ending up in the bass drum. They got so many phonecalls and complaints that they didn't show 'Big-Jesus', which wasn't quite as overt, but was equally disgusting. In a subtle way I think 'Big-Jesus' was even worse, a kinda grinding performance.

"Tracy was this great big black slug coming out of the bass drum. It was horrible. We'd been on the ferry from England all night drinking, we hadn't had any sleep and we got to the TV station at 8am, had breakfast, kept going. Both of the cameramen were gay, y'see, so they were having a great time and thought it was brilliant so it got shown. It didn't get shown again in a hurry.

"We got rid of Phill and went to Berlin. I suppose we thought there was something more to be done. Even though it was stagnating, we thought there was something more to be gotten out of it. It must have been in the air, because we didn't discuss those things very much."

Rowland: "Things may have been stagnating, but only in comparison to our usual ferocious rate of change. The Birthday Party thing only lasted three years."

Mick: "I liked Phill in a basic way, he just acts like an idiot most of the time. He's kinda difficult to deal with. He's a really good drummer in some ways. He was really good early on, but as things progressed through '81 and '82 he wasn't keeping up and I had to work out most of his drum parts and stuff. Phill's personality was very different from the rest of the group. He'd be happy in lots of groups. He was into rock 'n' roll. He had a good understanding of what we were doing but he was kinda more of a fan in a way. And as a personality he just wasn't cool enough.

"Nick wanted to get rid of him in early 1980, before going to England. Nick found it difficult having this character around. We parted company with Phill because the group had started losing certain creative juices. We were getting a bit jaded, a little slower creatively, so we used Phill as an easy scapegoat. Phill had to go, because we weren't writing many songs, decided we'd go to Berlin and continued. It doesn't make much sense, I know. It was a good shot in the arm for us, it put us in a position where we had to do something. It was the right thing to do."

Phill: "When Tracy came back, things weren't great. He stayed at my place for quite a while . . . he and Kate (Tracy's longtime girlfriend) living in my kitchen, which had a kinda family room.

"It was getting to be really hard work, particularly for me. I had a lot of insecurities then; not enough faith in my own ability to be with those people and do what I was doing. I was only 23. The rest of the band came on strong, man, they came on like they knew something you didn't know, that's hard shit to deal with. I felt the band was getting information from somewhere else and I wasn't tuned in to it because they were always telling me that. We lived in separate houses, only coming together for rehearsals or gigs.

"Earlier, in Australia and initially in London, we lent each other records. Working in Missing Link, I saw what everyone bought, I listened to everything that came in and we passed records around. That communication deteriorated, so I was working on stuff that was stylistically not correct for the band.

"In rehearsal, I never seemed to be able to come up with what they wanted. I'd always been able to come up with something really good, with something different, challenging, to see if we could make it happen and work; that was the idea of what we were supposed to be about. In the end, I was trying to play more complex rhythms, but they probably wanted less, more space. I could play what they were coming up with, but Mick's approach was different, less schooled.

"The move to Berlin . . . I let it be known that I didn't think it was a good idea. Nick said he wanted to make uh, like Leonard Cohen, only more down. He may've been taking the piss, but I didn't want to do that sort of music. From my perspective, I felt the situation was out of control. We'd started off with such a wonderful purpose. I knew that in the middle of all this I was powerless, but, shit happens."

The Birthday Party returned to London in the second week of July to break the news to the London music press. Around this time Nick announced to the band that he was writing a novel. Amrik Rai's interview appeared in the *NME* of July 31, 1982, and indicates that the split was mutual. Phill was definite that the split was the best thing for him, which it probably was. Nick, Mick, Rowland and Tracy were on the verge of reinvention – their biggest influence was still themselves.

Berlin was the only other city they'd discovered that was sufficiently like Melbourne for garrulousness and open-minded creativity. There were considerable advantages: reminding them of home without being home; relatively cheap food, alcohol and accommodation. Berlin's artistic community was well-established. Surrounded by the grim, drab austerity of East Germany, with a sense of the rebellious outcast about it, Berlin was also the home of Malaria!, Die Haut and Einsturzende Neubauten.

Mick: "Berlin started because our tour took us there, and we discovered we had a lot of friends there. Whenever we'd go there we'd have a great time, and we have a lot of contacts there; we realised it was kind of an alternative city, for alternative people. It was like a city with a nationality; definitely German but with expatriates from all over Europe, America, everywhere. Berlin was a magnet for people who wanted to get away from their own country.

"People in Berlin felt more like the way people are in Australia – not so hung up or always worrying about success. They're fairly cut off in Berlin; a lot of what they do, they can't possibly expect to be a huge success, they're doing it for the same reasons people here in Melbourne do things, because they want to. You all go and drink at the same bar and get drunk and meet everyone; everyone's in several fields, it doesn't get as subdivided as the rest of Europe."

They intended to recreate the band in a more even-keeled fashion, in which everyone had an equal opportunity. It was directly opposed to the star-system perpetuated by the music press, who seek out entertainers, novelties, or the next Sex Pistols.

Mick: "A common thing the UK press does is to take an idea that you give them. When they write the article, they make it their own idea. They did this with us; we ended up sounding pretty dumb; all the most interesting things we'd say became the writer's ideas. So the article would be positive, but it'd be excruciatingly embarrassing to read this false representation of ourselves. The *NME* keep doing it again and again.

"The *NME* article by Amrik Rai, who's a little scumbag, and I hope you quote me – he's the epitome of everything I hate about journalists . . . the *NME* wanted to do an article on us just after 'Junkyard'. It wasn't a backlash they were trying to set up, they were trying to get some balance. I think they'd sent Amrik a couple of our records but until then he'd never heard us. He showed up having listened to 'Prayers', which was a year and a half old. He didn't know 'Junkyard', and we were about to part company with Phill and go to Berlin. Amrik sat with Nick and

Rowland quoting lyrics from 'Prayers'. You can imagine what their response was: 'This guy's a fucking idiot, get out of here'.

"The *NME* was still influential, it moulded a certain area of the public's opinion about what was happening . . . and here's this turd who's heard 'Prayers On Fire' the night before, and he was going to write the definitive article for the year in the *NME* on The Birthday Party. We were furious, it was such a fucking insult.

"We started threatening him; we should have stolen his cassette player and broken it. We salvaged the situation, because I took him aside and said, 'Look, Amrik, in about a month Phill's out of the group and we're all moving to Berlin. Now do you want to start again?' "

Phill: "If you say a couple of wrong sentences, they'll be the ones that will get published, out of context, misrepresenting your direction and intent. It happened time and time again. We'd go, 'Fuck, how could they've printed that?! That's not what I was getting at at all!' It happened to Nick incessantly. If Nick felt that the guy doing the interview was wasting his time, he'd try and get it over with as quickly as possible by offending them, or by saying 'That's a stupid question'."

The last gig with Phill was at The Venue, in London on August 16.

Phill: "My last gig was treated as a five-way split; I got a fifth of the money from the door receipts; about £400. Mick and I calculated that, from what we considered the first official gig of The Boys Next Door, we'd done like 437 shows."

Rowland: "Butler Rep from the Psychedelic Furs was there, wearing pink trousers and a yellow shirt. He came up to Nick and I, and in his thick London accent, he 'Fawt that Nick and I and himself and possibly Elvis Costello, are the only four literate song writers in rock'. Nick's response to this was to grab the cigarette out of his mouth, have a drag out of it, grab the can of beer out of his hand and have a swig out of it, put the cigarette in the can and hand it back to him. Then we walked off. In other words, 'No! You'rc wrong! There's only three of us!' I mean, what are you supposed to say to that? 'Yes, you're right?!' The ridiculous thing is that Nick does like a lot of the lyrics on their first album, largely because of the repeated use of the word 'stupid'."

Phill: "I got a call from The Furs' manager asking me to come down for a session. I felt like I wasn't very good . . . I had a poor self-image because the guys I'd worked and lived with, done everything with for the last eight years of my life had said, 'We don't think you're the right guy to be in the band'. I'd said, 'Fuck, that's fine, I don't want to live in Berlin'."

To his surprise, Phill found a gig with The Psychedelic Furs, who insisted that he was the drummer for them. The Furs toured the world during 1982 and '83. Set to record on the Furs' next album, Phill argued with their producer over the drums. He wanted live, the producer didn't. The producer wanted him and a couple of others to play; Phill wanted to play himself. Richard Butler and John Ashton decided, with the producer's intervention, that he wasn't the drummer for the album, firing him.

Phill subsequently returned to Australia, playing with Melbourne's Blue Ruin, which he left around 1990 after several years and a couple of overseas tours. Phill played in The Sunday Kind from late 1993 to August 1995.

In removing Phill, The Birthday Party hoped to reinvent, and improve upon their creation. Without him, they could never have come up with the complexities of their prior achievements; in adjusting, they found that more space existed within their older songs. Nevertheless, a large part of the audience reacted in the same way whether they played 'Junkyard' or new material. This ran counter to their expressionist ideals; they felt uncomfortable.

Mick was much more effective playing drums. Stripping down their sound, so used to an intense overload of sensory input, must have been a joy. Their balance had shifted emotionally, and musically. With Phill gone, Mick exerted greater influence on the rhythm section, and offered more creative input into newer songs. Mick projected a musical cohesion, a solid glue, while Nick led their actual direction.

The rhythm section became more direct, more powerful, allowing Rowland more space to play in. Instead of filling up this new space with fiddly stuff, he pulled everything down to a skeletal minimum, allowing the guitar to sweep through the band like a drunk tornado. This focused more attention on Nick's vocals, and the new setting alone made them that much more powerful.

The intention was to allow a more direct input from everyone instead of just Mick and Nick. While in Berlin, shortly after Phill had left, they recorded a couple of songs with Anita on vocals, 'The Fullness Of His Coming' and 'I Killed It With A Shoe', for Monogam Records (headed by Elizabeth Rekker). 'Fullness' was issued on a Monogam sampler and on Anita's 'Dirty Pearl' CD. Rowland recalls that 'Shoe' was "the most remarkable vocal performance he'd ever heard; there was no distinction between the lyrics and what she was singing . . . it was a very vivid song of betrayal."

It was no secret that Nick was sexually opportunistic on tour; this was regarded as Nick being Nick. Anita and Nick apparently had a fairly open relationship, yet not a very easy one.

Rowland: "I can recall Anita saying, 'You don't really want me to come on tour, do you?', and Nick responding, 'Yes, I do, I really want you to come on tour', and Anita, 'You're just saying that; you don't really'; back and forth until everyone's in the van and driving out of East Berlin, when Nick turns around and says to Anita, 'You do know I can't pay for you, don't you?', and because Anita had no means of support, she had to get out."

Continuing to perform and tour, they slowly realised that the situation must draw to a conclusion sometime soon, even though for many of their European dates they were playing better than ever.

Rowland: "We went to Greece in September 1982 to play this festival. We were to play on the first day, then New Order and The Fall the third. We flew from East Berlin via Hungary to Greece. We were in the Hungarian airport for eight hours, I think, just drinking, and Nick met these two truly appalling Australian hitchhiking 'gals', and they got completely pissed together.

"When the promoter arranged the tour, he pleaded with us not to bring any drugs with us. When we got off the plane there was like *four photographers taking photos* (this had never happened to them before, and never would again – RB), taking photos of us getting our luggage, snap-snap-snap; like The Rolling Stones coming to Melbourne in 1964.

"This man appeared, our promoter's cousin, who worked in Customs and Immigration; if we followed him we wouldn't have to go through Customs. We were whisked through, probably because the promoter was terrified we'd have guitar cases crammed full of heroin. We got out of the airport and were greeted by this huge fat man who announced himself as Adonis, our driver. We arrived at our hotel, everyone was completely fucked and desperately wanted to go to bed. I remember looking at the front desk and seeing Nick standing there with the girls, and I went upstairs and went to sleep.

"About an hour later the desk rang up Minou, our tour manager, saying 'Can you please do something about this man?' Nick was standing down there, *demanding* that these two girls be allowed to share his room. The hotel said, 'Fine, if you'll give us whatever amount more to pay for them', and Nick was saying, 'No!' So Minou, falling back on her femininity, rang up Mick; 'Please, Mick do something about this, it is terrible!' So Mick gets up and goes down there and says, 'You *fucking cunt*! Get into *fuckin' bed* and *go to sleep*!'

"And Nick goes, 'Right! I'm leaving the band!', picks up his little briefcase and marches out into the night!

"The next morning, a policeman found him asleep under a bush in a park, and moved him on. He was so pissed, his memory of the last day was completely clouded, and he thought he was still in Berlin. Getting on a bus, he tries to pay German marks, and he's saying, 'Codbusitor?' which was where we lived, and he didn't speak any German, and the driver's going, 'What?' in Greek. Nick ended up wandering around for an hour, eventually realising that this is not Berlin, and he's sitting at this train station, and he looks up.

"Directly opposite him is this hotel, and we all walk out the door and down the steps. The next day the newspaper headlines read, 'Punk Rock Star Found Asleep In Park!' So we were on the front page of the Greek daily newspapers for two days in a row."

Mick: "Everyone was on stage at the end of the concert in Athens, it was like a party. It was also in defiance of the security who'd been throwing people off the stage. Eventually Nick walked up and pushed one of these security people out of the way, and the whole crowd went totally crazy."

By September, Rowland's 'Still Burning' was added; another indication of their need for new material, and of Rowland's natural desire to express himself more fully within the band. His 'Dim Locator', played regularly from late 1981 to early '82, although difficult for Nick to sing so low and make the lyrics comprehensible, was also added.

Rowland: "This huge, incredibly opulent venue, The Sector, offered us an enormous amount of money to play. The gig was scheduled in about three months, so on the strength of this we'd go there about four times a week and drink for free. Eventually they got so sick of us they decided they didn't want us to play there at all, although they'd put up posters for the gig all over Berlin, me and Nick sleeping next to each other.

"When they said they didn't want us to play, we said, 'Well, we've got a contract', so they said, 'We'll pay you', and paid us the big amount of money. Then we insisted they give us the rider as well, so we went away loaded with all this alcohol and cash."

Nick's new songs were also being added to the set. Initially shaky, 'Sonny's Burning', 'Deep In The Woods' and 'Fears Of Gun' all appeared. His new songs were more powerful and had greater scope than anything they'd done previously; Mick's reliable and simple presence seemed like the eye of a hurricane. The older songs they retained acquired a new, different, power and inspiration, mocking the slowly disintegrating nature of their internal affairs. The band became tighter, and a hell of a lot more powerful, much more direct.

Rowland: "We were in Berlin, sitting around Christof Dreyer's flat, bored out of our minds, and Nick goes, deadpan, 'Hands up who wants to die?' Which I thought was great. I thought that part of my job in The Birthday Party was to encourage that side of Nick's expression, because Mick tried to temper it in a more logical direction.

"That was a really great thing about The Birthday Party, this contradiction between dumbness and obvious intellectual capacity; rock music should be like that. Dumbness is an essential part of rock music. I think all art should contain those contradictory elements of life, because nothing is ever as black and white as it may appear, you can't get away with portraying things as one-dimensional."

Keith: "We were going to do a country single with Tracy, a Merle Haggard song, 'Branded Man'. I wish we'd done it, it would've been great. We had a great cover for it, Tracy in his cowboy hat with a slab of beer under his arm. Tracy was a real character and a fantastic bass player for a guy who never gave a shit about anything."

Occasionally Nick would express an interest in the music of one of Rowland's songs – 'These Immortal Souls', for instance – but not the lyrics. As far as Rowland was concerned, the two went together or not at all.

It looked as if they were moving forward, although they didn't return to the old days of fast and furious turnover. Still linked to the old band, the resulting dissatisfaction was partly responsible for the band's slow collapse. Subsequent to the release of 'The Bad Seed', the still-grasping crowds continued to physically hurt Nick considerably more than he hurt them.

But they'd made their choice, as they made all their choices, for better or for worse, married to their music.

IV

Four Bad Seeds?

IN OCTOBER 1982, they returned to their new home, Berlin, to record 'The Bad Seed' EP.

Rowland: "Mick had this idea – which I found really strange – that we should change the name of the band for one record to 'The Bad Seeds'. I couldn't understand what the point of it was. I didn't want to disown what we'd done in the past, I thought it was confusion for wilfulness' sake. It may have defined the break from Phill, but I don't see that it served any real purpose, yet he seemed to think that it was really important. If we hadn't been doing any of the old songs then that would have been different, but our sets were at least half our old songs."

It would have been the perfect time for them to change their name, signifying a new start in the band's life, but in the end they took the path of least resistance, relying on the security of the devil they knew rather than the devil they didn't.

Rowland: "'The Bad Seed' EP is my favourite record of The Birthday Party, and the one I had least to do with writing, but I think it's got the best guitar playing I ever did in the band on it. I always preferred the guitar I did on other people's songs rather than on my own. When it was my song, my guitar was an integral part of the structure of the song; when it wasn't, I could do something that was completely at odds with what the rest of the group were doing.

"One of the great things about 'The Bad Seed' is Mick's sense of rhythm. There's this particular sort of groove which is a Mick Harvey groove, which is a really fantastic thing. Mick's influence grew because in playing the drums he was doing something which was entirely his own area, which he did in incredibly singular fashion, and he exerted a lot more influence over the band; and secondly because he became Nick's prime collaborator.

"But he wasn't in command. He wasn't telling anybody else

what to play; I still did what I did. When Phill left, everybody achieved greater freedom, the idea being that everybody would have their own area to work in that was specifically theirs, so everybody's input would become greater. While the songwriting credits became more Nick and Mick's, everyone's personal input was greater."

Nick was intent on creative control over his own work, which would mean creative control over the group's; but he hadn't staked out the territory as his and his alone. Mick and Rowland still considered themselves integral members of a working, reasonably balanced group, not backing musicians.

Genevieve: "Rowland and Nick spent a lot of time together in Berlin in 1982 – they had a lot of major pastimes in common, and were staying in this warehouse for four months."

Nancy Pew: "I think in a lot of ways Tracy wasn't allowed to contribute to the band as much as he could've. I don't know whether he ever talked with anyone. I think he felt to some extent that he was pushed down. Nick was the major creative force, and maybe Tracy didn't present himself, because he wasn't pushy about showing what he could do."

Instead of talking about the situation, conversation slowed to a crawl. The drunken Aussie larrikin sheen was beginning to look a bit worn.

Presumably Nick decided to do the 'Bad Seed' EP cover because no-one else had. As Rowland recalls, Mick thought at first that Nick's cover was ridiculous and offensive, and everyone regarded it as silly. Nick had responded to the way the world perceived the band: four pale mugshots framed by a giant swastika. "What other symbol fits around four photographs?" he would innocently enquire. A crucifix, Nick, but no-one mentioned that.

Anyone genuinely offended by the swastika would probably never become aware of the EP anyway. The intention was not to offend, but to tease; nevertheless, the swastika resonates with strong taboos. Originally designed to celebrate the life force, the swastika in the twentieth century has a perverse magnetism which creates a response. Confined to their bubble, The Birthday Party had cracked another little funny, but like so many of their self-aware jokes, it backfired because few people recognised it as a joke. The sacred heart with the torch and barbed wire, all pastiches of Nick's own interests, merely enhanced the band's reputation as an evil, bloodthirsty barbarian horde come to raze the village to cinders. The swastika itself should no more be representative of evil than the cross, crucifix or the wheel, all being symbols which predate Christianity.

Most onlookers believed that they were about to split, yet 'The Bad Seed' is one of their finest records; original, well formed, powerful and abrasive. The Birthday Party had moved into an unconfined space, giving room for grand, spectacular songs; giving rein to the pent-up emotion which had encased them in eight months of grind and travel.

Most of the songs seem to deal directly with the expression of evil, of a temptation given in to. 'Deep In The Woods' concerns an itinerant who kills a woman under the belief that he 'loves' her. It is the act of killing a woman that he loves; for him, killing is an expression of his 'love'. The song focuses on the killer's grief for those he has killed, and on the fact that he will kill again.

'Sonny's Burning' appears to be about the torture of a young man, 'Sonny', as he hangs, presumably, from a tree or roof-beam, and the development of evil as the torturer goes about his hobby.

Nick's early life seems to have been spent fighting for spiritual independence, so it's no surprise that he wasn't too intimate with those around him. This reflects in his Dadaesque lyrics. In 'Fears Of Gun', Nick conceals himself in a character, Gun, so as to express his dissatisfaction with himself. This song concerns an alcoholic who beats his wife, again, apparently as an expression of love or desire.

'Wild World' describes sensuality. None of these songs make the killer or the drunk bully attractive or even interesting. Yet Nick became firmly stuck with the reputation of writing "woman-killer" songs. Oddly, no-one complains about country music songs which describe how some redneck's baby done gone left him 'cause he slapped her around some.

'The Bad Seed' does not glorify evil but comments on its methodology and motives; at people who feel no guilt for their actions because they have no empathy with others. The EP implies that evil is not a natural state as such, that we gravitate to this state through experience, ultimately corrupting ourselves. Focusing on the protagonist allows the pain and confusion, the mortality, to show, particularly in 'Deep In The Woods'.

Nick's use of language is ambiguous, twisting the meanings of the song and the feelings of the listener around. There are several conflicting moralities here. As the title suggests, somewhat tongue-in-cheekily given The Birthday Party's violent reputation, some people are just born bad, and grow up worse. The 'Bad Seed' joke is that the band were all fairly normal in most respects, certainly not what you'd call evil. Wayward, naughty, given to playing and acting up, taking too many 'recreational' substances, but, not actually *bad* or *evil*; perhaps too absorbed in what they were doing, but essentially harmless.

After 'Bad Seed' was released, The Birthday Party left 4AD because they didn't feel 4AD were prepared to promote them in the way they wanted. 4AD would always advertise their bands in block adverts, and The Birthday Party wanted to take their creation as far as they could, and they couldn't see that happening if they were lumped in with the 'indie' philosophy. Discussions through Chris Carr with Mute gave rise to a contract for the publishing rights to raise some money, and Daniel Miller, who'd been the first person to show interest in 1980, suggested that he represent them in future, so they signed with Mute.

Meanwhile Nick's songs 'Mutiny In Heaven', and 'Swampland', covertly about Nick's experience of The Birthday Party, were both turning into wordy epics. Nick also had a bad habit of losing the manuscript of his novel.

Rowland: "He lost the novel probably only about once or twice, but it seemed like many more. But he would have lost it many more times if we hadn't picked it up for him. I didn't have a real conception of how much work had gone into it, but I realised that it was a really careless act to leave it lying around. It must've been incredibly painful for him to find that he'd lost it.

"We'd be in a cafe, and he'd get up, walk out and leave his cigarettes on the table. I'd put them in my pocket and walk out, and about an hour later he'd go, 'Where are my cigarettes?' and I'd say, 'Here they are, Nick'."

By November, 'Wild World' and 'Pleasure Avalanche', had been added to their set; by January, 'The Six Strings That Drew Blood' and 'The Friendcatcher' were added again. Their new songs allowed them to drop much of their older material for the first time. The older songs retained were 'Hamlet', 'Big-Jesus', 'Dead Joe' and 'Six Inch Gold Blade'.

Returning to London on November 21, they recorded their last Peel session the next day. Mick and Nick's 'Sonny's Burning', 'Deep In The Woods', and 'Pleasure Avalanche' were recorded with Rowland's 'Marry Me (Lie! Lie!)', which they never performed again. Rowland later recorded it with These Immortal Souls. After two gigs in Scotland, their last gig of the year was in London at the Ace Cinema in Brixton. The vicious circle of violence continued, a circle which none of them wanted to continue, yet none had sufficient desire to halt.

Mick: "*Whatever You Want* (at the Ace Cinema, Brixton) is another time where television didn't work for us. They invited us to mix the songs we wanted mixed, so we watched the whole concert and we chose the best songs, 'Sonny's Burning' and 'Hamlet'.

"They spent the afternoon trying to talk us into using 'Fears Of Gun' because it's 'good television' and Nick's 'Jesus' t-shirt gets ripped off at the end. So they showed 'Hamlet', and 'Fears Of Gun' mixed fairly averagely. And we'd mixed 'Sonny's Burning' as well which was great."

The band were now struggling to force a new beginning and to gain a new validity while maintaining their own standards and integrity, under the scrutiny of increasingly doubtful London music papers.

After the Ace gig, Nick went to Aachen to record with Die Haut, before returning to London around Christmas. The music for the best of the four songs, 'The Stowaway', was apparently taken from Bowie's 'Putting Out The Fire (With Gasoline)'.

The Birthday Party decided to use London as a base for now; Berlin had served its purpose.

Mick: "We were never particularly popular in England because the English are so concerned with style and fads. We just didn't fit. I can't exaggerate this, it's so pervasive a part of English life. They were quite confused about us; the people that did like us were the people who weren't interested in any of that shit. I'd actually get asked quite often, 'What are you, are you a rocker or a punk?' "

"They tried to push us into [Goth], make us something so they could understand it, so that people knew what to wear to our concerts. Most of the goth people didn't really like us because we didn't do the right thing. The gothic elements of what we do and did are there, but the superficial goth thing didn't have a lot to do with us."

Rowland still had problems. Nick still had problems. Mick grew impatient with the lack of creative follow-through in the new, improved Birthday Party.

By the new year, there was less strain and struggle between the bass and drums; they became smoother, clearer; flowed more naturally. Rowland filled up larger spaces between the vocals and the rhythm section; his music became much more flexible and powerful. The musical balance between the members was a great improvement.

Phill: "Rowland wasn't a great technical guitarist; but he invented his own thing which he was great at, and that was what made him a great guitarist."

After a 10-week tour of Holland and England, they took a brief break. Looking back over their cuttings, it's difficult to obtain a balanced view because Nick is usually the one quoted at length. While Nick's talents certainly deserve scrutiny, The Birthday Party were not one man, but five, then four, and each held a position of some strength. The press view was *acutely* coloured.

The group couldn't cope with the demand or the change. In many ways their creative survival depended on the tension between them; pushing to make their creative mark on songs. More and more, Rowland *didn't* push against Nick and Mick, failing to counter-balance a creation which was becoming too one-sided. There was no 'scapegoat' within the band. Phill had served the purpose of an organic safety-valve; without that valve, much of their integral creation was threatened and consequently became strained.

Unsure of their ability to exist without a fifth member to spar against, Rowland, Nick and Tracy were uncomfortable without Mick's physical presence alongside them, although Mick's drumming had tightened their sound.

Rowland: "We'd been used to being in a band where we had two guitars, or guitar and keyboards, and I don't think we realised the strengths of the four-piece line-up. The songs were a lot more mature and we ceased to have anything to do with pop music. We'd broken out of the 'Junkyard rock monster' thing which, for a long time, seemed like we were never going to get out of.

"In a way, getting Jeffrey Wegener to play in the band was a step backwards because the two EPs we did as a four-piece were the most powerful, most condensed things we ever did."

Jeff was still playing in The Laughing Clowns at this time, so they couldn't have kept him anyway.

Mick: "The band liked the idea of having me play guitar as well as drums because it was important to some of the older material, so we got Jeff in because he was available; everyone liked the idea when we did 'The Bad Seed'. We toured Holland with Jeff in January '83. I played drums on four or five of the songs in the set, the ones in which I'd always played drums in."

After Jeff's departure, Rowland's 'Say A Spell' was added to their set, as well as Nick's 'Swampland', which he was still working on.

Rowland planned another band – These Immortal Souls. He intended the line-up to be built around instruments with more air or atmosphere about them: Genevieve on piano, Rowland on guitar, Barry on double bass and Jeff on drums.

Nick and Lydia concocted the idea of doing some performances together, with Nick reading his stories, Lydia some of hers, perhaps with some of Lydia's friends. Lydia also intended opening for The Birthday Party in America as well, doing her songs perhaps with Rowland on sax, with a cassette player for backing. Neither of these ideas came to pass.

With splintering interests, the band couldn't maintain maximum creativity and stay together. Was a hiatus the answer?

In Glasgow and in London, people still lined up in the front row to be bashed about the head by Nick; to be punched, kicked, spat on – responses which do nothing to endear the bashed to the basher. This clamour for punishment, apparently their only way of gaining attention for themselves, created a potentially lethal situation. The band could do nothing to stem the tide of sacrificial goats herding towards the front for a blessed mike-whipping. Nick was responding in whatever way he felt justified, like a hired sadist, which escalated the brittle nature and fragility of their performances.

Rowland: "This guy came up to the front of the stage and

demanded that Nick have a fight with him. Nick ignored him for as long as he could, but they ended up rolling around the stage punching each other a few times, I can't remember how it stopped. Then this guy came backstage and it was, 'Now we're all great mates and we're equals'.

"Our response was, 'No, we're not equals. You're some thick bastard who thinks that it's great to have a fight, and we're The Birthday Party. There's a considerable difference there.' It was like a male bonding session as far as he was concerned."

Small wonder that, dissatisfied with their crowds' response, they became contemptuous of them. Mick had taken over the role of organiser – the tours, the equipment – as well as performing. More practically minded, he was in a perfect position to see their progress and development with a more open mind. Well used to making decisions, it's no surprise that Mick reluctantly and painfully decided to draw the veil over the band.

In February 1983, Mick phoned Nick, stating, in part, that for The Birthday Party to continue was futile from a viable, creatively challenging point of view. Nick agreed, and so Mick contacted Rowland, who also agreed. Tracy went along with their decision; it's quite probable that Tracy was equally as fed up with milking a limited opportunity.

The reason for Mick's decision was that little new material was being produced; the tensions inside the band which had always produced a workable result, were pulling apart. The *dynamic* balance had gone; only habit and gritted teeth were holding them together. It was very hard to contemplate breaking up what had been their lives for eight years; naturally, their feelings were mixed but Mick was right in his decision; a valid creative future seemed impossible. Everyone was drifting just too far apart.

Nick was becoming more distant, partly because his contribution was constantly analysed, partly as a result of an increased interest in his writing, by which he hoped to go beyond the confines of 'rock-lyrics'. Nick's writing was being produced less with the group in mind than for his own literary ambitions.

Mick, Tracy and Rowland found the constant movement – London, Berlin, London, interspersed between touring – disconcerting and distracting. Nick and Rowland had taken their initial creative competitiveness to an extreme which hindered the band's continuing creativity. Both had altered greatly over the past year. Little direct dialogue concerning the future of the band had passed between them, which was dangerous since they were supposedly the band's major contributing writers.

Tracy or Mick could have written songs, but they both probably realised that Nick wanted to sing what he was comfortable with, and it would have been too much trouble to simply demand inclusion when Nick's material was so good. Mick was well-established writing music for Nick's lyrics by now, and he found that this role best suited him.

Tracy was his own man, not competing to get his own work heard. Tracy usually got along with everyone, probably because he realised that competition would be pointlessly divisive. "Tracy often spent large amounts of time either by himself or in silence, for the most part just getting on with the job, and perhaps as a result didn't pick up as much of the unspoken tension below the surface," Rowland recalls.

With the exception of the already booked American tour, there were no new, untrained crowds for the band to provoke. Provocation was their fuel, it broke down barriers and prompted re-examination of moral and actual behaviour. This is what modern art attempts to do: The Birthday Party had found a connection between their music and art itself.

Mick: "Ken West, the promoter in Australia, started making offers about coming to Australia, monetary enticements and stuff like that. I think Nick, Rowland and Tracy wanted to go back to Australia anyway, hang around, take drugs and go to parties and see their mums.

"Ken would've made some offer of what sort of money they would make, which of course they definitely wouldn't 'cause that's always the case with tours. So they started ringing me saying, 'Look, can't we go to Australia and do this last tour', and I said, 'No, I'm not interested, I don't see that it'll present any challenge to the group at all. We'd be going over old ground and I don't see any reason to do it; I won't be going'.

"But Rowland and Nick kept ringing me up, and we had incredibly long conversations every day about it, and eventually Nick said, 'Well, Ken needs an answer today, we need to say yes or no to it today, what do I tell him?' I said, 'Well, you tell him what you want to, I'm not going' . . . 'Look I need to tell Ken today what's happening' . . .'Well you tell him what's happening,

I don't know'. And Nick eventually said, 'Well do I tell him yes?', and I said, 'If you want to, you tell him yes'.

"So Nick went, 'Right, okay, great', hung up and rang Ken and said 'Yes', and presumed that I'd agreed to do the tour, which was remarkable. I knew that's what he'd done, I knew that he'd decided that that was me saying yes. An amazing interpretation of the conversation, but I knew that it'd get there somehow.

"I heard they did some good shows in the end, but there was a hell of a lot of drug taking. That's all I really heard about that tour – that and the New Zealand tour being picketed by feminists."

Rowland: "Mick does say this, that going back to Australia for that tour was going backwards because there was no challenge. Now, excuse me, but has Mick never played in Australia again? I don't understand that. If he was looking for challenges, I can't think of anything more challenging than keeping that band going."

In the meantime there was the American tour.

Mick: "That last tour of America was about the best tour we ever did."

Tony: "The last time they played America they made a great impact, because no-one had seen anything like them."

Ross Waterman: "They were reaching a point where their music was pretty extreme, they were trying to create a massive, sheer wall of sound, a sort of cacophony."

Rowland: "As a four-piece, to a large extent, we had a new lease of life; gigs were much more enjoyable than they'd been for a long time, the new songs were really great and there was a general sense of freedom. That American tour, I thought, 'This is what rock gigs should be like, this is the real thing.' We had finally matured, this was the point where we had finally got rid of any real influence that any other groups had had on us. We had started operating from our own reference points."

The music press in America stay on the mainstream, or fixed to genres that sell, like heavy metal. There was no real national, influential music magazine which looked at both the mainstream and the underground. Although they were still relegated to the invisible underground, there was an increasingly intense buzz about The Birthday Party which permeated the underground culture.

Since 1981, the American underground had undergone a massive transformation. There were more people interested in pushing music into areas of expression not currently acceptable. The Birthday Party had long since declared their intentions, and the underground had responded with emotions which were clearly appreciative.

The intention was to stay together long enough to record one more record, a double EP rather than an album, perhaps with a gatefold sleeve, tour Australasia, and split. The record was to allow everyone a chance to get their ideas down on vinyl one last time, to create a minimum of conflict.

America, while allowing the band to play to an unaccustomed audience, also served to highlight their problems; by the end of the tour, despite playing better than ever to a totally fresh crowd, the band were worn ragged from the same things which caused them to musically click on stage.

Ralf S: "I tell you, Mick and Tracy create between them the ugliest thunder imaginable, the sounds of war. Rowland fly-fishes this black, fast-running stream, jostling for space and frequently overriding as aggressively as he can manage. Itself a phenomenon, Tracy's bass is a sinuous artillery barrage, and certainly what he produces sounds nothing like the bass guitar."

Jo C: "I saw them in Chicago in April . . . Christ, the size of them. An omnipotent sound, forcing numbness on the rest of our bodies as we forget the world for an hour and are grasped by this captivating beast of noise. A chaos I can live with, drunk or sober, and these slide together like group sex, everyone's hands on everyone else.

"Nothing they've recorded prepares me for the fearsome gnarled mesh that is The Birthday Party. Successfully grandiose in scheme yet down to earth, with a deceptively casual manner. Faces in the crowd, except for Nick's outrageous hair. On stage, a force of sorts gets up like an unnoticed devil and takes over.

"Drums juddering at our skulls' insides, Rowland's guitar yowling like a vexed cougar, these sounds threaten each other in a totally unearthly manner. Nick is left to find some middle ground from which he abominates us. Timing becomes a strange joke and the band are splayed like moths on pins in an endless mirror.

"The crowd were noisy and responsive, reminding me of the gentry in Europe in the 1700's who went to insane asylums for amusement on Sunday afternoons. I didn't expect to see 'Dead Joe' or 'Big-Jesus-Trash-Can', but they've gained an acceptable, moving grandeur which hunches its way on stage, familiar and known, until the raggy old cloak is thrown off and a once familiar body is desperate again. More than ever we lose ourselves in the tragic grind and scrunch, the apocalypse of Tracy's bass slithering around us like an oily grunting machine."

While in LA Nick saw the Elvis Presley movie, *This Is Elvis*. He told several magazines that he watched it over and over. Nick had been performing to his own standards for some time, trying to establish a medium between the compromised performance that the crowd clamoured for, and representing his own personal situation many times larger.

Elvis struggled to establish a happy medium between what he wanted to be and what he was expected to be. *This Is Elvis* shows Elvis run-down and fighting to be what he was supposed to be, and failing because he was not the public Elvis. His hypnotic public decline was emotionally powerful, captivating, and it follows that Nick's public position, with all it's contradictory forces, would present a similarly powerful spectacle.

After the US tour, they flew to Berlin to record at Hansa Ton-Studios. Proceedings were overseen by Blixa Bargeld, who somehow kept the band mostly together. They were exhausted and depressed, the tension sometimes at flashpoint. Blixa tried to organise the recording as nothing would be done without the band being corralled into a working situation. Because of the lack of communication within the band, and the unresolved disagreements, the resulting tracks were confused and sketchy. They needed more work.

Rowland: "Mick fought tooth and nail throughout The Birthday Party to get things under control; he was livid about Nick singing 'that fat cunt behind the screen'; he just thought it was gratuitous.

Mick was adamant; he was not touring Australia. Frantic arrangements were made; the Australian tour was rearranged, initial Sydney dates cancelled; Des Heffner, their stand-in drummer, was recruited by phone. The last gig The Birthday Party played with Mick was at The Electric Ballroom in London on April 26, 1983.

It was an appropriate end for the band, stuffing up in a snarl of their own volatile personalities; the very thing which made them such a brilliant and emotional proposition on stage in the first place.

The next day everyone except Mick left for Australia. After a couple of days they flew to New Zealand for the first gig of the tour. Every band has someone who's regularly late for the plane. Tracy, according to Rowland, didn't see the need to rehearse, believing it could all be done at soundcheck.

Rowland: "Tracy was always a bit weird on tour . . . Tracy missed the flight, finally arriving the next day, so we went on with an hour's rehearsal and did a really rotten gig."

They'd rehearsed 'Hamlet', 'Deep In The Woods', 'Wild World', 'Junkyard', 'Six Strings', 'Sonny's Burning' and 'She's Hit'; later adding 'Jennifer's Veil'.

Dave Graney: "The story of people leaving Australia (and seeking fame and fortune) is pretty boring in the end. They have to leave to get some sort of audience to sustain their wild sort of fantasies. It's a boring story, but often true; it's repeated over and over.

"I'm only saying this 'cause The Moodists were lionised by the British press for a couple of weeks, so we completely sold out to them. Their stupid story of, 'Oh, aren't the Australians brutes, they don't like beautiful music, but we English can appreciate it', and we completely fuckin' went along with it!"

Rowland: "[Towards the end] Nick sat backstage with his head in his hands saying, 'I just can't do it'; he was under an enormous amount of pressure. As the band went on, the press ceased to perceive us as a band and we became 'Nick Cave . . . and those other guys'.

"Mick maintains that Nick felt that as the public perceived him as the prime mover behind the band, that everything the band did emanated from him, he should therefore have a much greater say over what happened in the band.

"I can understand it, but as we never paid too much attention to what people said in the first place I don't see why it should be that big a problem. I think it only became a problem because there were already other problems within the band, like we didn't give Nick enough support, or enough distance between what people were saying and himself . . .

". . . there were lots of times when we fought, but it was only really towards the end when the toll of it all began to interfere. We used to play a lot, but we'd never really get anything for doing it, and there was the toll of working very hard and never achieving any real reward for it. The Birthday Party was this grinding treadmill of touring and staying in these crap hotels yet reaping all this critical acclaim. Acclaim doesn't pay the bills.

"The Birthday Party was a way of life, we were all completely committed to the band; we went to wherever the band had to go, and lived in really horrible conditions for the band, all relatively unquestioningly. And we got nothing back for it except some good reviews.

"We were burning ourselves out for something which seemed at the time to be giving us very little in return. When we lost the support of each other, it ceased to be *us against the world* and started being *oneself* against the world including *these guys*. It happened in its most extreme form when we were recording 'Mutiny!' Everybody was far more isolated and alone than they'd ever been before.

"During the history of the band there'd been lots of different factions within the band of me and Nick, and Mick and Nick, and Nick and Tracy, and me and Mick Harvey and so on. These factions were extensions of our social behaviour; like if Nick and I hung out, we'd write songs together. At the end there weren't any factions, it was just everybody split into four different little chunks. If there was any faction, it was Nick and Mick, but even that wasn't a social thing, it was just band-related.

"All these things came down at the same time and the band ceased to be fun; we really needed to stop doing it for a while. I wanted to have some security in my life and not live in fucking poverty and travel around all the time. We were constantly struggling to survive, day in, day out. Towards the end, we had something to do for the band virtually every day . . . I don't really have any regrets, but we were all young, and youth has an innate sense of immortality. I had the feeling that musical success and acclaim would always be there; The Young Charlatans were an immediate success within a small sphere as well. I didn't realise how lucky I was to be working with this group of people until after it was all over. During the last tour, we were panicking a bit, it was really going to happen, and none of us knew what we were going to do afterwards."

A contract means you've got people to pay, and you're *on.*

You're *obligated* . . . Their last gigs were played for very demanding and musically literate crowds. The more The Birthday Party performed, the more of an obligation, the more habitual that repeated performance became. Once Nick's performances became definable, he was pressured to behave in a preordained manner – even from audiences who'd never seen them before.

Phill: "Certain people have got the 'it factor', charisma. When they walk down the street, people turn, 'That person's got presence'. When these people get up on stage and do their thing, people are affected; that person belongs up there, but Joe Bloggs doin' it looks stupid. Nick has that appeal; always has had."

Tony: "They had more fun than almost any other people I've met. They were having a great time, and they knew how to enjoy themselves. I've seen Nick fairly miserable after gigs, being rude to people, and things like that cause stories, but they don't see Nick the rest of the time. Nick would be the one to really 'upvibe' everyone. If everyone's tired and fed up with touring, Nick will do something funny to entertain everyone.

"At Melbourne's Tullarmarine airport, a popular TV current affairs host well-known for taking public moral stands was in the newsagents, and Nick was pinching books madly, and the host was looking at him, and Nick turned to him and said, 'Uurrgh, you're fuckin' XXXXXX! *Uuuurrrgh!* I hate you!', and the host was getting red in the face, getting really angry. We expected to see him on telly going, 'Punk Rockers! Shoplifting! Insulting innocent members of the public!' Nick with his pointy shoes and his green suit!"

Wendy: "Many bands tried to imitate The Birthday Party. They failed because their inspiration was The Birthday Party and rock 'n' roll. The Birthday Party's inspiration was not.

"Their video 'Pleasure Heads Must Burn!' was released, and even at their most dogged or hounded they were extremely entertaining. I've seen much better performances, but as a relic, it captures the transfixed audience well; idolising, waiting for the band to spark or intimidate them rather than responding to the music. To someone who'd never seen them before, it must all look a bit mysterious."

These final gigs were strange; wonky, rotten gigs where cues were missed alternated with brilliant ones, a brittle hurricane of self-conscious pisstaking. A spectacular divorce; a public spectacle beyond analysis.

Mute issued this statement while they toured Australia: "In view of events this year, it has become obvious that new challenges are needed to sustain our creative vitality. Rather than continue regardless of our better judgement (ie, for the money or through lack of daring) and diminishing the impact of our work, it has been decided to end The Birthday Party. Individual plans are not definite at this time but we hope this decision will prove as productive as is its intent."

The final Birthday Party tour was five gigs in New Zealand, three in Sydney, one in Perth, and two in Melbourne.

Rowland: "The tour was organised by Ken West. The money we were paid for that tour, what I believe happened is that we did about 12 gigs, and I believe grossed about $80,000. I think we were giving ourselves a wage of $250 a week. At the end of the tour we were given $700 each, I think.

"I could be wrong, but I remember walking out of the meeting completely fucking devastated because we'd worked so hard, it was the last tour, and none of us knew when we'd be earning any money again. That tour was incredibly destructive in a personal sense to Nick, Tracy and myself, we were all completely fucked. We'd been trying very hard to leave behind a very lasting impression, and it was physically and emotionally exhausting.

"Nobody explained to us what happened. I felt that the money had either been mismanaged or that we'd been ripped off. I'm not saying that Ken West did rip us off, because I don't know. We had to do another show to have money in our pocket when we got back to England.

"Bob Gosford was our tour manager on that tour, who gave himself massive pay rises, and nobody was telling us. He also decided that he wasn't going to lift anything, so we hired someone to lift the stuff that Bob wasn't going to. Nobody told us that, either. I think Bob saw himself as the sixth member of the band, and his job was shepherding us around and consuming any drugs that we might not.

"To receive so little for all that effort . . . where the only money you ever make is from playing gigs – Keith didn't pay us any royalties for some time – and people are continually telling you how fucking magnificent you are, and you get no real money from it, it just beggars belief.

"$250 a week was the most the band ever made, and the last gig we ever did in London I think we walked away from it with about £600 each. I made more from that gig than I did at the end of the whole Australian tour. The music business is run in a medieval and absurd way, everybody gets paid more than the band which is ridiculous. Apart from sweatshop workers, I can't think of any comparable industry where the person responsible for the whole industry existing receives such a pittance."

The Melbourne gigs were billed as their last, but they did a second 'final' gig on June 9 to raise money to return to London to finish recording and remixing in August. The engineer in Berlin had added some of his own flourishes to the tracks so that most of them would require re-recording and remixing. They decided to salvage four songs, keeping the backing tracks. The old unresolved conflicts hindered the process; Rowland and Nick painfully, barely speaking, hammering again and again at songs which seemed like they'd never come together.

Nick was unhappy with his lyrics, so he was rewriting them. Such a complex way to solve a simple problem, but they couldn't go down to Mrs Pew's shed and pound away until they got it right. The Birthday Party was like a clockwork mechanism made of old brittle china, slowly crumbling away until its working parts are no longer recognisable for what they were.

Nick scrapped most of his lyrics to 'Mutiny In Heaven', which had been rewritten several times, and waited for Rowland to add guitar to the backing track. Rowland wanted Nick to add some vocals, so he'd have some direction, and so the fuming, squabbly struggle continued, with Rowland passing the responsibility to Nick, and vice versa. Both were knackered and wiped out creatively. One night Nick sat up through the evening, finally producing the lyrics.

Rowland: "Working on 'Mutiny!' was a nightmare. I'd done four or five hours of guitar overdubs, I'd worked out three or four completely different things which I played over a very skeletal track. I'd play one which would be rejected by Nick ad infinitum.

"Eventually I said I can't keep coming up with things and hope that I'll play the right one. So I went out to the hall and sat down. Blixa came out and asked to borrow my guitar, so I gave it to him, packed up and left, because I thought it was the last day of recording and we'd never brought an outsider in to replace one of us. It wasn't the last day as it turned out, but I didn't find this out until much later. I picked my guitar up about two weeks later."

The songs were mixed and sent to Mute for release in late November 1983. Of the original Hansa recordings, 'Six Strings' and 'Pleasure Avalanche' were released on the later CD of 'Mutiny'. Nick's embryonic 'From Her To Eternity' and 'Wings Off Flies' were very different versions from their final forms, and the several takes of 'Mutiny' originally recorded remain unreleased.

'Mutiny!' was released by Mute Records in November, 1983. The comical cover is Nick's painting of an Anita Lane design, using brutal images to spell out the title. Journalists leapt at the swastika. In context, it was one symbol among many; scaffold with noose, a coffin. The cover points clearly at the folly of relying on the importance of a symbol, ignoring the reality of what it symbolises. Each symbol relates directly to The Birthday Party.

Nick's songs favour his developing narrative style. 'Mutiny In Heaven' is the most impressive. An uncomfortably jolly, predatory bass line juggernauts smugly through the waves thrown up by Nick's drama. The 'Punishment? Reward!' refrain saws across the grain of Christianity; and Nick enunciates an emotional, moral and philosophical dilemma. There is a distinct similarity to William Blake's concepts of Innocence and Experience.

'Mutiny!' is the dizzy nadir at which The Birthday Party halted. Nick's work is awash with characters displaying obsessive, compulsive behaviour, much like his own wilful lifestyle. The endless howl of 'Swampland', and 'Mutiny's equation of guilt and pain with pleasure and sensuality are almost unbearable. Maintaining both distance and familiarity, he continues his fascination with human motivation and behaviour.

The victimisation in 'Swampland' relates directly to The Birthday Party. 'Jennifer's Veil', depicts the returned lover and the townspeople after an act of mob violence. Rowland's 'Say A Spell' is an intense and rich evocation of love and desire which provides startling balance and perspective to the EP, a very different philosophical approach to Nick. Its open and personal nature, almost confessional, emphasising Rowland's vision of the helplessness of personal experience.

In early 1985, Keith issued the live album, 'It's Still Living'; on the back cover is a mysterious message to Paul Goldman, stating that proceeds from this record will go towards the making of the Birthday Party documentary. This, according to Keith, was a dig at Paul, who shortly after the record came out, had sold the rights to the 'Nick The Stripper' video which Keith had paid for.

Paul Goldman: "Tracy rang me up and said he was going to kill me . . . I didn't know the album had been released; I just got a lot of threats from Nick, Mick and Tracy. All I'd wanted to do was document the band, and Keith had been very co-operative in giving me money (as far back as mid-1979). I think he gave me $1,000 for 'Nick The Stripper', but that went nowhere; I had to borrow the equipment from Swinburne, I stole the film stock and a few of my friends were suspended. I destroyed equipment, I lost it, I begged, borrowed and I worked all summer to get some capital so I could do things again because I was paying for a couple of bands to record. Chris Carr rang me up (the Birthday Party's publicist in London) and asked me if they could use 'Nick The Stripper' on their compilation, and I asked if I'd get any money, and he said, 'No'."

Rowland: "We never received any money for it either."

Tracy decided to do an arts degree at Monash University, and performed so well that the University put him in the Honours stream. After a brief tour with Chris Bailey's Saints in February 1984, Tracy sold his bass, intending never to play again.

The circumstances surrounding Tracy's death have been distorted. The press erroneously implied that it was somehow linked to a rock 'n' roll lifestyle. Many people still believe this.

The truth is that Tracy became an epileptic. He had his first seizure just before Christmas, 1985. His shocked family took him to hospital; no medication was prescribed. Early in the new year Tracy had three more seizures. The doctor attending the third prescribed him medication.

Eventually doctors realised that Tracy had a recurring problem, and prescribed him medication to be taken daily. The impact on his family was tremendously stressful and distressing; living with the tense, unpleasant knowledge that he might have another, perhaps fatal, seizure at any time. They did everything possible to assist him when he was in the grip of a seizure.

After a year and a half of petit and grand mal seizures, and dislocating his shoulder at least five (excruciatingly painful) times , Tracy died of an epileptic seizure on November 7, 1986.

The coroner declared the cause of death to be "epilepsy". The pathologist who performed the autopsy noted later, in conversation with Fiona Pew, that the medication level in Tracy's blood was down, and the cause of death was simply that his heart had stopped. As Tracy would stop breathing during a seizure, this makes sense. He was alone at the time of his seizure, with no-one available to assist him.

There is no medical evidence that Tracy's 'rock 'n' roll lifestyle' was in any way responsible for his death.

V

From The Ashes
(August 1983–1996)

After the 'Mutiny!' sessions in London, Nick went to Rotterdam for a guest appearance with Die Haut, then returned to Berlin to record with Jim Thirlwell, Mick and Blixa, and, after Jim left, Barry Adamson. Nick had been rewriting his songs to a point just short of a story, developing his ideas, pursuing subjects to their fullest.

Mick now refused to write music for him, because Nick's main interest was his writing, and the last few years had sapped his love of music. Mick's standpoint forced Nick to take more interest in making music to complement his lyrics.

'Wings Off Flies', 'A Box For Black Paul', 'St Huck' and an embryonic 'From Her To Eternity' were recorded at London's The Garden, to be released as an EP titled 'Nick Cave – Man or Myth'.

Nick had seen Black Paul once, at a distance; but 'A Box For Black Paul' is about the breakup of The Birthday Party. Nick took the man's nickname because he liked it; Paul's initials are 'BP', so the title is 'a coffin for The Birthday Party'.

Nick wrote 'Wings' with Jim Thirlwell, inspired by a song title that Pierre (Peter Sutcliffe) did with one of his bands. 'Saint Huck' suggests Nick's interest in the blues and its mythical birthplace, America's south, with lyrical nods towards William Faulkner and Herman Melville.

Although these recordings certainly use the style and structure to advantage, they are not blues songs; his own material has been welded onto a loose extrapolation from the blues. This should have provoked hot debate: was Nick's blues the real McCoy, or just a clever fake with a patina of experience? The press missed their chance; only descending in 1985, when Nick's interest was so obvious they couldn't ignore it.

'Wings Off Flies' deals with the random uncertainty and

emotional violence of love, presented in an ironical, fatalistic manner. 'Saint Huck' finds Nick lurking behind Mark Twain's country boy who encounters temptation and eventual moral corruption "in the great grey greasy city".

The EP was initially planned as a one-off, perhaps followed by some gigs. Nick knew he had to assemble people around him who could construct a vehicle for his songs without the conflict of interests that existed with The Birthday Party. He stated in interviews that he didn't envisage starting up his own band, although the thought must have occurred to him, as it had to the journalists. The Immaculate Consumptive – Marc Almond, Jim Thirlwell, Lydia and Nick – played in Washington and New York over the Halloween weekend.

Nick then returned to Melbourne, partly to visit his mother, partly to follow up the production of his plays; a grant had been promised in Australia to no avail.

Mick also returned to Melbourne, keen to seek out Simon Bonney. After rehearsing, Mick and Simon went into the studio for some demos in January. Nick had by then asked Mick to be in his band; due to Mick's commitments to The Bad Seeds in 1984, it was almost a year before Crime and The City Solution (III) surfaced.

Rowland: "After The Birthday Party I sat around and watched television for a long time. I did some recording with Gen(evieve), Jeffrey Wegener and Chris Walsh which was fairly disastrous. Mute didn't think it was disastrous. But it didn't turn out anything like what I wanted it to, and that really destroyed my self-confidence because I was basically in charge and the whole did not equal the sum of its parts. It was common in The Birthday Party for one person to dominate and direct a particular song. I was working with three extremely talented musicians, and it just didn't gel at all."

Chris was in The Moodists, Jeff was with The Laughing Clowns. It's possible the necessary focus simply wasn't as full as it might have been had they been rehearsing in a shed in suburban Melbourne.

Apart from filming The Birthday Party, Paul Goldman and Evan English had been making video clips for better-known bands. In 1982 they had suggested to Nick that he write a screenplay, soundtrack, and perform in it. This screenplay proved unworkable, and Nick started to develop it into his novel.

'Mutiny!' had been released, so it was in Nick's interest to play. Nick asked Mick and Tracy, and Barry Adamson who was also in Melbourne. Mick thought Plays With Marionettes guitarists Hugo Race and Edward Clayton-Jones were also good choices. Needing to rid himself of the expectant, clamouring mob who were there for the myth, Nick had to battle the mob, better his weighty reputation and move on.

After a few weeks of rehearsal, 'Nick Cave – Man Or Myth' (the title comes from the book his father edited, *Ned Kelly, Man or Myth?*), played in Melbourne and Sydney in January. The set included 'Pleasure Avalanche', 'St Huck', (Leonard Cohen's) 'Avalanche', (Elvis' hit) 'In The Ghetto', 'Jennifer's Veil', 'Wings Off Flies', 'A Box For Black Paul', 'Mutiny in Heaven', 'Swampland', (John Lee Hooker's) 'It Serves You Right To Suffer' and (Screamin' Jay Hawkins' hit) 'I Put A Spell On You'.

At The Venue, Melbourne, on January 13, 1984, Nick kept coming to the monitor at the front of the stage where I was. He pulled my hair four times, and rested his hand and leaned his full weight on my head, twice. He poked my forehead to lay emphasis during 'I Put A Spell On You'. I was amazed at the deceptive manner in which he had expressed himself; apparently one thing to observers, and quite another to me.

The highlight came when he was teetering on top of the monitor during 'St Huck', and some idiots grabbed him, trying to haul him in. I batted one guy's arm aside, and as Nick was released, he lurched backwards towards Hugo. I didn't think he'd be able to right himself, and would have fallen heavily. As he fell, his right arm went out towards me, and without thinking, I grabbed it. I found myself holding his arm, forming a climber's grip, but Nick didn't leave it at that. He used my weight and grip to haul himself back up the way he'd come, arching as he came . . . all this while still singing . . . he hadn't stopped or missed a beat. We hung on like that for a while until he'd used up the effect, let go and walked off to another section of the stage.

As he left the stage, Nick looked up with an expression I'd never seen before or since on anyone – his eyes were wide open, and very bright and intent, like a glittering demon. He flicked some of his scotch at the audience with a tight little smile, and left.

k arrived in London in February. Mick, Hugo and Barry over, and Blixa was also asked to play. By March, Nick had new songs he wanted to record: 'The Moon Is In The Gutter', 'Well Of Misery' and he'd finished 'From Her To Eternity' and 'Cabin Fever'. With the four covers, Nick had enough for an album.

Undecided, they played twice as 'Nick Cave and The Cavemen', and 'Nick Cave and The Bad Seeds'. The London press thought 'The Nick Cave Experience' was a good idea.

By the end of April, Nick's band comprised Barry Adamson on bass and keyboards, Blixa on guitar, Hugo Race on guitar and Mick Harvey on drums, although Blixa couldn't play at their first few gigs. They recorded a Peel Session to generate interest in Nick's new band, recording 'I Put A Spell On You', 'St Huck' and 'From Her To Eternity'. This was Nick's last Peel Session . . . he found the producer difficult to work with. Used to Tony Cohen who didn't tell bands what to do, it didn't turn out very well.

Until early June they toured Europe followed by America. These gigs in England and Europe marked a turning point for many of Nick's horrorshow fans. Some were abusive, but many were prepared to listen to the new songs with an open mind. On the tapes, the mood of the crowd is sometimes intense, and Nick guides the set along a path that goes against the crowd. When this happens, the crowd becomes less surly; partly due to the disgruntled leaving and partly to Nick winning the crowd over.

'From Her To Eternity' was released by Mute during May, 1984.

Mark: "Anita Lane appears on the cover, yet she doesn't play on it, or have anything to do with the recording process. The album concerns the death of The Birthday Party, and Nick's relationship with Anita. He's showing homage, a token of recognition, of her importance to his writing over the previous years.

"In 'Avalanche', Nick sings about the expectations of the crowds who gathered for The Birthday Party; it could have been written for him, so closely does it dovetail with the Catherine Wheel of anticipation and greed.

"The LP reminds me of Edward Hopper's paintings; archetypes of America and jumping out with a startling, wearying familiarity. 'St Huck' we all know from the tabloids, from our day to day lives. 'A Box For Black Paul' . . . the lynch mob is an axis upon which America turns – particularly politically. Blixa adds abrasive, intrusive, splintery detail to the insidious black landscape which throbs, moans, murmurs, tides, and flows over the listener.

"'Cabin Fever': the motion of the song swings and lurches like a rotten corpse hanging from a ship's mast. The tone is alien and sodden, the subtext is the voyage of The Birthday Party and the demise of his relationship with Anita (although he makes it clear she will always be a part of him). 'Done is the kissing, now all that remains/Is to sail forever upon the stain' could apply to both subjects, as could the last four lines.

"Nick wasn't 'the captain', the leader of The Birthday Party, but one force which exacerbated their wayward course. Here the self-described captain decides to sail on, in spite of the pain of separation. Nick deliberately walks towards the introspection and devilry of the talking blues. 'A Box For Black Paul' can be accepted for its story, but it too tells the bitter, doomed story of The Birthday Party.

"The weird double helix '. . . why should ah dress his wounds/ When he has murdered my dress nightly/Right across the floor?' . . . murder being a simile for sex; Nick links murder and sex to The Birthday Party on stage, 'nightly/Right across the floor'. The instantly recognisable characters remain in these narratives like semi-literate echoes of Tex Avery brawls, painstakingly shaped, crudely enough drawn so that the stories fill us with conflict; moral, spiritual, mercantile. For example, 'Armies of ants wade up the little red streams/Heading for the mother-pool/O Lord it's cruel! O Lord it's hot!/And some of those ants they just clot to the spot' – surely this is the crowd's behaviour at gigs, feeding themselves to death on the band's mortally wounded torso. Nick calls them 'ants', they move in an army, not like individuals.

"By taking the well-worn image of The Birthday Party which was something of a cliché, and placing it in the context of a persecuted man in an isolated village, the cliché gains fresh, intriguing resonance and the band is symbolically given a decent burial.

"'St Huck' is an intensive, implosive tale depicting loss of innocence, impending moral corruption; human weakness in the face of temptation. 'Saint-Huck-A-Saint-Elvis' reflects Cave's own experience; Nick spoke of the later Elvis doing shows that were a titanic struggle; bearing in mind that Elvis also had an obligation to live up to a reputation. Nick's characters are helpless to their desires and perceptions; their experience corrupts them no matter how they strive for a balance. Nick's refining the expression and structures he used in The Birthday Party, in greater detail, with more thought to content; lyrically and musically.

"Take 'From Her To Eternity' . . . where desire for someone becomes so intensely obsessive that when this person – the object of desire – is somehow attained, the actual *object* changes its desirability, because the reason for pursuit has been realised. That is, the unattainability of an object or person provides the reason for desire. Politically, we are looking at why we do what we do."

Mick: "It's alright for a first album, it's patchy and strange, and everything's done in a completely different manner to how we'd worked before. Some of it worked, some of it didn't. 'Cabin Fever' doesn't really work, although it's got some great things about it. The same about 'From Her To Eternity', it's actually just a kind of mess.

"That's not to criticise the songs, just the way they were handled or recorded, whether they were effective. 'From Her To Eternity' is a great song, the version in *Wings Of Desire* is a lot stronger than the one on that first album."

The critical reaction was overall positive, but many were confused with this 'new' direction of Nick's. The American tour ended at the end of June. Hugo went back to Melbourne and formed The Wreckery; Blixa returned to Berlin; Barry to Manchester; and Nick went to LA.

Paul Goldman: "Evan English and I were living in LA, we'd been working overseas for about a year, and decided to come back to LA to live, so Evan got us a place in West Hollywood, and my girlfriend moved in. Nick had just finished a tour with the Bad Seeds, and Nick lobbed in, decided he was going to stay there with us because we asked him to. Nick had an idea for a film . . ."

Rowland: "He'd been writing it since 1982."

Paul: "He had no evidence of it, just some notes."

Rowland: "Well, he lost the manuscript twice when I was in The Birthday Party."

Paul: "I think he told us he was writing a novel, and I'd heard of it before; whenever we'd sit down and talk with David Thompson, Nick would talk about writing a novel, that that was one of his ambitions."

Rowland: "He was obsessed by this Dadaist short-story called *Humulus The Mute* for a long time, which is this very long shaggy-dog story."

Paul: "He talked about *Swampland*, and Evan, who's incredibly driven, said, 'Fuckin' let's do it, then!' We talked about it for a couple of weeks and did other stuff. Henry Rollins started coming round, and Jeffrey Lee Pierce, and all these fucking LA punks would sit at Nick's knees, and Evan and I would be driven into the backyard and watch the sun set. It was a really distressful time for me, there was just crap going on. I hate LA and I hated being in the house. Nick was a pretty bad fucking addict at the time, and Nick and Evan were taking just tons of speed, and Nick would be going out scoring all the time, and we'd have to drive him downtown, wait in the car for him. Evan and I weren't taking heroin, I've never taken any fucking drugs in my life. We'd drive down these streets at idling speed with these guys pushing the packet through the crack of the window and Nick pushing the money out at the same time, and two times out of ten Nick would be ripped off. There'd be ten guys crowding round the car, offering Nick a taste . . . and then we'd drive down another street 'cause Evan would want to score some grass. I went to some un-fucking-believable places to get drugs that I never used! We went downtown to an area where Nick regularly scored at, and when we got to the street, a block of flats, this fucking huge building, was going up in flames, there were fire engines, police cars and ambulances in the street, and we still drove down the street and scored.

"We'd go out once a week on these food excursions to these huge ten acre food barns and we'd say to Nick, 'You can buy anything you like', and it was madness. We'd have trolley after trolley filled up. And then Nick became obsessed with cooking, so he and Evan would cook all day, and Nick would make these chicken wings with so much fucking chilli on them that you'd take one bite and run into the toilet or you'd shit your pants. We'd buy five bottles of Jalopeno peppers and Nick'd sit in the backyard with me and we'd have these competitions of who could eat the most Jalopeno peppers, but Nick would be stoned, so . . ."

Rowland: "He'd be anaesthetised!"

Paul: "We had cable put on, and Nick would be watching the same movie all night . . ."

Rowland: ". . . and waking up every now and again and seeing another bit of it!"

Paul: "And we were writing the whole time, but it was Evan who cracked the whip. *Swampland* is Nick's idea, but we co-wrote it, we gave ourselves a third of the film to write each. Nick would outline the whole story in quite a lot of detail, Evan and I were fascinated, loved the character of Euchrid Euchrow. Evan can't find his copy of the script, and I have the only copy in existence. We wrote that script together, and there are ideas in the finished novel that are just not Nick's; no-one on God's earth will believe that they're not Nick's, but I know what happened. Nick outlined the story in detail, but when you're writing, you just change things, you're going to have new incidents.

"Nick's story is couched very carefully (in Iain Johnston's book); we didn't understand his writing so he read it to us. It makes us sound like we were just paying the rent, supporting this creative genius. At the time, Nick was fucked out on drugs, barely fucking able to do anything, and Evan, Evan alone, was the person driving that project. Ask yourself, why until that period, after two years of supposed talking and writing, was there no evidence of it? I know that he lost manuscripts, but the person who said, 'This is a good idea, we're paying a lot of rent here, let's do something. You're at loose ends, Nick, you've got no tour commitments, you're not recording'; that was Evan.

"Evan's a shocking fucking writer but has got better, and he wrote some great stuff for *Swampland*; and I've always written, and I jumped in and started writing. Nick would read our stuff and rewrite it, and at the end of his stay there, which was about three or four months, we paid a typist to type it all up, this script which was written by the three of us. I know there's a lot of my ideas, and Evan's, in there. Evan's absolutely livid, and he was very upset that Nick didn't include him in the dedication to *And The Ass Saw The Angel*. A film script is often written by a group of people, and *Swampland* isn't *And The*

Ass, but he wasn't writing a novel *And The Ass* at the time, he was writing a film screenplay called *Swampland.*

"At the time we were paying for his drugs, for his rent, his food, everything. We just took him in."

Robert: "Hang on, in Iain Johnston's book, the story is that Nick put his money in Evan's bank account so that Nick would go to Evan to get his own money."

Rowland: "This is a year after The Birthday Party. We were making £80 a week at the end of The Birthday Party."

Robert: "Can I ask you where all the money was coming from?"

Paul: "Yeah; from my father, and from Evan and I. We'd been making music videos, making quite a bit of money for bands like The Pale Fountains, Spear of Destiny, Aztec Camera, Berlin, Elvis Costello, Soft Cell."

At the Lhasa Club on August 1, Nick read an extensive *Blind Lemon Jefferson* and *Euchrid The Crow King*, both relating to his novel. Over the years Nick would do many such readings, and still does.

Mick: "Nick has great natural ability with words, and the way he uses them. That's why the offer was made to write a book. He had the offer from a publisher who wanted to publish his novel before he'd started writing it, who realised Nick was a wordsmith who would write a really good novel."

By October he, Blixa, Barry and Mick were rehearsing the new album when Nick was called upon to do a brief tour of Europe. With their current album released six months ago, and no new record, they had nothing new to promote. Recording sessions were rearranged, but Nick was not keen to do the tour. An indication of his state of mind could be found in the song, 'When The Sun Goes Down (And My Work Is Done)'. Dated October 30, 1984, the day the Italian tour was to have started, it's in Nick's collection, *King Ink.*

Mick: "1984 and '85 . . . it was settling down when Barry left for good which threw it all into confusion again for a few years until the more permanent line-up we now have. Barry, Thomas, me and Blixa was a group that was very strongly behind Nick."

From Italy the band arrived in a freezing London, probably still jet-lagged, to do a show at the Electric Ballroom the next day, November 7. The day after the Ballroom, they were off to Amsterdam to finish the tour.

Antonella Gambotto from *Zig-Zag*, an alternative music magazine distributed in Europe and Australia, went to Amsterdam with them. According to her book of interviews, *Lunch of Blood*, she "was born in Sydney on 19 September 1965". She would have been barely 19 years old at the time of the interview.

Genevieve: "The atmosphere backstage was strange . . . Antonella tried to approach Nick and he'd been very dismissive.

"I went to the toilets, and she came in after me, asking me what was the best way to get on with Nick, and was he really an arrogant bastard who didn't give a shit about anybody. So I said facetiously, 'He has a heart of gold, really', which later ended up being misrepresented in her article.

"She sat in front of the mirror and she started ripping her dark greyish t-shirt over her nipples; not quite on the nipple, but so that when she moved around the nipples would show; and then she did a few more strategic rips like over the belly-button, and ripping the neck of the t-shirt so that the neck went really big and pulled it down so that she was showing her *décolletage* and the shirt was just hanging off her shoulder.

"She was quizzing me as she was touching up her face; I can't remember what she said, but the idea of it was that she wanted to sleep with Nick and she was going to . . . so I was going to give her no help at all! She was saying, 'Do I look alright? Do I look alright?' while she was ripping her t-shirt, so I didn't say anything. I just thought, 'Give it your best shot, dear, I know exactly what's going to happen'."

Rowland: "She was very young. I think she was supposed to interview Nick before the gig, which she didn't. I was told that she piled into the car Nick was in after the gig, and Nick was saying, 'Can you just go away?', and she affected drunkenness to the point where you don't take any notice of what anyone says.

"They got to the place where Nick was staying, and she didn't have a cassette for the cassette player, and she didn't have any batteries. So Nick went around hunting for batteries and cassettes and by that time it was like three or four in the morning, and I think he eventually told her to fuck off, called her a cab, and she scuttled off into the night. It was just this stupid little episode which she decided to blow out of all proportion in her interview."

The *Zig-Zag* interview was scathing. If the reader could read this interview, it doesn't seem very clear-headed. This interview and the interview which appeared in her book are substantially different – in the former, she seems to have little grasp of Nick's basic history; in the latter, she provides the details clearly. There's a dramatic difference in structure and direction between the *Zig-Zag* version and the one in her book, although Nick looks ridiculous in both.

Finishing the tour, Barry, Blixa, Mick and Nick went to Hansa Ton-Studios in Berlin to record Nick's new album before returning to London for mixing.

'The First-born Is Dead' was released by Mute in June 1985. The opening song, 'Tupelo', is a magnificent epic; the rumbling, chugging bass evoking the dark mood of the valley, with the guitars equally as descriptive. Nick tells the story of a Biblesque storm assaulting the town of Tupelo, which lifts when 'the King is born . . . no bird can fly, no fish can swim . . . until the King is born' (recalling The Birthday Party's 'Cry'). Apart from the implicit 'second coming of Christ', the 'king' here is Elvis Presley, who was born in Tupelo.

Elvis had a twin brother who died at birth, hence the title of the album; the first-born child is dead, and the second-born lives. The first-born is The Birthday Party, now dead; Cave clearly wants to be accepted for who he is, as a newborn child is accepted, without prejudicial treatment or reference to the past, comparing himself more specifically with Elvis. The king, 'carries the burden outta Tupelo'; Nick still carries the public's perception of him in The Birthday Party, so he's referring directly to his audience when he sings the last line, 'You will reap just what you sow'.

Blixa's building chaos guitar towards the end of 'Train Long-Suffering' is overladen with his unique, overwhelming slide; without Blixa the album would have significantly less dimension.

'Black Crow King' asserts Nick's artistic independence. Concerning a mythical god who watches over a valley and describes what he sees, the god concludes that he will outlast the valley's inhabitants. Nick uses the classic blues call and response structure, but only by a leap of the imagination could this be called blues.

References to Nick's audience continue. 'I am the king' recalls 'Junkyard'. Nick mocks the expectant throng by adding, 'I am the king of nothing at all'. His references to 'a company of crows', and the line 'I am the keeper of the nodding corn' are a nasty observation on the goths who attended his gigs, swathed in black with stacked hair.

The second side is an absolute killer. 'Wanted Man' was a Bob Dylan song from a Johnny Cash album. Nick wrote several more verses and upped the tempo, turning an average song into a intense and bitter lament. Nick refers to his status as a 'wanted man', particularly in the closing lines 'But the one place I'm not wanted lord, is the place that I call home'.

'Blind Lemon Jefferson' paints a bleak picture of another mythological figure. Cave implies that Jefferson's life, rich with experience but blighted by poverty and incapacity, allowed him to remain uncorrupted. This preserved his essential human purity, implying that Lemon has retained his balance with God and the universe. Recalling the Book Of Job, Jefferson is a saint, or close to it. Nick is writing about the state of innocence itself. Looking back at 'Black Crow King' and 'Tupelo', Jesus is the ultimate innocent. Very Blake.

William Blake argues that without the perspective experience provides, good and evil do not exist, yet a purity of spirit can. Nick Cave implies that this purity is somehow immortal, transcending life and death. It's not the concept itself which is so striking, but Nick's apparent adoption and subsequent use of it as an integral part of his work.

'Knockin' On Joe': a lament which sits back and unfolds its woes against a gorgeous melody; then the bitter and ironical, self-parodic 'Wanted Man' which pokes fun at the expectations of the listener (again). Instead of ending the album with an uptempo trouser-strainer, Nick pulls out 'Jefferson', a drawn-out reflection on the inevitability of death.

Mick followed up his intention of recharging Crime and The City Solution in February, and suggested that Rowland and Harry Howard would be good additions. Recordings and rehearsals began in March.

Rowland: "Mick rang me up and said that he and Simon Bonney were putting something together; I think he said it was a core of him and Simon and they wanted to use different people to play with them. I was surprised because I always felt that

Mick found me a frustrating person to work with and he wasn't that happy with my guitar playing . . . that he felt I tended to dominate anything I worked on, sound-wise; and that I wasn't versatile."

Crime continued for some years, and were a mighty force.

Zig-Zag's March issue included Antonella 'Black's article, portraying Nick as a rude, absurd cartoon character, who dribbled and had a bad drug problem. Nick had had a heroin habit for about two and a half years now, but it wasn't preventing him from producing challenging music and performances. He became markedly more hostile towards the music press after this interview, which also annoyed a large section of his increasing fanbase, although some readers were confused. The Seeds were on the eve of a tour of England, with a new record to be released, and Crime were about to come out. There were other interviews and incidents which irritated Nick no end, but this one stands out like a beacon.

Blixa wasn't free until the end of May, so Mick eventually suggested Rowland, who played guitar during their April tour of England. Barry was unable to come, so Christoph Dreher was recruited. Die Haut's Thomas Wydler became their permanent drummer at the beginning of this tour, freeing Mick Harvey for a variety of other roles.

Every Bad Seeds album except for 'Your Funeral, My Trial' has been accompanied by a tour. Being mobbed in Japan accompanied their first dates there in November, followed by Nick's first gigs in Australia with The Bad Seeds and recording 'Kicking Against The Pricks'. Perhaps because Nick had some new songs but wasn't happy enough with them to record them, it was intended to be a double album of covers. Nick's mum, Dawn, guests, as do Rowland and Tracy.

After the recording, everyone headed for Berlin in March 1986 to finish mixing. The single 'The Singer' b/w 'Running Scared' and 'Black Betty' was released in May 1986.

Phill: "Nick gleaned things from all sorts of places. I remember driving around Holland with Anita in the van singing 'Black Betty'."

Blixa had stolen a copy of Tim Rose's solo album from a radio station during 1985, and Nick was impressed by Rose's versions of 'Long Time Man' and 'Hey Joe'.

'Pricks' was released in June, and Nick finished his songs, so they recorded another album, 'Your Funeral, My Trial', in July and were filmed for Wim Wenders' film *Wings Of Desire*.

'Kicking Against The Pricks' is a reference to Nick's critics (such as Antonella) and his expectant audience. His most commercial album to date, most critics were on-side with his interpretations.

As they toured England, a flexidisc was given away at some gigs. 'Scum' – a very funny 'put-down' song – was recorded during the 'Funeral' sessions. In giving 'Scum' away exclusively in England, Nick clearly wanted to make sure that the music press got the message. The lyrics are printed in the endpapers of Nick's book *King Ink*. 'Your Funeral, My Trial' was released in November 1986 in the form of 2 x 12″ EPs.

Mick: "When The Birthday Party sold 10,000 records, I just thought that was 'so' many records. Now we expect to sell more with every release because it's gone that way with every Bad Seeds record except for 'Your Funeral . . .' because it came out two months after 'Kicking Against The Pricks', there was no tour and hardly any promotion. The cover looked similar to 'The Singer' 12″, so nobody knew it was a new record."

'Your Funeral . . .' was Nick's most cohesive album, quite commercially acceptable. The gentler, more melodic structures flow like wings through air yet maintain a powerful atmosphere. The title again refers to expectant crowds and media hoopla; Nick's album titles almost always refer to how he perceives himself in relation to the world.

Nick continued writing his novel for most of 1987. VPRO TV's 'Stranger In A Strange Land' filmed in Berlin and Hamburg in March, was aired in May. Nick's romantic, dreamy melodies became more clearly defined in 'Stranger', recognising the beauty exposed by reflection. The compilation 'Smack My Crack' was also released; Nick read *The Atra Virago* from his novel. In September, he was being filmed as Maynard in Evan English and Paul Goldman's film *Ghosts Of The Civil Dead* at Port Melbourne. Nick improvised his own lines. Mick, Nick and Blixa made the soundtrack with some of the music being taken from backing tapes used at Nick's readings. Barry left after the 'Funeral' sessions, Kid Congo Powers joined on guitar and Mick swapped to bass.

Mick talked about staying committed to the Seeds and Crime.

Mick: "It's not a matter of commitment to one or the other; it's just what I do. A few people have asked about that, but it's not an issue with me . . . I don't think about it, I just do it. I do almost the same thing in both groups. I stopped managing the groups in the middle of 1991, which is the same as The Birthday Party; my main job in The Birthday Party was arranging stuff, the music, co-producing the stuff with the engineer. That's always been my main job with Crime and The Bad Seeds too. I'm always there as the co-producer or something, and arranger and occasionally I co-write songs or whatever.

"We did a great version of 'Black Betty' in Italy which went for about 15 minutes, because Nick was really drunk and was improvising, so we kept going. It was much faster, and we had a stage with wooden floorboards so everyone was stomping . . . I think he went straight into some other song and we had to start playing it, thinking, 'What is he *doing*?'

"The best thing about that night was when Nick left the stage, walked through the audience to the band room, got to the merchandising table and started selling the t-shirts, so it was mayhem, total mayhem. There was a partition between the band room with the merchandising stand on the other side. We were in the band room, and the walls were squashing inwards, and the room was getting smaller and smaller, the crowd were crushing the table and Nick just . . . he was so drunk, he'd decided to enjoy the concert for a change.

"I don't know how many gigs he actually enjoys. He says he doesn't enjoy very many of them, but I don't know how true that is. I think he exaggerates."

Drugs appear to eradicate feelings of inadequacy. Nick Cave is often portrayed as a man driven to create, but it's more likely he's *fleeing* from failure. Long-term, a user's perspective is as streamlined, fast-tracked and sedentary as any 'nine to fiver'. Australian punks hated the 'nine-to-five' lifestyle, it had nothing to offer them. Drugs offer a quick alternative, a rebellion which can be fun, and because emotional and physical addiction can become involved, addicts often deny they have a problem; no addict likes to think of themselves as weak-willed. Nick was busted in London on possession of heroin and, since he'd apparently had previous convictions, was ordered to undertake detoxification or face conviction. Not a good reason to undergo detox.

In April 1988 Nick gave a reading at ID's, Melbourne.

Ross: "I was standing three feet away from him; ID's was a very small club, only about 100 or so could squeeze in there. He was reading from *And The Ass* . . ., concentrating on the words. His face was so beautiful and poetic, serene as the light fell onto it; you could see how much genuine emotion he was putting into this reading; not something that you'd usually see him do on stage."

King Ink, a collection of Cave's recorded lyrics and poems was published by Black Spring in May 1988. Mute released 'Tender Prey' in July; initial copies had a 12″ of Nick reading four pieces from his novel, which were reissued on CD with the Italian book, *Nick Cave*, by Andrea Cangioli and Maria Alessandra Scalise (Stampa Alternativa – Nuovi Equilibri, June 1995).

Mick: " 'Tender Prey' was such a hotch-potch. I couldn't get any perspective on it at all. I like it now, it's a strong record.

"The first day I think we recorded eight songs but five were instrumentals, like Burt Bacharach pieces, of which we could only use one ('Slowly Goes The Night'). Nick didn't know what to do with them because he couldn't write any lyrics for them. It was recorded in six or seven different studios in four different countries over about six months, with everyone um, y'know, drug excess. It was a total nightmare to make that record, but we knew there were a lot of good songs there so we kept going at it until we'd finished it . . . some nights Nick is totally disinterested in playing . . .

"If he doesn't feel well or inspired, I'd rather he did a bad show than pull off some slick professional thing, it's a lot more honest. It's always been a part of what we do. The good nights make up for the bad nights. The kind of good nights we have wouldn't happen if we were slick . . .

Nick was described by a friend in 1981 as 'a really nice guy with a few weirdy bits'.

Mick: "Well, he is a very nice guy, but very few people get to see it because they always throw something on him before he has a chance to be himself, and then he just shuts off, and then it can get worse . . . so people have these weird encounters with him and think he's a freak, or a total bastard or whatever . . .

"The most blatantly bad interview was the famous 'Jack Barron' article. It was so transparent; anyone with half a brain thought 'This guy's fucked up his interview with Nick and he's covering his tracks.' The most blatant part was the opening where Jack describes Nick trying to beat him up, which was so funny 'cause Nick basically did beat him up.

"Jack turned up in Amsterdam (in July 1988) to do an interview with Nick, and offended Nick in about five minutes by harping on about drugs and pestering him about his drug problems and his personal life, and Nick going, 'Fuck you, fuck this, I'm not doing this interview, that's the end of it, piss off'. Then our fucking press agent wouldn't leave it alone, he kept rearranging, saying, 'Look, are you going to talk to Jack tomorrow', and Nick'd go, 'No, I'm not fucking talking to Jack'.

"We went over to Hamburg for another gig, and lo and behold, who turns up – Jack Barron . . . with our press agent going, 'Please Nick, please, you've got to talk to him'. Two days later, Jack's in one corner trying to talk, and Nick's sitting at the bar going, 'No, I'm not fucking talking to him. I'm not talking to this fucking idiot', but eventually relents, and goes, 'Okay, okay, I'll talk to him.'

"He sat down to talk to Jack again, and Jack started the same shit again . . . I think Nick picked up Jack's bag and threw it out the door, so Jack would go outside to get it, and Nick just started kicking him when Jack got out. Jack was terrified, I think.

"Jack's alright. He's a bit of a silly man. Nick and him made up. Forgave him for being such an idiot. He was just misguided, but it was his own fault; it was a stupid way to behave to Nick. And a stupid way to write an article about what happened, too; everyone could tell he was bullshitting, everyone could tell the article was really mendacious and it reflected badly on him."

'Tender Prey' is a classic Seeds album, with some exceptionally powerful and emotive songs, less verbose than his previous work. The title comes from Patricia Roberts' 1983 novel, *Tender Prey*, which inspired Nick to write 'Watching Alice'. 'Tender Prey' contains one song which is clearly about heroin addiction – 'Sunday's Slave' – disguised as a comment on daily routines. Nick successfully completed a detoxification program in August, and this marks the end of Nick's public life where innuendo regarding drug abuse was rife.

The February 1989 tour of America was filmed by Uli Schuppel, resulting in a black and white cinema verité documentary, *The Road To God Knows Where*. American magazine *Reflex* was given an out-take from 'Pricks', 'Rye Whiskey', for release as a flexidisc.

In April Nick made his first visit to Brazil, where he fell in love with fashion designer Viviane Carneiro, and, after a brief holiday there, continued the tour. Viviane, whom Nick later married, is the mother of Nick's son Luke. Nick's novel was released in August, and promoted by a few signings and readings.

And The Ass Saw The Angel was published by Black Spring Press in August 1989. Nick's expansive character Euchrid reveals his personality by his indirect self-revelations. Functioning in a world of actions and motives peculiar to himself, he is capable of extreme violence committed in a manner removed from the world, as if watching an unfolding film involving a fictional identity. Euchrid is highly believable, made more intriguing with the knowledge that elements of Nick's own personality must be seeping in, more than his interviews reveal.

Elements from 'Prayers On Fire' to 'Tender Prey' are all here, forming twisted chunks of the book's structure. Some events are wry to the point of deformity. The refrain of the drowning man from 'Swampland'; and the heavy, drunken atmosphere which hangs fearsomely above our heads on 'The First Born Is Dead', treads throughout.

Nick lets the meaner side of his humour out; Euchrid's outlook on life winds the reader tight like a screw. The humour is crude and slapstick, and Nick repeatedly shoves moral opposites against each other.

A fascination with aberrant behaviour within a Biblical community forms the background, while the ritualistic isolation of the individual is the foreground. Giving the text an archaic, hillbilly feel, Nick creates a vivid image of the isolated community – he makes up words from Greek and Latin roots and 'anglicises' them, and the book becomes more of an adventure to read.

The Bad Seeds returned to Brazil in October 1989 to record 'The Good Son'. Released in May 1990, it was accompanied by the usual slog around Europe, Japan, Australia and America.

Mick, despite playing and touring with two bands, also found time to contribute to many other artist's projects, writing soundtracks, producing records, contributing music and encouraging many artists, from Anita Lane, to The Cruel Sea and Once Upon A Time. Mick released his second solo album, 'Intoxicated Man', in November 1995.

Nick enjoys collaboration with other artists: Anita Lane and Lydia Lunch we know about, but in early 1988, Nick suggested a duet with Reels singer Dave Mason.

Dave: "We were talking about doing a duet. But he wanted to do a cover version, and I wanted to do an original song, so we put it back."

Later in 1990, rumours of a Kylie Minogue/Nick duet began to surface, and by 1992 it was reported that they'd recorded a session together.

Kid Congo Powers returned to The Gun Club, and Conway Savage was recruited from Dave Graney's White Buffaloes for piano. Mick moved back to guitar with The Triffids' Martyn Casey on bass, giving them a permanent touring line-up; subsequent albums find The Seeds more comfortable with this line-up.

Ross: "Nick takes the purest parts of what he's done previously and re-uses them in a new format. Over the years you can see cycles where you can pick up threads that go through the music. An artist needs to include certain things they're interested in; Nick's interest in religious iconography has tempered and changed as he's moved through different cultures, like Brazil."

Robert: "Has the attention directed at Nick gone to his head?"

Mick: "It's kinda what he'd been angling for anyway; he was always the singer, so it's the logical thing. I think it's what he expected.

"I don't know about 'going to his head'; that's usually used to describe someone who doesn't cope with it well when it occurs; whereas Nick didn't cope with it before it happened, so there was no difference. He has exactly the same kind of arrogance and ego that he had before he had notoriety or fame; he's the same as he was at school. He's never pretended that things are otherwise, so I've always known where I stand with him. He's very egocentric, but he's also very caring about people around him. I'm not saying he's selfish; he hasn't changed, even recently since he's got a lot more money. He doesn't care for that, although he's quite glad that he's not poor anymore.

"He's very ambitious and wants to be very successful in the creative fields that he enters. He has more drive to get success than I do.

"Famous people don't have a good time of it, it makes life quite impractical . . . they go out in public and they get pestered all the time. It makes them aware and self-conscious all the time which makes it harder to know whether you can trust anybody around you. Nick's always had the ability to express himself in a way that's effective on certain levels; he'll continue to do that because he's just expressing himself – if people continue to recognise that, then it's not going to be changed by him being famous."

Ross: "I think it's good for artists to have someone like Mick around to bounce ideas off, maybe he can point out something which no-one else can. I think that's valuable to artists. It makes them a bit more critical of what they're doing. Mick's influence is as musical director; he takes a central role in the band."

Andrew: "I imagine that if Nick didn't have the consistency of at least one person who has worked with his music, then the musical side of Nick's work would be quite different. Nick plays piano, organ and guitar on the records, but Mick's a better musician. That's given Nick the opportunity to see possibilities."

Mick: "I think Nick went in to do 'The Good Son' wanting to have things organised before we went in, which is why he's writing all of the songs now; he wants to turn up and have something organised. It was a turning point for him in that sense."

Ross: "Does he have a clear idea of what the songs are about after he's written them?"

Mick: "I don't know, you'd have to ask him what they're about. No, he doesn't tell me. I have to guess for myself. Sometimes I think I have a clearer idea of what they're about than he does. Sometimes I'll say something about what the songs are about, and I'll see Nick looking at the lyrics and trying to work it out, so I don't know what he thinks they're about.

"I think he writes them, and has some idea about them, and then he lets go of it, and they become an entity unto themselves and he doesn't worry about the meanings of everything that's going on in there."

* * *

'The Good Son' flirts with the structure of the mainstream while remaining a considered, implosive force. Nick's unique vocal phrasing is drastically pared down. With plenty of time to write before going into the studio, his lyrics are simpler, less convoluted, rather than overwhelming the listener with a rich landscape of meaning. These songs are codes or ciphers for a magnitude of blue devils, attempts to meld with the shabby and vainglorious crown of mainstream rock. It's a lesson in extrapolation – a hint of Cash, a blur of Dylan, and a dash of Presley, without an obvious and grating pigeonhole.

With rousing harmonies and yearning vocal choruses, 'The Good Son' possesses a tender refractive melancholy which lingers like *déjà vu*. The songs move lithely on stage, with a greater intensity, a rush of solitude and reflection. 'The Good Son' reveals a prism of emotion, like a prehistoric insect held motionless in amber; past and present suspended as some icon of future memory.

Mick: "I think a lot of people think ('The Good Son') is less deep in meaning than usual, and I think that's an error because they're seeing the superficial effects. It's also musically deceptive; we've tricked them into believing it's a 'soft' record, which it isn't.

"I've always felt that my groups should be able to be perceived in several different ways. Usually they aren't, for practical purposes, by the press.

sb "For me, with any real music it's always following a feel; you have to get inside the song . . . and push it into a . . . that's hard to describe, it's very . . . it's almost impossible when you're on tour to not start going through things by repetition. You learn ways that you can do the songs where they're effective that way, and especially on nights where you're physically exhausted because you've been on tour for a few weeks . . . you do use repetition, and you can get away with it very well, as I've learned over the years. It's hard to tell the difference.

"The best gig is when there's a really good feel going on . . . it's the same in the studio; the best music is produced by running with the feel of the music. It's not to do with calling out the tricks that you know can work, because that doesn't impress us. If we've done it before, it's not interesting, it doesn't surprise us. So it's always by running with the feel of the music, and something new coming out of the different atmospheres you're working with.

"It changes with every tour. The tour starts, it can have a certain freshness at the beginning of the tour, and by the time you're on your 50th concert of a very similar set, it . . . becomes harder to get back to the spontaneity of things happening by accident which is more likely to happen when you're not that well-versed in the songs . . . we're very rare amongst most groups I know in that we don't rehearse properly before we go on tour, and that sometimes shows, particularly in our early concerts. This means that for a portion of the tour, from about the fifth concert to about the twentieth it gets very exciting. I think of it that way anyway. We don't rehearse ourselves out of the songs, that's for sure.

"If a song is an easy one to play, then it becomes harder to get into. If you have to put a lot of effort into it to get a good version going then it's not difficult; if you start slacking off the song just stops working, and becomes like a nightmare. Too much adrenaline around to tolerate, somehow.

"You just have to really go for it. Some songs require an energy level; a dynamic range which is such that you really have to be in there to keep the song working. It's exciting every time that it does work because you know there are times when it doesn't work, and everybody's dynamic range is fucked up and different from each others. You do lose it some nights, so when you do get it again, it's a great feeling.

"Take the version of 'The Mercy Seat' we were doing in 1990. That was quite hard to pull off, it had a lot of subtleties which required a great deal of energy but a lot of subtlety in the way it was delivered. It was the opening song, and also a big risk 'cause we had to pull it off every night. Going out every night stone cold and to have to start with that was a real test – which we pulled off most of the time. It's something which really puts you on the spot. It's a good thing to do every night, gets the concert going in a good way, too.

"We're not going to make some horrible video that misrepresents us to become popular. We've never done that, we've tried very hard not to do that, and sometimes gotten close to getting messed up with that. I'd like to think what we do in The Bad Seeds, and what I do in Crime, is very original and different to what anybody else does. The Bad Seeds records might become more acceptable to a broader base of people, I don't know. I don't think our records sound like anybody except us, and they can be very varied in themselves."

"I don't look forward to (touring) with as much enthusiasm or freshness as I used to. I'm very well-versed, I've been practically everywhere I've wanted to go; that used to be an incentive. Now it's . . . yeah. But once you're up there playing it's better than ever; it depends on how well the group's playing.

"Our popularity has been steadily on the increase since 1980. Each new record becomes our new best-seller. Tours likewise. In Greece 'The Good Son' went to Number two on the official chart. Two sold-out concerts (5,000) in Athens. Italy we do better all the time. 'From Her To Eternity' sold 2,000, 'The Good Son' passed 15,000."

The Seeds made demos for the new album in London in February 1991, also recording a somewhat inebriated 80 plus minute version of Leonard Cohen's 'Tower Of Song' (later edited) for the Cohen compilation album, 'I'm Your Fan'. This clearly marks a much looser period for Nick, the next five years see him increasingly joining a disparate selection of performers on stage and in the studio.

The album, 'John Finn's Wife', was recorded in New York and Los Angeles, in November and December. For the first time Nick acquiesced to Mute's request to use a producer. Despite initial enthusiasm, Mick and Nick realised that some of it would have to be re-recorded, so, while in Melbourne, Tony Cohen effected a rescue with skilful remixes and some re-recording in January 1992.

The re-titled 'Henry's Dream' is full and powerful, away from the somewhat subdued tone of 'The Good Son'. After many months on the road, the band were a very tight unit.

His song 'Christina The Astonishing' is based on the entry in Butler's *Lives Of The Saints* – Christina The Astonishing appears on July 24. Christina is purely innocent, hailed as a saint, and does her best to escape the "stink of human corruption". There is also a link between Christina and the Jim-Thompsonish character Euchrid (from Nick's novel) – the mad are often regarded as touched by the hand of God; the purest example of innocent. Again, very Blake.

'When I First Came to Town' is often considered to be about Nick's experiences as a performer, his arrival in Brazil and so on, which probably was his initial inspiration. What is interesting is his description of how the townspeople 'wash their hands of me' – a common, but significant figure of speech. Pontius Pilate washed his hands of Jesus, and Nick has linked himself with Jesus for years, to the extent of wearing a childish, white t-shirt on stage with that single name on it. Jesus is the ultimate innocent, crucified not for his sins but for all humanity's . . . William Blake also bases his concept of Innocence on Jesus. Does Nick consider himself fundamentally innocent?

Another drinking song, 'Brother, My Cup Is Empty' is also revealing – the bar-room hustler is on the make for another drink, and spins some emotive yarn, gets his dollar and turns on the sucker, 'Now kiss my ass and leave'. Does Cave identify with the bar-room hustler, spinning some dramatic tale to a captive audience, taking the dollar, 'now kiss my ass and leave'? He is quoted (*Nick Cave*, Stampa Alternativa, 1995) as admiring Dylan's attitude to performing a rotten gig and taking the money, not caring about the response of the crowd, and doing a great gig when he feels like it. Surely the ease with which money can be acquired should *not* be a deciding factor in art? So is Nick touring for the love of it, or because it's an 'easy' option?

'Henry's Dream' concerns sin and purity – balancing the human need to sin with the inevitable retributions or torments which follow. 'John Finn's Wife' introduces a perpetrator who considers murder a justifiable act, that his actions are perhaps *inevitable*; it's the inevitability of people's behaviour about which Nick circles, like a moth around a flame. 'Straight To You' is similar, the couple are so shunned for their actions (which aren't entirely clear) that even 'heaven has denied us it's kingdom'.

In September, Nick rehearsed with Shane MacGowan and Rowland for a special charity gig in London. A duet with Shane and Nick, 'What A Wonderful World' was released at the end of November.

Rowland still lives in St. Kilda, Melbourne, and plays with a number of artists, including These Immortal Souls, and occasionally performs solo.

Rowland: "Australia is my home because it feels like home. It's a place where you're in touch with life; it's alive, it's a hot place, there's trees, mosquitoes. Although Melbourne is a city, you're not out of touch with nature, whereas London is like something that's dead or dying."

The Seeds' November 19 gig at the Amsterdam Paradiso was recorded for a live album. The tour ended with 'The Big Day Out' package in early February 1993. Iggy Pop, Mark Arm (Mudhoney), Thurston Moore and Kim Gordon (Sonic Youth) all joined The Seeds for encores on this tour, Nick carrying a limp Pop across the stage like a corpse.

By the end of January The Seeds had recorded at least ten songs, demos for the new album. The live recordings were produced by Tony Cohen, and 'Live Seeds' was released in September 1993. More demos were recorded during 1993, and recording started in London in August and finished off in Melbourne over Christmas. In between, Nick was a special guest on Die Haut's 'Ten Years of . . .' tour.

'Let Love In' was released in April 1994, followed by the inevitable world tour. Jim Scavlunos, of Kid Congo's band Congo Norvelle, was added to the band as an additional percussionist just prior to the two-month Lollapalooza tour; during which Nick sang with The Flaming Lips and L7, and vice versa.

Several songs on 'Let Love In' reflect on the wisdom of marriage or love. In 'I Let Love In' the singer's loved one trashes his vulnerable, sinful past, and 'Do You Love Me?' describes a matrimonial bondage. In the video clip, the realm of meaning is expanded further; a familiar experience for prostitutes is for clients to ask, 'Do you love me?' On stage, is Nick asking the crowd if they love him? The resonance of the chorus is not in the question, 'Do you love me', but in the continuation, 'Like I love you?' More than anything, Cave is dealing with an essential human frailty on 'Let Love In', the fleeting nature of love. He hasn't strayed from his usual themes, but, probably with his new experiences of marriage and fatherhood, found space to expand his artistic enquiries.

'Lay Me Low' and 'Thirsty Dog' also look hard at mortality, love and desire; in 'Thirsty Dog' he sings, 'I'm sorry I ever wrote that book/I'm sorry about the way I look'. Much of this album is autobiographical; however Nick has a knack for writing about himself without appearing to. For example, 'Loverman', like his earlier 'Hard-On for Love', links sexual desire to evil and is a classic rock device, but the brooding, obsessive nature of the song tends to make the concepts Nick evokes more visceral, more immediate.

The singer dies in 'Lay Me Low'. 'All the stories will come out . . . my friends will give up the fight/They'll see my work in a different light.' Not many artists beg the question of their own death, yet Nick does it in three other songs here: 'Thirsty Dog', 'Jangling Jack' and 'Loverman' in which he spells out the title cheer-leader style. Although live, he changed the original lyric of 'M is for Murder Me' to 'M is for Molest Me' – obviously he was unwilling to confront his mortality in such an immediate manner! It's not the first time he has called for his own death, either; 'Zoo-Music Girl's 'Oh God please let me die beneath her fists'; 'Swampland's 'Come my executioner'; and Maynard's invective from 'Ghosts', 'Kill me! Kill me!'

Nick's version of 'Mack The Knife' was included in the film about Kurt Weill, 'September Songs'. The single 'Loverman' was released in July, and 'Red Right Hand' in October. Recording with Kylie Minogue finally came together over Christmas 1994. 'Where The Wild Roses Grow' was released in October 1995, coinciding with her new work.

The two other songs on the CD, 'The Ballad of Robert Moore and Betty Coltrane' and 'The Willow Garden' are noticeable in their simplicity, carried with little descriptive embellishment; the opposite of 'Henry's Dream', which returns to the lengthy novelesque vignettes visited on 'Your Funeral, My Trial'. 'Robert Moore', a sordid bar-room brawl over an uncaring, mercenary woman, is cartoonish in tone; 'the man with wingnut ears', indeed!

Also that Christmas, the band were busy on 'The Murder Ballads' album, recording with a number of friends including Polly Harvey; and Melbourne band The Dirty Three, whom Nick had accompanied on their tour of Australia's Eastern seaboard in January/February 1995. Every time Nick is in Melbourne to tour or record, he lays down a challenge to musicians to better him, to perform to their fullest. He is now much more confident of his ability as an artist – he's progressed significantly from the Eighties, when he spoke of "wringing the towel dry" after each album. Justification of this can be found in his willingness to expand his talents by working with other artists in fields different from his own; for example, joining The Dirty Three in London to play in the silent film *Joan Of Arc* in August.

By June 1995 the band were in Melbourne finishing off the

album, originally titled 'Lovely Creatures'. This title was discarded when it was pointed out that, with a body count of 86, it could be interpreted as a reference to the killers, not the victims. Nick's original design for the album cover was a drawing by an American schizophrenic artist by the name of Henry who painted in a naïve style; apparently the women he painted had male genitals.

SBS (Australia's alternative TV channel) presented a documentary on Nick, shot in Sao Paulo and interspersed with archival footage. In August, Nick guested twice with Kylie at two European festivals. He separated from Viviane and now lives in Notting Hill in London. By October, he was filming and working on the soundtrack of John Hillcoats' new film.

Rowland: "Nick's music has a big 'fuck-you' element to it, but it's often submerged. He doesn't express that side of his personality that much – he can write good, literary, angry songs."

Nick may now have a highly successful music career, but without The Birthday Party, things might have been very different. Without the chemistry of intense personality clashes which defined and fuelled the band, it is unlikely that Nick would have risen this far. His gift for artistic cataclysm and his powerful curiosity and imagination were matched early on with an overwhelmingly self-destructive, attention-seeking urge.

'Murder Ballads' was released in January 1996 and for the first time Nick had an album in the mainstream charts. He's returned to his roots yet again; the album reeks of overkill – and for good reason. Nick is milking his violent, bad-boy reputation once again and, as usual, the last laugh seems to be on us. With each record, Nick seems to go full circle in his own self-determined way. He will remain a fascinating artist, intriguing, bewildering, aloof and quite probably rich. He's worked harder than most for it.

Paul Goldman: "Nick's always traded on his bad boy reputation. Nick's very clever at mythologising himself, he's done that since the start."

Rowland: "From the first time I met Nick he had black hair. Tracy had green hair the first time I met him. Tracy and Nick were an incredibly formidable pair when they were together, their whole attitude to the world was 'Fuck You!', and they brought that out really strongly in each other. They were both very intelligent and well-read, but their combination was a denial of that, and they'd be completely the opposite of that. I was in a car with Graham Peters and Simon McLean from our band The Obsessions. We pulled up at the lights, and a car pulled up behind us, and these people got out and started running towards our car; it was Nick and someone else. The lights changed, and we drove off, and Tracy, who was driving their car, also drove off and left them stranded there in the middle of the road.

"Nick thought I was a big poof. He grabbed me and threw me against the wall and demanded to know whether I was 'a punk or a poof', and then did it again the next time he met me."

10/96 (25969)